A Research Agenda for International Political Economy

T0327574

Elgar Research Agendas outline the future of research in a given area. Leading scholars are given the space to explore their subject in provocative ways, and map out the potential directions of travel. They are relevant but also visionary.

Forward-looking and innovative, Elgar Research Agendas are an essential resource for PhD students, scholars and anybody who wants to be at the forefront of research.

Titles in the series include:

A Research Agenda for Political Marketing
Edited by Bruce I. Newman and Todd P. Newman

A Research Agenda for Public–Private Partnerships and the Governance of Infrastructure
Edited by Graeme A. Hodge and Carsten Greve

A Research Agenda for Governance
John Pierre, B. Guy Peters, Jacob Torfing and Eva Sørensen

A Research Agenda for Sport Management
Edited by David Shilbury

A Research Agenda for COVID-19 and Society
Edited by Steve Matthewman

A Research Agenda for Civil Society
Edited by Kees Biekart and Alan Fowler

A Research Agenda for Tax Law
Edited by Leopoldo Parada

A Research Agenda for Food Systems
Edited by Colin L. Sage

A Research Agenda for International Political Economy
New Directions and Promising Paths
Edited by David A. Deese

A Research Agenda for International Political Economy

New Directions and Promising Paths

Edited by

DAVID A. DEESE

Professor of International Politics, Department of Political Science, Boston College, USA

Elgar Research Agendas

Edward Elgar
PUBLISHING

Cheltenham, UK • Northampton, MA, USA

Published by
Edward Elgar Publishing Limited
The Lypiatts
15 Lansdown Road
Cheltenham
Glos GL50 2JA
UK

Edward Elgar Publishing, Inc.
William Pratt House
9 Dewey Court
Northampton
Massachusetts 01060
USA

Paperback edition 2024

A catalogue record for this book
is available from the British Library

Library of Congress Control Number: 2022943312

This book is available electronically in the **Elgar**online
Political Science and Public Policy subject collection
http://dx.doi.org/10.4337/9781800884120

ISBN 978 1 80088 411 3 (cased)
ISBN 978 1 80088 412 0 (eBook)
ISBN 978 1 0353 3901 3 (paperback)

Printed and bound by CPI Group (UK) Ltd, Croydon, CR0 4YY

Contents

Contributors

Mark Abdollahian, Clinical Professor of Computational Analytics and Data Science, Claremont Graduate University, USA

William Akoto, Assistant Professor of International Politics, Department of Political Science, Fordham University, USA

Puspa D. Amri, Assistant Professor, Department of Economics, School of Business and Economics, Sonoma State University, USA

Ida Bastiaens, Associate Professor, Department of Political Science, Fordham University, USA

Celeste Beesley, Assistant Professor, Department of Political Science, Brigham Young University, USA

John Connolly, Professor of Public Policy, School of Education and Social Sciences, University of the West of Scotland, UK

David A. Deese, Professor of International Politics, Department of Political Science, Boston College, USA

Corinna Dengler, Assistant Professor, Department for Socioeconomics, Vienna University of Economics and Business, Austria

Eunyoung Ha, Research Fellow, The Institute for Welfare State Research, Yonsei University, South Korea

Wei Liang, Gordon Paul Smith Professor of International Policy, Graduate School of International Policy and Management, Middlebury Institute of International Studies, USA

Nicholas R. Micinski, Libra Assistant Professor of Political Science and International Affairs, The University of Maine, USA

Evgeny Postnikov, Senior Lecturer in International Relations, The School of Social and Political Sciences, The University of Melbourne, Australia

Aaron Schneider, Professor, the Leo Block Chair at the Josef Korbel School of International Studies, University of Denver, USA

Emily Scott, Lecturer in International Development, Development Department, University of Birmingham, UK

Hanna Völkle, Research Associate in Political Economy and Feminist Economics, The Berlin School of Economics and Law, Germany

Gary Winslett, Assistant Professor, Department of Political Science, Middlebury College, USA

Zining Yang, Adjunct Professor, Department of Economics, La Sierra University, USA

Preface

This book project identifies and assesses not only key "gaps" in international political economy (IPE) scholarship but also the most promising work that addresses and goes beyond them. Our goal is to explain the most important emerging and required research in the field. The chapters that follow address these research areas in four parts, or key pathways in IPE. Each pathway highlights some of the most promising and potentially important research areas in international political economy. The authors cover new and emerging areas, while also addressing promising offshoots from longer-standing research directions. These four parts are socio-economic inequality, externally triggered crises, change in the fundamental nature of IPE, and the underlying ideas and perspectives that shape the thinking and scholarship of the field.

First, three chapters probe the most promising lines of research on the crucial interconnections of globalization and socio-economic inequality. Next, three chapters investigate our understandings of how externally generated financial, health, and migration crises affect political economic systems worldwide. Third, five chapters map out the most promising research on fundamental changes in the nature of the IPE field itself. These address core changes driven by technology, power transitions, the geography of trade, new foreign aid channels, and economic espionage. A final, fourth section explores the deep roots of the western, white, male orientation of traditional IPE research, and the alternative perspectives of decolonial and feminist ecological thinkers.

The first part emphasizes socio-economic inequality because it reflects the damage done to societies worldwide by technological change and failed national policies, e.g. inadequate regulation and excessive reliance on markets, but also aggravated and accelerated by economic and financial globalization. This fundamental inequality opens up globalization for scapegoating by populist politicians and parties, and undermines the minimal education and training level of societies that enables them to benefit from globalization. Inequality also occurs across societies, leaving some behind even as many have caught up in relative terms. In the end, inequality erodes trust, positive international interconnections, and the collaboration required in order to sustain effective international order. Eunyoung Ha explains how the global production network has increased the demand and income of relatively skilled workers in emerging markets as well as advanced economies while it also concentrates the perverse effects on certain social groups, firms, industries, and regions. She points to crucial research on the central role of governments in mitigating these effects, as well as the constraints on fiscal resources and the efficiency pressures of the global market. Ida Bastiaens and Evgeny Postnikov assess the importance of future research on developing states' trade policy preferences and practices, in order to understand how by far most leaders, governments, and regional organizations worldwide engage in trade and production, and pursue agreements among themselves and in the WTO. In this way, they highlight work that digs deeper than the prevailing theoretical assumptions and trade policy models. Celeste Beesley and Ida Bastiaens explain the urgency of work on variables such as race, inequality, and welfare state compensation that mediate the intersection between political participation and IPE. They argue for scholarly attention on a wider range of forms of political participation and different aspects of globalization, e.g. financial, immigration, trade, and investment. Indeed, when citizens actively engage in the range of political activity, political elites are more likely to address public grievances on globalization.

The second IPE research pathway, externally generated crises, whether financial, health, or migration, reflects the reality that globalization has deeply destructive as well as positive effects and implications. At the regional even more than global level, more intensive international interactions have accelerated the number and destructiveness of external crises on national social-economies. Governments and governance worldwide struggle to cope with this new reality, and if these efforts are not successful these crises have the potential to escalate to uncontrolled levels and undermine the foundations of the current international system. Chapter 4, for example, outlines four prominent existential threats, and the ways in which the IPE field might help address those. Puspa Amri outlines how the 2008–2009 global financial crisis surprised scholars, illustrating starkly the limitations in predicting their outbreak and spread of crises and understanding their political drivers. She pinpoints crucial necessary research on government behavior, political institutions, and economic policies that will contribute to predicting, avoiding, and mitigating future banking and currency crises. John Connolly explains the One Health approach to emerging infectious diseases at the animal-human interface, which applies multi-sector collaboration to reveal the underlying causes of disease outbreaks. Crisis governance, both preparation and response, with One Health can lead the way to a new political economy of health security. Nick

Micinski explains how states conceptualize migration as a strategic resource in power relations and regulated it with development aid, earmarked funding, delegation to international organizations, externalization, and refugee commodification. He highlights research on who pays for, and benefits from, the international migration regime, and how it provides a venue for states and IOs to test new forms of governance.

The third research pathway is how the IPE field is itself evolving in fundamental ways, indicating how scholarship must adapt and catch up with technology and geopolitics, as well as related social, economic, and political change. Mark Abdollahian and Zining Yang explain how rapidly evolving technologies, information environments, and great power competition are defining the future environment for IPE. They emphasize new and emerging research on how transformational computing power, big data, AI, and computational social science enable and empower actors to anticipate and shape change in IPE. Wei Liang probes great power competition by advancing and advocating research on US–China decoupling, including the role of corporate interests and the failure of neoliberalism to anticipate US–China trade wars. She investigates the failure of the liberal world order to accommodate different political economic systems, and advocates a "middle," more inclusive pathway. William Akoto asks how technological advances and heightened international economic competition accelerate the understudied area of cyber economic espionage. He explains the crucial role of scholarship investigating the motives for this espionage, how governments respond to it, and how it is affected by economic interdependence. Gary Winslett explains the interaction of technological change and the geography (especially clustering) of trade, or specifically how "superstar" firms and cities capture job, wage, and investment growth, thus benefitting from globalization while other areas are left behind. He emphasizes that the political backlash against globalization is due more to educational and rural-urban inequality than the China Shock. Emily Scott advances a new research agenda for "local aid," aid given as directly as possible to actors and capacities in the local community. She outlines five promising research avenues: (1) systems of exclusion of local actors; (2) alternative aid sources; (3) new players to support localization; (4) effects of aid on developing state capacity; and (5) where aid actually ends up sub-nationally.

The final, essential part of the book explains how the underlying white, male, western ideas and perspectives have shaped the IPE field, for example leaving key blind spots around the natural resource, food, biodiversity, and climate crises, and excluding women as anything approaching equal leaders in IPE decision making and leadership. Corinna Dengler and Hanna Völkle connect gender and IPE, in part by focusing on a feminist–ecological IPE perspective.

They apply this ecofeminist perspective to explain the multidimensional, intertwined, and dynamic crises confronting IPE. They highlight an urgency for research on society and economy as embedded and embodied, and IPE as gendered and ecologically sensitive. Aaron Schneider presents a decolonized approach to development—a relational view from the South of community interactions with the natural world and the global system. It replaces binary and hierarchical North–South relations with a focus on authentic cultural values as reflected in embryonic alternatives such as key ideas in Morales' program (2006–2019) in Bolivia and "Buen vivir" from Bolivia and Peru.

PART I

Introduction

Introduction to *A Research Agenda for International Political Economy: New Directions and Promising Paths*

David A. Deese

Introduction

The human species occupies only a relatively trivial time period in the overall history of the earth—about 200,000 years of the earth's 14,000,000,000 (billion)! After only a miniscule fraction of those 200,000 years—the past 250 since the Industrial Revolution began—humans are on track to create as much damage to the earth's fundamental systems as most of the past brutal shocks from asteroid collisions and violent eruptions from deep inside the earth. In other words, human-induced change now rivals most of the profound natural upheavals since the origin of the universe (Christian 2018).

International Political Economy (IPE) as a field has emerged fully on the scene only over the past half century since the early 1970s. Triggered in part by scholars' observations of growing "interdependence" in the early 1970s, it has largely evolved around the traditionally defined sub-areas of trade, money, finance, multinational corporations, and development (e.g. Oatley 2019), until the 1990s when it also focused on economic and financial "globalization." At the same time, IPE has tended to incorporate both western, white, male perspectives and the capitalist model of "development." A leading outcome of this white, patriarchal, market orientation of the field has been a substantial degree of blindness, or at least apathy, to the socially destructive elements of the predominant western capitalist development model (Paterson 2020; Dengler and Völkle this volume; Schneider this volume). In this context, it is important that scholars continue to research and explain whether the destructive dimensions of politically regulated capitalism have resulted more from the inherent nature of capitalism (and its drive for growth), or from the lack of socially embedded, carefully regulated capitalist economies. In either case, it seems clear that the IPE field must transform or reorient key foundational elements of its groundings if it is to help salvage the basic planetary systems that humanity is so relatively rapidly destroying.

Why, more specifically, is this reorientation or transformation in the IPE field necessary? Scholars, research centers, and think tanks that focus on human existence and existential risks to humanity generally agree on the five to ten greatest existential threats. These threats cluster around three areas—(1) the climate crisis and the overlapping degradation of natural resources (especially water) and ecosystems (biodiversity), as well as resulting food insecurity; (2) technology and weapons (nuclear war/winter, biotechnology/ engineered pandemics, cyber war, or uncontrolled new technologies such as super-intelligence/AI); and (3) the political or governance failure to recognize and address these threats (Commission for the Human Future 2020; Statistica 2020; Beard and Holt 2019; Global Challenges Foundation 2021; Future of Life Institute; Sanberg 2014). IPE as a field of study has core responsibilities to reorient and help address especially the first and third of these areas. IPE research and policy prescriptions are essential to understanding how political economic systems can address the climate crisis, natural resource and biodiversity loss, and food insecurity. Equally, the field is absolutely central to assessing international and global governance failures and prescribing pathways to reform and renovation. IPE should lead in the process of offering creative, productive responses to the fundamental failures of western, patriarchal, capitalist models of global governance and development.

IPE as a core required and "socially responsible" field of inquiry—outline of this book

What are essential areas of inquiry where IPE research and prescriptions can help address these crises over the required time frame? The chapters that follow address several fundamental dimensions of these crises along four key pathways of IPE research. Each pathway highlights some of the most promising and potentially important research areas in international political economy. Some chapters cover new and emerging areas, while others address promising offshoots from longer-standing research directions. These avenues or directions are socio-economic inequality, externally triggered crises, change in the fundamental nature of IPE, and the unconventional perspectives of decolonial and feminist ecological thinkers.

First, three chapters probe the most promising lines of research on the crucial interconnections of globalization and socio-economic inequality. Next, three chapters investigate our understandings of how externally generated financial, health, and migration crises affect political economic systems worldwide. Third, five chapters map out the most promising research on fundamental changes in the IPE field itself. These address core changes driven by technology, power transitions, the geography of trade, new foreign aid channels, and economic espionage. A final section explores the deep roots of the western, white, male orientation of traditional IPE research, and the alternative perspectives of decolonial and feminist ecological thinkers.

This introductory chapter applies one theoretical approach—international and domestic political-economic leadership at mainly the individual level. Individual political leadership can only contribute so much within the constraints of bureaucratic politics, national economic and industrial structures, political institutions and electoral processes, and public values and opinion. However, it is the one key driver, along with policy entrepreneurship by civil society groups, that can shift policies over the required time frame of months to a few years instead of the medium and longer terms. This compressed time frame is essential to redirecting public policy in ways relevant to addressing existential crises. This chapter defines political leadership, with emphasis on the less studied, individual level, in its four main modes, in order to explain where additional research is crucial to addressing the governance, climate, natural resources, and biodiversity crises. It also emphasizes the critical roles of women as leaders in these areas, as indicated by various lines of research.

Defining political leadership in five components

A leader presents and explains in persuasive rhetoric a policy based on her ideas reflecting values important to collective interests and political institutions. In domestic political leadership, it is the collective interests of her society, whereas international leadership includes broader cross-national or international interests. Leaders pursue collective or public goods formulated as morally neutral, if not positive goals advancing social well-being, i.e. achieving a public purpose or policy rather than seeking mainly individual power, status, or reputational advancement (Deese 2008, 2018). This is emphasized as one important way to distinguish leadership from other forms of bargaining behavior (Skodvin and Andresen 2006).

Second, leaders apply personal energy, competence, intelligence, vision, commitment (or positive ambition), tenacity, and rhetorical skills. Leaders are better informed than those they are attempting to persuade (Skodvin and

Andresen 2006). These capabilities are applied to persuade would-be followers and bargain in making deals and building coalitions, while aiming to limit the growth of opposing coalitions. Building coalitions and managing networks of support is a crucial dimension of both political leadership and policy entrepreneurship. Thus, leadership is assessed and measured in terms of how often and consistently an individual or state advocates for the proposed policy, as well as whether the policy or measure is enacted. Reimer and Saerbeck (2017) call this "policy entrepreneurship."

Third, political leadership is the capability to recognize an individual's (or state's) status and position in history. "Men make their own history," Karl Marx observed, "but they do not make it as they please; they do not make it under self-selected circumstances, but under circumstances existing already, given and transmitted from the past" (1852, p. 329). In other words, leaders must be able to size up supporting and opposing actors and institutions, and capitalize on existing circumstances. More specifically in Skowronek's (1997) terms, leaders are likely to find themselves positioned in an established political regime that is resilient or vulnerable to disruption, and they may end up continuing it (articulating) or replacing it (reconstructing) with a new one. Leaders have a vision of their place in history and how that opens and closes opportunities for change, or what are called "windows of opportunity" in the policy entrepreneurship literature. They try to capitalize on external shocks to strengthen supportive coalitions and undermine opposed ones (Aklin and Urpelainen 2018). This leadership element is measured in terms of whether an individual or state recognizes an opening for policy enactment, as well as the timeliness of actions taken.

The fourth component is a leader's judgment and prudence in decision making and adjusting to setbacks and failures. Leaders must be ambitious in seizing on political opportunities, while also recognizing when compromise is necessary and appropriate. Prudence includes recognizing persistent criticism and blockages, understanding when flexibility and humility are essential to compromise, managing constraints, and gaining policy acceptance. At the same time, it requires the judgment to discern when to persist with an unpopular policy and respond with firmness and "education" from the top down, just because it is the right thing to do. Mere popularity without morally positive policies and purposes, or with only "symbolic" instead of substantive policies, is a perversion or pathological practice.

The fifth, final element of leadership is building and maintaining trusting relationships with superiors and peers, especially elected leaders and representatives, ministers, and other officials and agencies most involved in the involved policy area. Policy outcomes surely depend on bureaucratic and institutional cooperation, in particular for implementation and compliance, from the national to local levels. Furthermore, leaders often seek opportunities to forge a small group of policy entrepreneurs, officials, or aligned national governments. If strategically selected, co-leaders establish critical connections to a range of different followers and groups, which enhances a leader's credibility, and expands the consensus group and the chances of achieving effective policy outcomes. This element is measured or assessed by the degree of legislative, bureaucratic, or consensus group support for the proposed policy, particularly for its enactment and implementation (Deese 2008, 2018).

The four modes of political leadership

When identified and assessed separately, each of these four modes of leadership can be compared and contrasted with each other. Particularly effective political leadership may involve different modes over time, but for analytical purposes only one mode is identified and explained at any one given time frame. Young (1991, p. 288) characterizes structural leaders as "experts in translating the possession of material resources into bargaining leverage." Material resources vary according to asymmetries among actors, and can include relative freedom from domestic policy constraints, leverage over the outcome of negotiations, and hard or soft power. Structural leaders leverage these asymmetrical forms of influence to catalyze policy outcomes. Kindleberger calls this "arm-twisting and bribery." Structural leadership requires deft use of education and public relations, and crucial traits such as integrity, flexibility, and compromise (Young 2001, p. 289). This is an "exclusive" definition of leadership, since it excludes coercion, or "… when someone forces others to do as he or she wishes or threatens to harm those who don't" (Malnes 1995, p. 96).

Directional leadership is shaping behavior by acting first, setting a clear, positive model for others to follow (Parker et al. 2014, p. 438; Karlsson et al. 2102, p. 48; Park 2016, p. 782; Gupta and Ringius 2001, p. 282; Underdal 1994, p. 185). They gain credibility and may communicate moral principles (Malnes 1995, p. 96). At the same time, their action may limit the set of options available to others (Schwerhoff 2015). In addition to taking credible policy actions at home, they initiate proposals bilaterally and multilaterally in order to catalyze bargaining or break deadlocks. One variation on this is "conditional leadership," where an actor catalyzes followers by forging cooperative, mutually reinforcing schemes based on promises of reciprocal action (Vanderheiden

2012). This is proposed specifically as a way to breaking deadlocks in global climate negotiations.

Intellectual leaders leverage "the power of ideas" to influence actors' understanding of problems and potential solutions (Young 1991, p. 288). Intellectual leadership by experts, academics, non-governmental organizations, or public institutions generates ideas, concepts, issue framing, negotiating approaches, or policy proposals that shape international negotiations at their origin or key turning points (Deese 2008, p. 24). Intellectual leaders are the least likely to be directly involved in the negotiation, and indeed can be difficult even to identify. Intellectual innovation most often originates with individual experts or scholars, and is introduced to the negotiation by an official or country delegation. Entrepreneurial and structural leaders regularly apply ideas, frames, and approaches without attribution to any specific source. Still, intellectual leaders are crucial to the success of bargaining, whether in the form of providing a timely op-ed article or media interview, or publishing the entire approach that enables a successful negotiation.

Entrepreneurial leaders help set the international or domestic agenda, draw attention to issues, innovate with policy options, and broker deals (Young 1991, p. 294). They provide negotiating skill, creative brokering, deal facilitation, and innovative solutions to blockages or deadlocks, for example by structuring incentives for parties, advancing mutually acceptable outcomes, and helping players visualize deals (Deese 2008, p. 36; Underdal 1994, p. 294; Young 1991, p. 288). They may create turning points in negotiations by suggesting issue linkages, possible trade-offs, and side payments. Individuals from states of any size or position, public international organizations, or international non-governmental organizations (INGOs) provide entrepreneurial leadership. They stand out based on experience, skill sets, political neutrality, insight, and respect developed over years of interactions, particularly in the issue area at hand. After decades of international climate negotiations, there is a substantial pool of actual and potential entrepreneurial leaders in this issue area. However, even the most recent UN COP26 in Glasgow clearly did not include a balance by gender in national representatives, or in developing-developed state participation in COP leadership roles.

The "demand" for research on political leadership in IPE

The next two sections illustrate how the study and practice of political leadership can help address existential crises. The first section briefly explores the puzzle of whether "capitalism" and market-based political economic systems are capable of coping with these crises, and if so, how they might do that. As Schneider and Dengler and Völkle emphasize in this volume, the question is whether existing political economic systems recognize, and can reflect, the fundamental ecological embeddedness of our societies. The spectrum of most likely, if not existent, political economic ideas and national policy agendas worldwide is herein divided into three separable approaches. First is what Schneider and the literature call "decolonial," and Dengler and Völkle label ecofeminist "alternatives to growth rather than growth alternatives." Second are the most socially embedded, ecologically sustainable democracies (or most coordinated market economies), the Scandinavian societies. Third is the market-oriented economies transitioning to green growth models that rely on "greening" capitalist systems, e.g. the EU's 2020 "Circular Economy Action Plan" within the European Green Deal initiative. In its specific terms, this section focuses mainly on "comparative political economy" because it covers the most fundamental elements of IPE, the types of national political economic systems that interact and intersect forming either collaborative or conflictual bonds that largely define economic and financial globalization. The puzzle at hand is how these systems will either evolve and help address the growing instability of globalization, or fail to adapt and end up accelerating the existential resource, biodiversity, food, and climate crises of our time (Deese and Biasi 2022).

Decolonial, ecofeminist political economy

The first, decolonial, ecofeminist approach or "cluster" is not fully implemented in any existing political economic system. A partial example was the structural leadership of the Morales regime in Bolivia, during its three terms (2006–2019), in land reform, indigenous rights, and redistribution. As explained by Schneider, it emphasized plural and relational values. It also applied what Dengler and Völkle highlight as ecological economics, anti-capitalist, and environmentalist perspectives (Himes and Muraca 2018, in Dengler and Völkle this volume). The idea of "Buen Vivir" in Bolivia and Peru does "not accept the concept of progress and its derivatives (particularly growth) or the idea that welfare depends only on material consumption" (Gudynas 2015, p. 202). Intellectual leadership along this path guided basic reforms in how societies approach consumption, environmental accounting, and taxation (Gudynas 2011, p. 446, in Schneider this volume). This is especially relevant in mitigating how crises reinforce social and gender injustices (Agarwal 1992; Harvey 2005; Roser and Seidel 2017).

This includes a range of literatures and approaches, but each emphasizes the failure of western liberal democratic political economies in practice, or capitalism more generally, to address the existential threats outlined above. Essentially, the focus is to research and model an IPE and political economic system that supports socially and ecologically progressive policies without at least economic growth, if not the capitalist framework. A crucial priority, based on relational and pluralist values instead of monetary ones, is to correct the deeply troubling degree of social-economic inequality across many countries, including many autocratic- and authoritarian-quasi-market economies.

Socially embedded, ecologically sustainable, market-oriented democracies

The second approach, as best exemplified by political leaders and parties in the Scandinavian region, most closely approaches socially embedded, ecologically sustainable, market-oriented democracies. They lead the way in maintaining relatively effective, comprehensive social policies, "greening" the political economy, and pursuing multilateral foreign policies. For example, Norway, Denmark, Finland, and Sweden ranked 1, 2, 3, and 5, respectively, in the 2020 "social progress index" (Social Progress Imperative 2021). In 2013–2014, Norway, Sweden, Finland, and Denmark were 5, 6, 8, and 9, respectively, in "social progress". Sweden, Norway, and Iceland are credited with the highest "family-friendly" policies in the OECD and EU (UNICEF 2019). Development Finance International and OXFAM's Commitment to Reducing Inequality Index (2017) integrates three indicators to address inequality spending on health, education, and social protection, progressive structure of taxation, and labor market policies. Sweden, Denmark, Norway, and Finland rank 1, 3, 4, and 6, respectively (Belgium and Germany are 2nd and 5th), which helps to confirm the social embeddedness of their political economies. The fact that Australia (14), Canada (15), and the UK (17) all rank well above the US (23) also highlights the striking lower level of US commitment to socio-economic equalization. In addition, Scandinavian leaders and societies sustain higher levels of multilateralism in IPE (Milner and Tingley 2013). For example, in foreign aid allocated by the OECD states, the multilateral and untied portions are considerably higher for the Scandinavian states than for the US and most others (OECD 2011a, 2021). Finally, these states also excel in their relative environmental performance. In their "environmental health" (40 percent of the overall environmental performance index 2020 (Yale Center for Environmental Law and Policy 2021)), which includes air quality, sanitation and drinking water, heavy metals, and waste management, Finland, Norway, Sweden, and Demark rank 1, 2, 3, and 8, respectively. The Climate Change Performance Index (German Watch 2022) reports Denmark, Sweden, Norway, and Finland as 1, 2, 3, and 14, respectively, among the 64 largest greenhouse gas emitting countries (Finland is weighted down by the energy use category).

IPE and comparative political economy research need to lead the way in understanding how these "social democracies" are able to capitalize on, or at least regulate, the effects of economic and financial globalization. In particular, does the clearly higher level of social progress reduce citizens' fears and concerns about economic and financial globalization? Which of their leaders and groups have been most instrumental in getting their policies on the agenda? As political parties turn over, which coalitions sustain the core social-economic agenda? In what ways do leaders and policies in Scandinavia provide viable models for leadership in societies at lower levels of income and wealth?

"Circular" or green growth transitions in market economies

With regard to political leadership in most other countries worldwide, it is essential to explain more fully why some publics understand that development and sustainability can be mutually reinforcing, whereas others perceive sustainability and growth to be in conflict. Societies in the former category, such as many in the EU and some in Latin America, as opposed to those in the latter, e.g. the US, tend to maintain greater stability of resource, energy, and climate policies in support of more sustainable outcomes. Even as elections shift governing coalitions between right- and left-leaning political parties, public policy is more predictable and private investment more stable in countries where economic performance, human development, and environmental protection are seen as mutually supporting, if not essentially the same thing. Indeed, most European political leaders, and those representing the EU in particular, help shape prevailing public opinion support for addressing environmental problems foremost by "changing the way we consume" and "changing the way we produce and trade," in addition to investing in R&D to find technological solutions, providing more information and education, encouraging businesses to sustainable activities, and introducing stricter environmental legislation and heavier fines for breaching laws (European Commission 2021). This reflects a fairly widespread understanding that existing economic practices are not sustainable. It is important to explain the leadership and political economy drivers that helped lift Morocco, Chile, and India to 8, 9, and 10, respectively, (among the 64 largest emitters) in the Climate Change Performance Index 2022. Indeed, Morocco is first overall in the sub-category of energy use and second in climate policy.

Just as intellectual leadership helped create the surge of neoliberalism in the early 1980s, leaders can also play a central role in shifting values and beliefs toward socially embedded, ecologically responsible policies worldwide. In order to do this, IPE and comparative political economy scholars need to either integrate, or be explicit about the differences among, three prevailing concepts—the "circular economy" (CE), bioeconomy (BE), and "green economy" (GE). CE emerged from work on urban "ecological industrial practices" of the 1970s–1980s, which was then applied in structural leadership by Chinese and EU leaders in the 1990s (D'amato et al. 2017; Frosch and Gallopoulus 1989). It emphasized "decoupling," or redesigning production to minimize inputs and waste. European, and some US, literature also encouraged leaders to emphasize BE-biological innovations in renewable resource and land use, especially in forestry and agriculture in more rural areas (Bugge et al. 2016; Kleinschmit et al. 2014; Pfau et al. 2014; Ollikainen 2014). Finally, the GE incorporates some ideas from CE and BE, and focuses broadly on socially, ecologically embedded development (without exploring degrowth) (D'amato et al. 2017; Barbier 2012). The UNEP drew on intellectual leadership from scholars worldwide to define GE in terms of human well-being in socially and ecologically embedded political economy (UNEP 2011).

A second critical line of research across IPE

A second critical line of research across IPE is the fundamental "demand" for women as climate and natural resource leaders. Indeed, women need to be equal holders of climate and resource leadership roles and positions for basic reasons of rights and ethics, social progress, effective public policy, and economic productivity. Substantial research highlights several key advantages that women offer in this regard, and the high opportunity costs of their constrained opportunities due to the social hierarchies, gendered norms and attitudes, and institutional rules (OXFAM 2013, 2021; World Bank 2012). Furthermore, international norms in this regard affect domestic policies by creating standards and expectations in global, regional, and local civil societies (Simmons 2009; World Bank 2012). Since women tend to approach problem solving more from a collective, than individual, perspective, they are inherently more likely to provide political leadership (Woolley et al. 2010). It is understood that on average women are more likely to make decisions that advance socially beneficial outcomes, and take positions based on ethics and honesty (Roetzel 2021). In light of this, the more women who have opportunities for senior positions in politics, public administration, business, and civil society organizations, the more political leadership and positive social outcomes will occur (Kwauk 2021). At the same time, it is important to not over-identify women with "social issues." As of 2010, women ministers were twice as likely to occupy a social as opposed to an economic position (World Bank 2012).

This may help to explain why countries in which women have higher social and political status are reported to have 12 percent lower CO_2 emissions (Kwauk 2021). More specifically, a study across 91 countries found that those with higher female representation in parliaments have stricter climate policies and lower emissions (Tanyag 2021). Additional research should be directed at explaining why a large sample of 130 countries showed that national governments with a relatively high representation of women in agencies and departments are more likely to ratify environmental treaties (Norgaard and York 2005). One hypothesis worthy of investigation is that women tend to provide entrepreneurial leadership from within administrations in guiding political appointees and cabinet heads toward joining and implementing environmental treaty systems. A broad review of 17 studies on conservation and natural resource management worldwide found that on average women tend to adopt innovation and preventative measures more readily than men. Specifically, the presence of women was found to enhance collaboration, rules, compliance, transparency, and conflict management (Leisher et al. 2016; Westermann and Ashby 2005). This is clearly an area rich for further work and understanding, as well as practical action (UN 2020).

Furthermore, women offer important intellectual, as well as entrepreneurial, leadership capabilities. Well over half of all 200 winners of the annual Goldman Environmental Prize (or "Nobel" prize for the environment) since 1990 have been women. Female leadership for the environment is also likely closely connected to values regarding human and ecological health (Deinenger and Liu 2009). For example, countries led by women are reported in a cross-national study of 194 countries to have enacted more effective responses to the pandemic (Garikipati and Kambhampati 2020). Indeed, US states led by female governors reported fewer deaths from COVID-19 (Sergent and Stajkovic 2020). Leadership in the corporate sector under crisis conditions seems to parallel these findings. A study of US corporate managers early in the pandemic found that women scored higher in most capability areas (*Harvard Business Review* 2020). Importantly these capabilities included key components of political leadership—motivating followers, taking the initiative, and communicating powerfully.

Leadership is emphasized and widely studied in the private sector. Research regularly reports benefits for companies and economies overall when women are empowered. For example, businesses with more than three women in senior "management" positions score higher on organizational performance (UN Secretary General's High Level Panel on Women's Economic Empowerment 2016). Companies with a female CEOs are reported to enjoy higher stock prices by 20 percent (after two years) (CNBC 2019). A study of 350 startups found that women-led firms earned over twice the dollar amount relative to the investments (Kapin 2019; CNBC 2019).

In light of these and many other findings, it is a crisis in a crisis that women are so poorly represented as heads of states and in the UN COPs. In recent years there have been only 26 female heads of government and state worldwide. Even worse, at the 2019 UN climate COP about 80 percent of the delegation heads were men.

Conclusion

In sum, what are the most promising insights and models for political leaders from the very limited experience with decolonial, feminist ecological political economy, the more extensive history of social-ecological embedded political economy, as illustrated in Scandinavia, and the much broader experience of greening political economies elsewhere? In what ways do they indicate how national and international political economy can address the dehumanizing growth in national and global inequality, which is also destabilizing economic and financial globalization? First, IPE scholars must dedicate much greater attention to the degrowth literature and movement, and more generally to the problem and politics of economic growth, with emphasis on the highest income states (Paterson 2020; D'Alisa et al. 2015; Kallis 2011). If blended with substantially accelerated rates of technological and socio-economic change, do the public policies associated with degrowth shift the planet to a relatively safe climate pathway? IPE research should help determine the likely and required rates of decarbonization in this pathway. Indeed, scholars should continue to question whether capitalism as a system, along with autocratic and author-itarian (and resource curse) systems with market-oriented sectors, are even possible without a fossil fuel foundation (Malm 2015).

Second, in both social-ecologically embedded economies and greening econ-omies worldwide, how can fossil fuel and other socially perverse subsidies in their several different forms be phased out on a timely basis? Comparative political economy and IPE research are essential to understanding the possible pathways for the energy transition generally, and electrification and "green hydrogen" specifically, as well as transitions to restorative natural resource and biodiversity policies. In what ways must the global political economy shift in order to enable these transitions? As argued by Paterson (2020) and illustrated by Bridge and Gailing (2020), IPE is central to investigating how the range of different financial instruments can most productively facilitate the transition to net zero economies. It is especially critical to ask how developing state governments can relatively efficiently and effectively facilitate green investment avenues and instruments to support economy-wide infrastructure development (Stern 2019). What are the key insights and lessons from the most successful states in the regulatory roles of central banks, and finance, environment, agricultural, and energy ministries (Dafermos 2021)? Finally, one very clear and critical direction for research is understanding how and why female leadership produces such socially positive outcomes for managing natural resources, addressing the climate crisis, and advancing human health. At the same time, there is more than sufficient scholarly understanding calling out for rapid increase in female roles at all levels of governance, elected political leadership, and global negotiations. Given our current, well-established understandings, it is completely counterproductive and even socially irresponsible not to have equal representation of women as top leaders of global negotiations and governing bodies for public health, environment, climate, the energy transition, natural resources, and biodiversity.

References

Agarwal, Bina. 1992. "The Gender and Environment Debate: Lessons from India," *Feminist Studies* 18(1): 119–158.

Aklin, M. and J. Urpelainen. 2018. *Renewables: The Politics of a Global Energy Transition*. Cambridge, MA: The MIT Press.

Barbier, E. 2012. "The Green Economy Post-Rio+20," *Science* 338: 887–888.

Beard, Simon and Lauren Holt (2019) "What are the Biggest Threats to Humanity?" BBC News, February 15. Center for the Study of Existential Risk.

Bridge, G. and L. Gailing. 2020. "New Energy Spaces: Towards a Geographical Political Economy of Energy Transition," *Environment and Planning A: Economy and Space* 52(6): 1037–1050.

Bugge, M.M. et al. 2016. "What is the Bioeconomy? A Review of the Literature," *Sustainability* 8: 1–22.

Christian, D. 2018. *Origin Story: A Big History of Everything*. Boston, MA: Little Brown, & Co.

CNBC. 2021. https:// www .cnbc .com/ 2019/ 10/ 18/ firms -with -a -female -ceo -have -a -better-stock-price-performance-sp.html (retrieved June 17, 2021).

Commission for the Human Future. 2020.

Dafermos, Y. 2021. Climate Change, Central Banking and Financial Supervision: Beyond the Risk Exposure Approach. SOAS Department of Economics Working Paper 243.

D'Alisa, G. et al. 2015. *Introduction of "Degrowth: A Vocabulary for a New Era."* Routledge, UK.

D'amato, D. et al. 2017. "Green, Circular, Bio Economy: A Comparative Analysis of Sustainability Avenues," *Journal of Cleaner Production* 168: 716–734.

Deese, D. 2008. *World Trade Politics: Power, Principles, and Leadership.* Routledge, UK.

Deese, D. 2018. "Ruling the Global Commons." International Studies Annual Convention, San Francisco, CA, February, 2018.

Deese, D. and S. Biasi. 2022. "Financial Crises and Trade Wars: Has Globalization Failed to Deliver?" in K. Zeng and W. Liang (eds.), *Research Handbook on Trade Wars.* Cheltenham, UK and Northampton, MA, USA: Edward Elgar Publishing

Deininger, K. and Yanyan Liu. (2009). "Economic and Social Impacts of Self-Help Groups in India." World Bank Policy Research Paper. Washington, DC: The World Bank.

Development Finance International and Oxfam. 2017. *The Commitment to Reducing Inequality Index: A New Global Ranking of Governments Based on what they are doing to Tackle the Gap between Rich and Poor.*

European Commission. 2021. Citizen Support for Climate Action: 2021 Survey.

Frosch, R.A. and N. Gallopoulos. 1989. "Strategies for Manufacturing," *Scientific American* 261: 144–152.

Future of Life Institute. https://futureoflife.org/background/existential-risk/

Garikipati, S. and U. Kambhampati. 2020. "Leading the Fight Against the Pandemic: Does Gender 'Really' Matter?" SSRN Abstract 3617953.

German Watch. 2022. Climate Change Performance Index 2022.

Global Challenges Foundation. 2021. Global Catastrophic Risks 2021: Navigating the Complex Intersections. Annual Report.

Gudynas, E. 2011. "Buen Vivir: Today's Tomorrow," *Development* 54(4): 441–447.

Gudynas, E. 2015. "Buen Vivir," in G. D'Alisa, F. Demaria, and G. Kallis (eds.), *Degrowth: A Vocabulary for a New Era.* New York: Routledge.

Gupta, J. and L. Ringius. 2001. "The EU's Climate Leadership: Reconciling Ambition and Reality," *International Environmental Agreements: Politics, Law, and Economics* 1.

Harvard Business Review. 2020. "Research: Women Are Better Leaders During a Crisis." https://hbr.org/2020/12/research-women-are-better-leaders-during-a-crisis

Harvey, D. 2005. *The New Imperialism.* New York: Oxford University Press.

Himes, A. and B. Muraca. 2018. "Relational Values: The Key to Pluralistic Valuation of Ecosystem Services," *Current Opinion in Environmental Sustainability* 35: 1–7.

Kallis, G. 2011. "In Defense of Degrowth," *Ecological Economics* 70: 873–880.

Kapin, A. (2019, January 28). "10 Stats that Build the Case For Investing in Women-Led Startups." Retrieved from https://www.forbes.com/sites/allysonkapin/2019/01/28/10

Karlsson, Christer et al. 2012. "The Legitimacy of Leadership in International Climate Change Negotiations," *Ambio* 41.

Kleinschmit, D. et al. 2014. "Shades of Green: A Social Scientific View of Bioeconomy for the Forest Sector," *Scandinavian Journal of Forest Research* 7581: 1–31.

Kwauk, C. (2021). "Why Captain Planet Should Have Been a Woman." https://www.brookings.edu/blog/education-plus-development/2019/03/28/why-captain-planet-should-have-been-a-woman (retrieved June 17, 2021).

Leisher, C. et al. 2016. "Does the Gender Composition of Forest and Fishery Management Groups Affect Resource Governance and Conservation Outcomes? A Systematic Map," *Environmental Evidence* 5(6).

Malm, A. 2015. *Fossil Capital: The Rise of Steam Power and the Roots of Global Warming.* New York: Verso Books.

Malnes, R. 1995. "'Leader' and 'Entrepreneur' in International Negotiations: A Conceptual Analysis," *European Journal of International Relations* 1(1): 98.

Marx, K. 1852. *The Eighteenth Brumaire of Louis Bonaparte.* New York: Die Revolution.

Milner, H. and D. Tingley. 2013. "The Choice for Multilateralism: Foreign Aid and American Foreign Policy," *Review of International Organizations* 8(3): 313–341.

Norgaard, K. and R. York. 2005. "Gender Equality and State Environmentalism," *Gender and Society* 19(4): 506–522.

Oatley, T. 2019. *International Political Economy.* New York: Routledge.

OECD. 2011a. *Development Cooperation Report 2011.* OECD Publishing.

OECD. 2011b. *Towards Green Growth.* OECD Publishing.

OECD. 2021. *Development Cooperation Report 2021.* OECD Publishing.

Ollikainen, M. 2014. "Forestry in Bioeconomy-Smart Green Growth for the Humankind," *Scandinavian Journal of Forest Research* 29: 360–336.

OXFAM. 2013. "Women and Collective Action: Unlocking the Potential of Agricultural Markets." Research Report. OXFAM International, UK, March 27.

OXFAM. 2021. "Social Norms Structuring Masculinities, Gender Roles, and Stereotypes." Research Report. OXFAM International, UK, August.

Park, S. 2016. "The Power of the Presidency in UN Climate Change Negotiations: Comparison between Denmark and Mexico," *International Environmental Agreements: Politics, Law, and Economics* 16: 781–795.

Parker, C.F. et al. 2014. "Climate Change Leaders and Followers: Leadership Recognition and Selection in the UNFCCC Negotiations," *International Relations* 29(4).

Paterson, M. 2020. "Climate Change and International Political Economy: Between Collapse and Transformation," *Review of International Political Economy* 28(2) 394–405.

Pfau, S.F. et al. 2014. "Visions of Sustainability in Bioeconomy Research," *Sustain* 6: 1222–1249.

Reimer, I. and B. Saerbeck. 2017. "Policy Entrepreneurs in National Climate Change Policy Processes," *Environment and Planning* C 35(8): 1456–1470.

Roetzel, J. (2021, June 22). "Why Women are Key to Solving the Climate Crisis." Medium.com. One Earth.

Roser, D. and C. Seidel. 2017. *Climate Justice: An Introduction.* Routledge UK.

Sanberg, Anders. 2014. "The Five Biggest Threats to Human Existence," *The Guardian,* Comment Network, July 21.

Schwerhoff, Gregor. 2015. "The Economics of Leadership in Climate Change Mitigation," Climate Policy 16: 196–214.

Sergent, K. and A.D. Stajkovic. 2020. "Women's Leadership is Associated with Fewer Deaths During the COVID-19 Crisis: Quantitative and Qualitative Analyses of US Governors," *Journal of Applied Psychology* 105(8): 771–783.

Skodvin, T. and S. Andresen. 2006. "Leadership Revisited," *Global Environmental Politics* 6(3): August.

Skowronek, S. 1997. *The Politics Presidents Make: Leadership from John Adams to Bill Clinton.* Cambridge, MA: Harvard University Press.

Simmons, B. 2009. *Mobilizing for Human Rights: International Law in Domestic Politics.* Cambridge: Cambridge University Press.Social Progress Imperative. 2021. Social Progress Index. September 10.

Statistica. 2020.

Stern, N. 2019. *Unlocking the Inclusive Growth Story of the 21st Century: The Drive to a Zero Carbon Economy*. London: London School of Economics and Political Science.

Tanyag, M. 2021. "We Need more Female Leaders in the Fight against Climate Change," *The Guardian*, Opinion, November 11.

UN. 2020. *Women and Girls: Closing the Gender Gap*. New York: UN.

UN Secretary General's High Level Panel on Women's Economic Empowerment. 2016. "Leave No One Behind: A Call to Action for Gender Equality and Women's Economic Empowerment."

Underdal, Arild. 1994. "Leadership Theory: Rediscovering the Arts of Management," in W. Zartman (ed.), *International Multilateral Negotiation: Approaches to the Management of Complexity*. San Francisco, CA: Jossey-Bass.

UNEP. 2011. *Towards a Green Economy: Pathways to Sustainable Development and Poverty Eradication: A Synthesis for Policy Makers*. UNEP.

UNICEF. 2019. "Sweden, Norway, Iceland, Estonia, and Portugal Rank highest for Family Friendly Policies in the OECD and EU Countries." Press Release, June 12.

Vanderheiden, S. 2012. "Coaxing Climate Policy Leadership," *Ethics and International Affairs* 26(4): 463–479.

Westermann, O. and J. Ashby. 2005. "Gender and Social Capital: The Importance of Gender Differences for the Maturity and Effectiveness of Natural Resource Management Groups." *World Development* 33(11): 1783–1799.

Woolley, A.W. et al. 2010. "Evidence for a Collective Intelligence Factor in the Performance of Human Groups," Science, September 30. DOI: 10.1126/science.1193147

World Bank. 2012. *Gender Equality and Development*. Washington, DC: The World Bank.

Yale Center for Environmental Law and Policy. 2021. *EPI 2021*. New Haven, CT: Yale University.

Young, Oran R. 1991. "Political Leadership and Regime Formation: On the Development of Institutions in International Society," *International Organization* 45(3): 288.

Young, Oran R. 2001. "The Behavioral Effects of Environmental Regimes: Collective-Action vs. Social Practice Models," *International Environmental Agreements* I(1): 9–29.

PART II

How and why globalization interconnects with socio-economic inequality within states

PART II

how and why globalization interconnects
with socio-economic inequality within
states

1. Globalization and income inequality

Eunyoung Ha

Over the last three decades, the global economy has witnessed rapid market integration. Both developed and developing countries, after removing their policy controls, have experienced unprecedented flows of trade and capital. This phenomenon, which is often termed economic globalization, has been accompanied by rising economic growth and substantial poverty reduction in many developing countries. At the same time, income inequality has significantly increased in many advanced economies and has remained high or even worsened in most developing economies (Milanovic and Squire 2005; Ravallion 2016).

The rising domestic inequality has created public skepticism about the benefits of globalization in many advanced economies. When most developed countries experienced stagnated real income growth and rising income inequality in the 1990s and 2000s, the public in these countries perceived free trade as a zero-sum game, in which the winners are developing countries and the losers are developed countries. There has been a widespread belief that workers in developing countries are earning higher wages at the expense of workers in advanced economies. Several scholars also regard global economic integration as a leading force to the changes in income inequality (Lakner and Milanovic 2016; Milanovic and Squire 2005). This has given credence to this popular belief, and often been cited as the cause of the current backlash against globalization in high-income countries, as revealed by the 2016 election of President Trump in the United States, the Brexit vote in the United Kingdom, and the rise of radical populist parties in Western European countries.

However, this popular belief about the winners and losers of globalization misses an important point: Globalization in fact generates winners and losers within both developed and developing countries. Economic globalization influences workers' earnings and employment within a country through various factors such as their working industries, firms, and locations of residence. The global production network has increased trade competition, foreign investments, and technological advances, which have increased the jobs and wages of relatively skilled workers in emerging markets as well as advanced economies. It has also provided global markets for mobile capital and enlarged capital profits relative to labor (Furceri, Loungani, and Ostry 2019; Jaumotte, Lall, and Papageorgiou 2013). Yet, the adverse effects of globalization are concentrated in certain social groups, firms, industries, and regions, often persistent or even magnified over time. The role of governments in income insurance and education is critical to mitigating these effects, but it is often constrained by the limited fiscal resources and efficiency pressures of the global market.

This chapter first examines the trends and causes of economic globalization in the last three decades. The second section reviews standard trade theories and discusses how the distributive impact of globalization can be perceived differently according to the relative and absolute measures of global inequality. The third discusses how increased flows of trade and investments are significantly intertwined with technological advancement, a key driver of income inequality, in both developed and developing countries. The fourth section focuses on how the effects of globalization can be concentrated in certain social groups and regions while persisting over time. The fifth discusses the importance of government policies and their constraints under the efficiency pressure of globalization. The final section summarizes my argument and discusses how public discontent over inequality catalyzes the backlashes against globalization.

I   The trends and causes of globalization

Economic globalization can be termed as "long distance flows of goods, capital and services as well as information and perceptions that accompany market exchanges" (Keohane and Nye 2000, p. 106). That is, it incorporates both trade and financial globalization. It also has two different dimensions: The de jure policy dimension that refers to the reduction of tariffs and the liberalization of capital accounts, and the de facto flow dimension that refers to the actual cross-border economic flows of trade and foreign investments.

Figure 1.1 shows the changes in *economic globalization* over the last three decades in four income groups of countries: high-income, upper middle-income, lower middle-income, and low-income groups. Economic globalization is measured by Dreher's (2006) KOF index of an economy's integration into the global market, which ranges from 0 (closed economy) to 100 (open economy). The figure reveals two important facts. First, richer countries on average continued

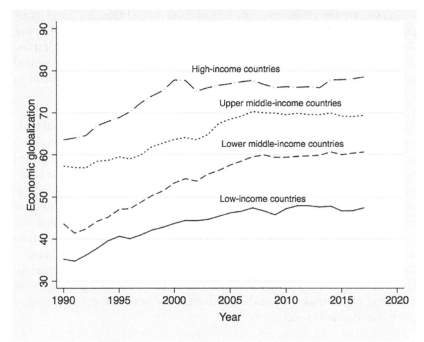

Note: Income group is divided based on the average gross domestic products (GDP) per capita (constant 2010 US$) from 1990 and 1994.
Source: Author's calculation based on World Development Indicator (WDI 2020).

Figure 1.1   Economic globalization by income group, 1990–2017

to have predominantly higher levels of globalization than poorer countries over the past three decades. Second, all four groups of countries have experienced a significant expansion in their domestic market integration into the global market. High-income countries continued to enlarge their level of economic globalization. In the same period, low- and lower middle-income countries rapidly caught up with top-income groups, by nearly doubling their level of globalization, while the process slowed down after the 2008 global financial crisis.

Global market integration in the last three decades was brought about by various factors, such as declines in transportation costs and declines in policy barriers through the General Agreement on Tariffs and Trade (GATT) and the World Trade Organization (WTO) (Baier and Bergstrand 2007; Bown and Crowley 2016; Goldberg and Pavcnik 2016). One of the most prominent causes is the decline in transportation and communication costs. For example, sea freight costs in the 1990s were only 20% of those in the 1930s. Air travel transport costs in the 1970s were also only 20% of those in the 1930s (Ortiz-Ospina, Beltekian, and Roser 2014). The development of the internet has, in the last few decades, also drastically lowered the costs of communication and increased the capacity of document sharing, video calls, and the remote control of management.

Another key reason is the reduction of policy barriers through unilateral trade reforms, bilateral trade agreements, or multilateral trade negotiations such as the GATT and the WTO. Most high-income countries, such as the United States, West European countries, and Japan, have already reduced their tariffs by the time a large number of developing countries started to join the international market in the 1980s. For example, the average import tariff rate in these countries fell from roughly 22% in 1947 to roughly 5% in 1980s (Bown and Crowley 2016). Still, developed countries have actively participated in bilateral and multilateral trade agreements such as the GATT, WTO, the Canada–United States Free Trade Agreement (CUSFTA), and the North American Free Trade Agreement (NAFTA). Their participation in trade agreements has expedited global trade by reducing uncertainty about trade policy (Handley 2014; Handley and Limão 2017).

On the other hand, China and a large number of developing countries have deeply integrated into the global market by participating in the GATT and the WTO. The process of their market integration was substantially facilitated by their participation in multilateral trade negotiations, particularly China's entry into the WTO in 2001. China's domestic growth has expanded the demand for commodities, which has increased the international trade of many commodity-rich developing countries (Costa, Garred, and Pessoa 2016; Hanson 2012). For example, China's trade (the sum of exports and imports) as a share of GDP increased from 21% in the 1980s to 40% in the 2010s. Mexico's trade share increased from 28% in the 1980s to 70% in the 2010s. India's trade increased from 13% to 42% in the same period (WDI 2021). The share of exports from low-income countries to low- and middle-income countries rose from 24% in 1994 to 42% in 2008, with half of this growth accredited to exports to China and India (Hanson 2012).

II   The winners and losers of globalization

Who are the winners and losers of globalization? According to the Stolper–Samuelson (SS) model in economics (developed from the Heckscher–Ohlin model), trade increases the relative return, e.g., jobs and wages, of the relatively abundant factors of the economy, e.g., capital, skilled labor, and unskilled labor (Stolper and Samuelson 1941). In general, developed countries are relatively more abundant in capital and skilled labor, while developing countries are relatively abundant in unskilled labor (see Kanbur 2015 for an overview of related theories). Therefore, developed countries will export more highly skill- and capital-intensive products, which have a comparative advantage in developed countries, while developing countries will export more unskilled-labor-intensive products, which have a comparative advantage in developing countries. Thus, increased international trade in developed countries increases the demand for and incomes of skilled workers, while reducing those for unskilled workers. The opposite will be true in developing countries, where the demand for and incomes of unskilled labor will increase relative to those for and of skilled labor and capital.

Similarly, capital openness in developed countries is expected to benefit skilled labor and capital relative to unskilled labor. The theoretical expectation is similar to that of trade liberalization: An abundant resource has a lower marginal return than does a scarce one. In general, developed countries have an abundant capital stock; thus, they have lower returns on capital relative to labor. However, the marginal product of capital increases as foreign investment outflows into developing countries and decreases capital stocks in developed countries. On the other hand, capital inflows in developing countries are expected to increase the demand for, and income of unskilled labor relative to skilled labor and capital. Foreign investment inflows increase the marginal return to labor by increasing the productivity of labor, which is equivalent to wage. As most foreign capital in developing countries will be invested in unskilled-labor-intensive products, the jobs and wages for unskilled workers are expected to grow relatively more than are those for others.

The classic trade models have received scholarly attention as China and other emerging market economies started to play a greater role in global trade (Eaton and Kortum 2002). The rapidly expanding trade flows and growth of China have brought domestic and international debates on distributive effects of globalization. Popular commentators and politicians have often stated that developing countries are winners of trade, while developed countries are losers. They argue that economic globalization has shifted relatively low-skilled jobs from advanced economies to unskilled labor-abundant developing countries. In other words, the jobs and wages of low-skilled workers in rich countries are squeezed by the increased import competition with lower-paid workers in poorer countries. The United States is often seen as the most pronounced example, where jobs for low- and medium-skilled workers are destroyed partly by the competition with China and other emerging market economies. Yet, other advanced countries have also experienced growing income gaps between the rich and the poor, which are often attributed to the impact of globalization (Bergh and Nilsson 2010; Gozgor and Ranjan 2017; Jaumotte et al. 2013).

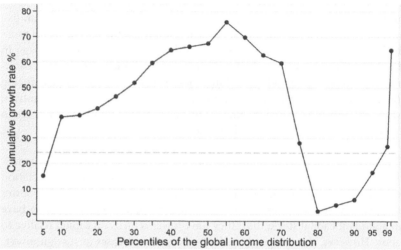

Source: Lakner and Milanovic (2016).

Figure 1.2   Global growth incidence curve, 1988–2008

Figure 1.2, the "Globalization Elephant Chart" illustrated by Lakner and Milanovic (2016), theoretically confirms this popular argument. The chart shows the global growth incidence curve, which reports the growth rate for each perceptible group along with the level of income distribution across the globe over 20 years (1988–2008). It reveals that the low to middle class of developing countries have gained substantially from globalization. In particular, the middle class in China, which is located around the global median (often called elephant's head), has gained the most amongst the global population. Second, the low to middle class in high-income countries, which are located around the eightieth percentile of the figure, has gained little from globalization. Third, the very top class in the rich countries, located at the top of the global distribution (often called the elephant's trunk), gained the most income shares in the globalized world market. This elephant chart has attracted significant attention in the mass media because it confirms the popular belief that the biggest winners of globalization are the middle class in developing countries and the very rich in developed countries, while the biggest losers are the poor and middle class in advanced economies.

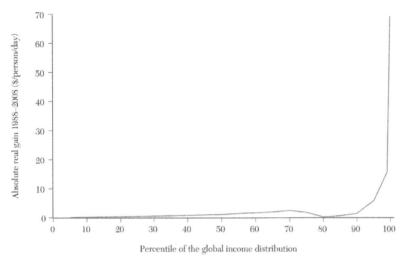

Source: Ravallion's (2018) calculation corresponding to the estimation made by Lakner and Milanovic (2016).

Figure 1.3   Incidence of the absolute income gains corresponding to Figure 1.2

However, the global elephant chart, illustrated based on relative gains, can look quite different when we use absolute gains as a measure of global inequality. Figure 1.3 shows the chart which Ravallion (2018) redrew based on absolute income gains. In the figure, the so-called elephant's head has significantly shrunken, while the trunk remains high. When absolute gain is used, the low to middle class in developing countries gained little over the 20-year period. This is because the underlying global distribution at the beginning was already so unequal. The average income per capita at the beginning of the period was $600 for the global median, but $39,000 for the global top 1 percentile. Therefore, even when the median and the top 1% of global distribution had the same growth rates, the former gained only an additional $400 over the 20 years, while the latter earned $25,000 for the same period (Lakner 2016). In fact, the top 5 percentile of the global population gained 44% of the increase in global income over the 20-year period (Lakner 2016).

As shown, the debates on globalization and inequality are subject to the choice of inequality measure. Different sides hold different ideas about how to measure "inequality." As such, the debates on distributive impact of globalization are closely related with our perception of individual welfare. In fact, the two figures for global inequality, shown in Figure 1.2 and Figure 1.3, treat the entire world as a single unit and characterize individual welfare as a function of individual income in the global market. Yet, most concerns about individual welfare remain within countries. This is because most policies are designed to address inequality at a national level, and individual well-being is affected mostly by localized inequality rather than global inequality. Important individual-level welfare losses such as relative deprivation and social alienation, as well as individual welfare gains such as the benefits of living in a richer country, are also closely related to within-country income inequality.

Economic globalization, in fact, generates winners and losers in both developed and developing countries. If we shift the analysis to the distributive effects of globalization within countries, we see that globalization significantly boosts the absolute incomes of the very rich, while having little impact on the poor in most countries or improving them in only some developing countries. Contrary to the expectation of classic trade theory, e.g., the SS model, several studies show that income inequality in developing countries has increased with the expansion of trade and capital openness (Ha 2012; Lundberg and Squire 2003; Milanovic and Squire 2005; Ravallion 2016). According to Ravallion (2016), developing countries have experienced rising income inequality, mainly because of the widening gap between the poorest and the average standard of living in developing countries. Also, the lower class in developing countries gained only modest income growth, which was just slightly above a survival level.

III   Globalization, technological development, and income inequality

The expansion of economic globalization is highly intertwined with technological development, which is one of the main causes of the rising income inequality in both developed and developing countries. In advanced economies, technology-biased change was seen as a major cause to shift the demand for less-skilled workers to skilled workers (Acemoglu 2002; Berman and Machin 2000; Card and DiNardo 2002). Technological development replaces manual, low-skilled jobs with automation, which increases the required job skills. This *skill-biased* technological development in advanced economies has caused deindustrialization, i.e., decline in the share of manufacturing sector in an economy, and enlarged skill premium—the demand for and income of relatively more skilled, or educated, workers as compared to unskilled, or less educated. The process of deindustrialization has been accelerated by the increased international competition (Rodrik 2021). As the market competition enlarged, investors and entrepreneurs in advanced economies reallocated their resources from declining, low-skill-intensive importing industries to growing, capital-intensive and high-skill-intensive exporting industries, which have a comparative advantage in advanced countries. As the market competition grows, firms in tradable sectors have strong incentives to replace routinized tasks with automation through technology and reduce production costs (Karabarbounis and Neiman 2014).

What is puzzling is that increased trade and foreign capital inflows have also enlarged income inequality in developing countries, which is contrary to the expectation of the conventional trade theory. This paradox can be explained by "technology-centered globalization," i.e., the technological advance of developing countries is accompanied by their participation in global trade (Ha 2012, p. 543). Foreign capital investments, particularly foreign direct investment (FDI) flows, have played a significant role in building global production chains and transferring technology and knowledge to developing countries (Hanson, Mataloni, and Slaughter 2005; Harrison and McMillan 2011; Muendler and Becker 2010). With the expansion of global production networks, manufacturing products are made through a sequence of stages, from raw inputs to parts and components, and then into a final product, where each country across borders adds value along the production chain. In the process of global production, advanced economies retain the production of technologically advanced, capital-intensive products (consistent with the SS theorem and the concept of comparative advantage). Yet, they shift to developing countries not only the production of unskilled-labor-intensive products, but also the production of intermediate products (also consistent with the SS theorem and the concept of comparative advantage). Although these products are unskilled-labor-intensive from the perspective of advanced economies, they are relatively capital-intensive and skilled-labor-intensive from the perspective of developing countries (Feenstra and Hanson 1995; Zhu and Trefler 2005). This technology-centered globalization has increased the relative demand for skilled labor and caused an increase in the skill premium (Conte and Vivarelli 2007; Fajnzylber and Fernandes 2009; Frias et al. 2018; Mazumdar and Mazaheri 2002).

Nowadays, most middle-income countries have shifted from low-skill-intensive industries to intermediate-skill-intensive industries, and low-income countries have become major exporters of intermediate goods (Cadot, Carrere, and Strauss-Kahn 2011; Schott 2003, 2004). In general, countries export different types of products according to their stage of development. Middle-income countries generally export goods that are intensive in human or physical capital (microchips, cars, and metals), while low-income countries generally export commodity products such as petroleum, copper, unwrought aluminum, tea, coffee, and raw cotton. Yet, with the expansion of the global production network, many emerging market economies have deepened their production capacity and evolved their product specialization to more capital-intensive and higher quality products as their economies grew. In fact, East Asian economies such as Hong Kong, Korea, Singapore, and Taiwan developed their productive capacity by first entering global production networks with product assembly, and later moving to input production and production design. China has embraced this process, and its top export goods nowadays are completed computers and computer parts.

IV   Globalization, the local labor market, and labor immobility

Although economic globalization may increase income inequality in the short term, the economic theory expects that the effects should dissipate over time, as capital and labor will reallocate across firms, industries, and regions. However, there is unbalanced mobility in the global market between capital and labor, and between skilled and unskilled labor. First, capital in the global market is disproportionally more mobile than labor. Nowadays, international investors and entrepreneurs are able to move for the highest returns on their investments because most countries removed controls over capital flows. As capital can move across borders anytime and anywhere, global actors such as multinational corporations and international investors have increasing power over states and people in terms of investment, production, distribution, and employment. The owners of capital, top income groups in both rich and poor countries, have seen their profits increase with the global technological change and rapid economic growth (Karabarbounis and Neiman 2014). Chinese billionaires, as well as American investors, are gaining enormous profits from their global reach. Indeed, capital has been the major beneficiary of globalization over the last two decades and led to greater inequality in both developed and developing countries (Bourguignon 2016; Furceri et al. 2019; Jaumotte et al. 2013).

However, labor, particularly unskilled labor, tends to be less mobile across firms, industries, and regions, as compared to capital (Attanasio, Goldberg, and Pavcnik 2004; Autor, Dorn, and Hanson 2013; Dix-Carneiro and Kovak 2017; Notowidigdo 2020; Topalova 2010; Wacziarg and Wallack 2004). In fact, the positive and negative effects of trade tend to be geographically concentrated in both developed and developing countries. Some regions have import-competing industries that lose the most from trade liberalization, while others may have more export-oriented industries that gain the most. Individuals residing in regions with a high concentration of import-competing industries face declining wages and jobs relative to those in other regions. For example, in a study of India, Topalova (2010) found that, after the trade reform in 1991, the regions exposed to import competition experienced relatively less poverty reduction than did less exposed regions. In a study of Vietnam, McCaig (2011) found that, after a bilateral trade agreement with the United States in 2001, Vietnamese families living in provinces with more export-oriented industries experienced greater declines in poverty relative to families residing in less exposed regions. In the study of the United States, Autor et al. (2013) found that regions that had mostly unskilled, manufacturing industries were most adversely affected by increased import competition with Chinese products during the 1990s and 2000s. The earnings differentials across local labor markets are presumed to dissipate in the long run, as workers adjust to the trade shock by changing their firm or industry of employment, or by moving out of locations with declining industries and toward locations with expanding industries. Contrary to conventional predictions, however, the evidence suggests the long-run persistence of the effects of trade shocks on labor markets in both advanced and developing economies (Autor et al. 2014; Dix-Carneiro and Kovak 2017).

Why don't people move across regions within a country despite the negative trade shock? There are various plausible reasons: Relocation costs, lack of information, and lack of required skill. First, moving is costly. Unskilled, poor workers may not have sufficient assets to finance the fixed costs of relocation. Second, housing availability is an important factor to explain immobility of low-skilled workers. Unskilled workers in the United States spend a significant portion of their incomes on housing. Because negative labor demand shocks significantly decrease housing costs in local markets, unskilled workers in the United States are less likely to migrate out of adversely affected regions than are college-educated individuals (Bound and Holzer 2015; Notowidigdo 2020). Third, individuals, particularly unskilled, less educated workers, may have fewer social contacts in growing regions and know less about alternative job market opportunities (Bound and Holzer 2015). Fourth, families and local communities may provide informal insurance to individuals, especially in developing countries where public social safety nets are weak. For example, families in India rarely move across regions because of caste-based informal insurance (Munshi and Rosenzweig 2016). Finally, workers who lose jobs in regions with more import-competing industries may not have the skills demanded by export-competing and expanding industries in other regions. For example, Young (2013) argues that the rural–urban wage gaps across the world reflect labor sorting based on human capital and skill, with skill-intensive production located in urban areas and unskilled-intensive production located in rural areas.

V   The role of government policy in the integrated market

The impact of globalization on within-country inequality cannot be separated from domestic policies that set rules to redistribute the benefits of globalization. Economists suggest that increased international trade and capital flows promote economic growth and aggregate national welfare, which can be shared with those harmed by globalization, and thus make everybody better off in the long term. Yet, the gains from globalization are not automatically redistributed without deliberate government policy changes. Government policies significantly influence market outcomes by setting market regulations and enforcing taxation and social policies to redistribute income from the rich to the poor. Although income inequality has increased in almost all countries, it still varies significantly across regions. For example, in 2016, the top 10% incomes as a share of total national income were 37% in Europe, 47% in US–Canada, 41% in China, and 55% in Brazil (Alvaredo et al. 2018). The wide differences suggest the influences of national institutions and policies.

In general, governments would have a strong incentive to moderate market income inequality caused by globalization (Gozgor and Ranjan 2017). In light of the increased inequality and job insecurity of international market fluctuations, the public would increasingly demand compensation and social protection. To avoid a public backlash against globalization, policymakers thus have a strong incentive to provide welfare compensation and cushion market dislocations (Cameron 1978; Garrett 1998; Katzenstein 1985). In fact, policymakers in established economies have expanded social welfare spending and redistributed the gained wealth to the losers of globalization to further market liberalization (often called "embedded liberalism") (Ruggie 1982). For example, West European countries such as Belgium, Denmark, and Finland have kept a lower level of income inequality by coordinating the economy and welfare system through democratic institutions.

However, in practice, compensating the losers does not always happen. Governments' political incentives and fiscal ability largely vary across countries. Some countries, particularly democratically underdeveloped developing countries, have less responsive political systems. They also have lower levels of fiscal revenues, and insufficient government budgets to build inclusive social safety nets. Because import tariffs have been easy tax sources for most countries, large-scale trade reforms often result in large losses of government revenue, except in some fast-growing emerging market economies (Ha and Rogers 2017; Rodrik 2021). Tax systems in developing countries tend to be insufficiently progressive, and often ineffective because they lack tax administrative capacity, with very high tax thresholds that prevent the application of the highest tax rates to the rich (Kanbur 2015; Lakner and Laderchi 2016).

Moreover, globalization puts "race-to-the-bottom" pressure on tax rates and social welfare systems (Busemeyer 2009; Genschel 2002; Rodrik 1997; Strange 1996). Traditional redistributive policies, such as generous social welfare programs and high levels of corporate taxes, can increase production costs and make markets and goods less attractive to international investors and consumers. In particular, increasingly mobile capital constrains governments' ability to raise the necessary tax revenues. To compete against trading partners and attract international investments, governments feel pressure to lower corporate taxes and thus downsize welfare programs. In fact, corporate tax rates in advanced economies have decreased due to tax competition, while the tax burden on wages has remained steady (Rodrik 2021).

Although globalization places some constraints on redistributive policies, the role of the government remains powerful, as it can significantly affect net income inequality with deliberate policy choices. Despite the efficiency costs of social welfare protection, a high level of income inequality can increase social instability and political inequality while hindering human development and economic growth (Alesina and Rodrik 1994; Case and Deaton 2020; Galor and Moav 2004; Persson and Tabellini 1994). Thus, policymakers must focus more on how to design compensation schemes that share increased wealth with the less fortunate, while also ensuring growth. For example, government investments in public education can help provide a larger number of highly skilled workers, which are in greater demand in tradable sectors of both developed and developing countries. Given that the losers of globalization are concentrated in certain social groups and regions, governments can also direct social protection and compensation to them.

VI   Conclusion and policy implication

This chapter has outlined how economic globalization, intertwined with technological progress, reallocates resources and jobs across firms, industries, and regions, benefitting certain social groups more than others. The main takeaways in this chapter are that: Globalization has brought significant benefits to open markets, but some gained more than others within countries. Although globalization enlarges national welfare, the increasing income inequality in either relative or absolute term can expand public discontent over free trade and capital (Burgoon et al. 2019). According to a recently published IPSOS (2021), the public support for globalization, trade, and foreign investments still remains strong even in the midst of the global pandemic. However, publics worldwide expressed significant concern over rising income inequality, e.g., 90% in Brazil, 81% in Germany, 70% in Britain, and 56% in the US. According to the PEW Global Attitudes surveys (Pew Research Center 2018), citizens in advanced economies have expressed increased discontent over the impact of free trade on earnings and employment opportunities. Citizens in emerging markets have also raised some concerns about the impact of trade on inflation, which can affect their real wages and incomes.

Economic deprivation and public discontent have been accompanied by the rise of populist radical parties and politicians, who carried anti-globalization, anti-cosmopolitan, or anti-international organization appeals (Burgoon et al. 2019). The backlash against international trade has recently been observed in high-income economies such as the United States, the United Kingdom, and other West European countries (see Winslett, Chapter 10 this volume). For example, in the 2016 presidential election, Donald Trump won the presidency by putting forward anti-globalization and anti-Chinese slogans. Yet, these phenomena are not limited to advanced economies; they are also widespread amongst high-performing emerging market democracies. For example, in the 2018 Hungarian elections, Fidesz (Hungarian Civic Alliance) openly raised the battle against foreign companies, the International Monetary Fund, and the European Union to end the subordination of the national economy to them. The populist parties and politicians often purposely directed the public discontent and resentment to anti-immigrant and ethnopopulist propaganda. And, most attracted to the anti-immigrant narratives were those who were harmed by or alienated from the benefits of market liberalization (Autor et al. 2020; Pehe 2018; Szczerbiak 2017).

Given the benefits of globalization, it is not in the best interest of anyone to undo market liberalization. Although the support of protectionism might be grounded in empathy for those less fortunate, market protection would not improve the lives of unskilled, poor people in rich countries. Rather, import tariffs would increase the prices of goods, and thus reduce their real incomes. Countries around the globe are in different stages of globalization. Thus, some might consider growth-enhancing effects to be more important, while others are more concerned about the distributional effects. Still, as more countries experience greater economic globalization and get deeper into the global production networks, the distributional issues of global trade and investment will become central policy issues.

References

Acemoglu, Daron. 2002. "Technical Change, Inequality, and the Labor Market." *Journal of Economic Literature* 40(1): 7–72.

Alesina, Alberto, and Dani Rodrik. 1994. "Distributive Politics and Economic Growth." *Quarterly Journal of Economics* 109(2): 465–90.

Alvaredo, Facundo, Lucas Chancel, Thomas Piketty, Emmanuel Saez, and Gabriel Zucman. 2018. *The World Inequality Report 2018*. Cambridge, MA: Harvard University Press.

Attanasio, Orazio, Pinelopi K. Goldberg, and Nina Pavcnik. 2004. "Trade Reforms and Wage Inequality in Colombia." *Journal of Development Economics* 74(2): 331–66.

Autor, David H., David Dorn, and Gordon H. Hanson. 2013. "The China Syndrome: Local Labor Market Effects of Import Competition in the United States." *American Economic Review* 103(6): 2121–68.

Autor, David H., David Dorn, Gordon H. Hanson, and Jae Song. 2014. "Trade Adjustment: Worker-Level Evidence." *Quarterly Journal of Economics* 129(4): 1799–1860.

Autor, David, David Dorn, Gordon Hanson, and Kaveh Majlesi. 2020. "Importing Political Polarization? The Electoral Consequences of Rising Trade Exposure." *American Economic Review* 110(10): 3139–83.

Baier, Scott L., and Jeffrey H. Bergstrand. 2007. "Do Free Trade Agreements Actually Increase Members' International Trade?" *Journal of International Economics* 71(1): 72–95.

Bergh, Andreas, and Therese Nilsson. 2010. "Do Liberalization and Globalization Increase Income Inequality?" *European Journal of Political Economy* 26(4): 488–505.

Berman, E., and S. Machin. 2000. "Skill-Biased Technology Transfer Around the World." *Oxford Review of Economic Policy* 16(3): 12–22.

Bound, John, and Harry J. Holzer. 2015. "Demand Shifts, Population Adjustments, and Labor Market Outcomes during the 1980s." *Journal of Labor Economics* 18(1): 20–54.

Bourguignon, François. 2016. "Inequality and Globalization: How the Rich Get Richer as the Poor Catch Up." *Foreign Affairs* 95(1): 11–15.

Bown, C. P., and M. A. Crowley. 2016. "The Empirical Landscape of Trade Policy," in *The Handbook of Commercial Policy, Volume 1A*, edited by B. Staiger and K. Bagwell. Elsevier.

Burgoon, Brian, Sam van Noort, Matthijs Rooduijn, and Geoffrey Underhill. 2019. "Positional Deprivation and Support for Radical Right and Radical Left Parties." *Economic Policy* 34(97): 49–93.

Busemeyer, Marius R. 2009. "From Myth to Reality: Globalisation and Public Spending in OECD Countries Revisited." *European Journal of Political Research* 48(4): 455–82.

Cadot, Olivier, Celine Carrere, and Vanessa Strauss-Kahn. 2011. "Export Diversification: What's Behind the Hump?" *The Review of Economics and Statistics* 93(2): 590–605.

Cameron, David R. 1978. "The Expansion of the Public Economy: A Comparative Analysis." *American Political Science Review* 72(4): 1243–61.

Card, David, and John E. DiNardo. 2002. "Skill-Biased Technological Change and Rising Wage Inequality: Some Problems and Puzzles." *Journal of Labor Economics* 20(4): 733–83.

Case, Anne, and Angus Deaton. 2020. *Deaths of Despair and the Future of Capitalism.* Princeton, NJ: Princeton University Press.

Conte, Andrea, and Marco Vivarelli. 2007. "Globalization and Employment: Imported Skill Biased Technological Change in Developing Countries." *IZA Discussion Papers* 1–43.

Costa, Francisco, Jason Garred, and João Paulo Pessoa. 2016. "Winners and Losers from a Commodities for Manufactures Trade Boom." *Journal of International Economics* 102: 50–69.

Dix-Carneiro, Rafael, and Brian K. Kovak. 2017. "Trade Liberalization and Regional Dynamics." *American Economic Review* 107(10): 2908–46.

Dreher, Axel. 2006. "Does Globalization Affect Growth? Evidence from a New Index of Globalization." *Applied Economics* 38(10): 1091–1110.

Eaton, Jonathan, and Samuel Kortum. 2002. "Technology, Geography, and Trade." *Econometrica* 70(5): 1741–79.

Fajnzylber, Pablo, and Ana Margarida Fernandes. 2009. "International Economic Activities and Skilled Labour Demand : Evidence from Brazil and China." *Applied Economics* 41: 563–77.

Feenstra, Robert, and Gordon Hanson. 1995. "Foreign Investment, Outsourcing and Relative Wages." *NBER Working Paper* 5121.

Frias, Judith A., David S. Kaplan, Eric Verhoogen, and David Alfaro-Serrano. 2018. "Exports and Wage Premia: Evidence from Mexican Employer-Employee Data." *CDEP-CGEG Working Paper #64.*

Furceri, Davide, Prakash Loungani, and Jonathan D. Ostry. 2019. "The Aggregate and Distributional Effects of Financial Globalization: Evidence from Macro and Sectoral Data." *Journal of Money, Credit and Banking* 51(S1): 163–98.

Galor, Oded, and Omer Moav. 2004. "From Physical to Human Capital Accumulation: Inequality and the Process of Development." *Review of Economic Studies* 71(4): 1001–26.

Garrett, Geoffrey. 1998. *Partisan Politics in the Global Economy.* New York: Cambridge University Press.

Genschel, Philipp. 2002. "Globalization, Tax Competition, and the Welfare State." *Politics and Society* 30(2): 245–75.

Goldberg, Pinelopi, and Nina Pavcnik. 2016. "The Effects of Trade Policy," in *The Handbook of Commercial Policy, Volume 1A,* edited by B. and K. B. Staiger. Elsevier (pp. 161–206).

Gozgor, Giray, and Priya Ranjan. 2017. "Globalisation, Inequality and Redistribution: Theory and Evidence." *World Economy* 40(12): 2704–51.

Ha, Eunyoung. 2012. "Globalization, Government Ideology, and Income Inequality in Developing Countries." *Journal of Politics* 74(2): 541–57.

Ha, Eunyoung, and Melissa Rogers. 2017. "What's Left to Tax? Partisan Reallocation of Trade Taxation in Less Developed Countries." *Political Research Quarterly* 70(3): 495–508.

Handley, Kyle. 2014. "Exporting under Trade Policy Uncertainty: Theory and Evidence." *Journal of International Economics* 94(1): 50–66.

Handley, Kyle, and Nuno Limão. 2017. "Policy Uncertainty, Trade, and Welfare: Theory and Evidence for China and the United States." *American Economic Review* 107(9): 2731–83.

Hanson, Gordon H. 2012. "The Rise of Middle Kingdoms: Emerging Economies in Global Trade." *Journal of Economic Perspectives* 26(2): 41–64.

Hanson, Gordon H., Raymond J. Mataloni, and Matthew J. Slaughter. 2005. "Vertical Production Networks in Multinational Firms." *Review of Economics and Statistics* 87(4): 664–78.

Harrison, Ann, and Margaret McMillan. 2011. "Offshoring Jobs? Multinationals and U.S. Manufacturing Employment." *Review of Economics and Statistics* 93(3): 857–75.

IPSOS. 2021. *Global Trends 2021: Aftershocks and Continuity.*

Jaumotte, Florence, Subir Lall, and Chris Papageorgiou. 2013. "Rising Income Inequality: Technology, or Trade and Financial Globalization?" *IMF Economic Review* 61(2): 271–309.

Kanbur, R. 2015. "Globalization and Inequality," in *Handbook of Income Distribution*, Volume 2, edited by A. B. Atkinson and F. Bourguignon. Elsevier.

Karabarbounis, Loukas, and Brent Neiman. 2014. "The Global Decline of the Labor Share." *Quarterly Journal of Economics* 129(1): 61–103.

Katzenstein, Peter J. 1985. *Small States in World Markets.* Ithaca, NY: Cornell University Press.

Keohane, Robert O., and Joseph S. Nye. 2000 "Globalization: What's New? What's Not? (And So What?)" *Foreign Policy* 118 (Spring, 2000): 104–19.

Lakner, Christoph. 2016. "The Implications of Thomas Piketty's 'Capital in the 21st Century.'" *World Bank Policy Research Working Paper*. No. 7776.

Lakner, Christoph, and Ruggeri C. Laderchi. 2016. "Pulling Apart? The Growth of the Super-Rich in East Asia and Pacific and Its Implications for Inclusive Growth." World Bank.

Lakner, Christoph, and Branko Milanovic. 2016. "Global Income Distribution: From the Fall of the Berlin Wall to the Great Recession." *World Bank Economic Review* 30(2): 203–32.

Lundberg, Mattias, and Lyn Squire. 2003. "The Simultaneous Evolution of Growth and Inequality." *The Economic Journal* 113(487): 326–44.

Mazumdar, Dipak, and Ata Mazaheri. 2002. *Wages and Employment in Africa.* Aldershot: Ashgate.

McCaig, Brian. 2011. "Exporting out of Poverty: Provincial Poverty in Vietnam and U.S. Market Access." *Journal of International Economics* 85(1): 102–13.

Milanovic, Branko, and Lyn Squire. 2005. "Does Tariff Liberalization Increase Wage Inequality? Some Empirical Evidence." *World Bank Policy Research Working Paper* 3571.

Muendler, Marc Andreas, and Sascha O. Becker. 2010. "Margins of Multinational Labor Substitution." *American Economic Review* 100(5): 1999–2030.

Munshi, Kaivan, and Mark Rosenzweig. 2016. "Networks and Misallocation: Insurance, Migration, and the Rural–Urban Wage Gap." *American Economic Review* 106(1): 46–98.

Notowidigdo, Matthew J. 2020. "The Incidence of Local Labor Demand Shocks." *Journal of Labor Economics* 38(3): 687–725.

Ortiz-Ospina, Esteban, Diana Beltekian, and Max Roser. 2014. "Trade and Globalization." *Our World in Data*. https://ourworldindata.org/.

Pehe, Jiri. 2018. "Czech Democracy under Pressure." *Journal of Democracy* 29(3): 65–77.

Persson, Torsten, and Guido Tabellini. 1994. "Is Inequality Harmful for Growth?" *American Economic Review* 84(3): 600–21.

Pew Research Center. 2018. *Americans, Many in Advanced Economies, Not Convinced of Benefits of Trade.*

Ravallion, Martin. 2016. "Are the World's Poorest Being Left behind?" *Journal of Economic Growth* 21(2): 139–64.

Ravallion, Martin. 2018. "Inequality and Globalization: A Review Essay." *Journal of Economic Literature* 56(2): 620–42.

Rodrik, Dani. 1997. *Has Globalization Gone Too Far?* Washington, DC: Institute for International Economics.

Rodrik, Dani. 2021. "A Primer on Trade and Inequality." *HKS Working Paper* No. RWP21–031.

Ruggie, John Gerard. 1982. "International Regimes, Transactions, and Change: Embedded Liberalism in the Postwar Economic Order." *International Organization* 36(2): 379–415.

Schott, Peter K. 2003. "A Comparison of Latin American and Asian Product Exports to the United States, 1972 to 1999." *Latin American Journal of Economics – Formerly Cuadernos de Economía* 40(121): 414–22.

Schott, Peter K. 2004. "Across-Product Versus Within-Product Specialization in International Trade." *The Quarterly Journal of Economics* 119(2): 647–78.

Stolper, W. F., and P. A. Samuelson. 1941. "Protection and Real Wages." *Review of Economic Studies* 9(1): 58–73.

Strange, Susan. 1996. *The Retreat of the State: The Diffusion of Power in the World Economy.* Cambridge: Cambridge University Press.

Szczerbiak, Aleks. 2017. "Power without Love: Patterns of Party Politics in Post-1989 Poland," in *Post-Communist EU Member States: Parties and Party Systems.* New York: Routledge (pp. 105–38).

Topalova, Petia. 2010. "Factor Immobility and Regional Impacts of Trade Liberalization: Evidence on Poverty from India." *American Economic Journal: Applied Economics* 2(4): 1–41.

Wacziarg, Romain, and Jessica Seddon Wallack. 2004. "Trade Liberalization and Intersectoral Labor Movements." *Journal of International Economics* 64(2): 411–39.

WDI. 2021. *World Development Indicators.* Washington, DC: World Bank.

Young, Alwyn. 2013. "Inequality, the Urban–Rural Gap, and Migration." *The Quarterly Journal of Economics* 128(4): 1727–85.

Zhu, Susan Chun, and Daniel Trefler. 2005. "Trade and Inequality in Developing Countries: A General Equilibrium Analysis." *Journal of International Economics* 65(1): 21–48.

2. Away from the Global North: new directions in the politics of trade

Ida Bastiaens and Evgeny Postnikov

Introduction

For decades, mainstream knowledge production in international political economy (IPE) has occurred in the Global North and/or relied on empirical assessments of these developed countries (Taylor 2005, Helleiner and Rosales 2017). Mantz (2019), for example, points to Eurocentrism and the resulting "colonality of knowledge" in IPE. Limited attempts have been made to expand the scope of mainstream IPE work (see Cohen 2014, Deciancio and Quiliconi 2020), despite calls for reconceptualizing the "international" in IPE to centrally include non-western peoples, knowledge, and histories (Mantz 2019) and become "global" (Helleiner and Rosales 2017). Within IPE, scholarship on the politics of trade has also focused on analyzing trade policies of developed nations, such as the United States and European Union (Taylor 2005). Yet, as Deciancio and Quiliconi (2020, p. 260) explain, "IPE in the periphery has been marked by the struggle for economic development, access to credit and foreign aid, debt payment, regional integration to access a better international insertion, and adding value to its exports. These concerns put the focus on different needs and required different approaches from those of developed countries to understand their realities."

As a result, in this chapter, we argue that it is time for IPE scholars to shift their North-centric focus and engage more with the politics of trade in the Global South. Given the increased importance of the developing world and emerging economies in global trade, neglecting their study risks omitting important trends in the North–South cooperation and can result in a failure to explain and predict the evolution of liberal international order and its institutional forms, including the global trade regime, at this critical juncture in history (see Hopewell 2021). The recent surge in economic nationalism and protectionist populism across the developed world underscores the centrality of the developing world for the future of economic cooperation centered around rules-based trade. Given the globalization backlash that is occurring in the Global North (Walter 2021), the South may emerge as a critical champion of the liberal order during the hegemonic interregnum or be a force of anti-neoliberalism. Thus, analyzing attitudes towards global trade in the Global South is paramount.

We suggest focusing future scholarly inquiry along the two interrelated dimensions: (1) understanding trade policy preferences in the Global South and (2) examining the emerging contours of South–South trade cooperation and policymaking, such as the proliferation of South–South preferential trade agreements (PTAs) and the role of developing nations in the World Trade Organization (WTO). Extensive research exists on societal and individual preferences in the North, shedding light on the recent turn towards economic nationalism. Yet, the endurance of international economic openness in the South, registered in public opinion surveys (Stokes 2018), calls for a similar focus on trade preferences of constituents and political and economic actors in the developing world. Concurrently, a better understanding of trade policy institutions channeling these preferences and shaping the form of South–South trade cooperation is also needed for a holistic view of the role of the Global South in world trade. Examining these empirical domains will expand our knowledge of the IPE of trade, and improve the generalization of existing claims, increasing the accuracy of deeply held theoretical assumptions and trade policy models.

Current scholarship on the politics of trade: oscillating between the North and the South

Extensive research explores trade liberalization, preferential trade agreement (PTA) formation and design, World Trade Organization (WTO) participation, trade preferences, and trade impacts in the Global North (Goldstein 2017, Kim and Osgood 2019, Milner 1999). A smaller yet still large and growing body of work explores similar issues of trade agreement design, participation, attitudes, and consequences of trade between the Global North and the Global South (Baccini 2019, Bastiaens and Postnikov 2019, Greenaway and Milner 1990). Economists explore the impacts of South–South trade (Bloomfield 2020, Goldberg et al. 2004, Gourdon 2007, Horner 2016, Kowalski and Shepherd 2008, Moncarz and Vaillant 2010), but the role of politics is often marginal in these analyses. Instead, the focus is typically on trade diversion, labor markets, or income effects. Yet, understanding public attitudes or how institutions mediate such trade effects is critical to understanding the broader welfare and trajectory of trade in the Global South (see Nielson 2003 for example). What have IPE scholars found on these issues to date?

IPE research on trade in the Global South often focuses on liberalization processes and institutions. Why and how Southern countries liberalize is a central theme of much IPE work. Internal factors like democracy (Milner and Kubota 2005, Eichengreen and Leblang 2008) as well as external ones such as international organizations or policy diffusion (Baccini and Urpelainen 2014, Mansfield and Reinhardt 2015, Simmons and Elkins 2004) are highlighted as determinants of global economic integration. Structuralist, Marxist, and Dependency theories center the study of trade in the Global South (see Deciancio and Quiliconi 2020, Helleiner and Rosales 2017): much of the Southern view thus critiques and challenges the mainstream neoliberal discourse and practices. Research on Southern participation in the WTO forums and WTO disputes and negotiations is also extensive (Busch and Reinhardt 2006, Bouët et al. 2005, Goldstein, Rivers, and Tomz 2007). Findings highlight increased acrimony and ineffectiveness at the WTO due to differing interests of the Global North and South (Goldstein 2017) as well as advantages of richer nations in the dispute settlement forum (Kim 2008, Bown 2005, see also Davis and Bermeo 2009). Finally, welfare effects of trade and trade agreements in the Global South have been explored by various scholars (Rudra 2008, Kim 2012, Peinhardt et al. 2019, Brandi et al. 2020, Desai and Rudra 2019, Greenhill et al. 2009, Cao and Prakash 2012, Neumayer and DeSoysa 2011, Bastiaens and Rudra 2018). The findings are overwhelmingly positive for labor and environmental outcomes, despite some debate (Mosley and Uno 2007), but they certainly are not regarding the fiscal budgets of governments. However, much of this work examines the effects of North–South trade or overall trade flows (in total or by sector), without disaggregating South–South trade relationships or trade agreements. Gamso (2017) is an exception. In fact, he finds that the aforementioned race to the top in labor is driven by a small group of countries and does not translate to South–South trade. Weaker domestic institutions protecting labor (see Rudra 2002) or less competitive pressure or norms for labor rights diffusion (Gamso 2017) are possible explanations for this finding.

The first agenda for future research: trade preferences in the Global South

Scholarship on trade preferences typically employs data solely or mostly from the advanced industrialized world (for example, Mayda and Rodrik 2005). The findings on the determinants of attitudes on trade has transitioned over time from one focused on income and employment to an exploration of non-material and consumption-based factors as well (see Norris and Inglehart 2019 for a debate of such determinants). Classically, scholars pointed to economic factors or the distributional consequences of globalization as the key to individual preferences on trade, using factor endowment (Heckscher–Ohlin) and sector specific (Ricardo–Viner) models (Rogowski 1987, Hiscox 2002). Baker (2003) advanced the debate by pointing to how consumption, not just skill, affects preferences on trade. Similarly, Mansfield and Mutz (2009) highlight how sociotropic welfare effects, not just egotropic gains or losses, can influence preferences on globalization. Yet, due to continuing puzzles concerning how individuals support policies against their economic interest, recent research extends this classic work by pointing to the role of non-material forces and characteristics on individual preferences on trade (Mansfeld and Mutz 2013). Scholars point to nationalism or fair trade values as influences of trade attitudes (Margalit 2012, Mansfield and Mutz 2013, Ehrlich 2018). Additionally, education as well as ignorance have been cited as explaining puzzling trade attitudes in the Global North (Rho and Tomz 2017, Hainmueller and Hiscox 2006). Government compensation policies can also play a role in boosting support for trade (i.e., embedded liberalism), following Hays et al. (2005) and Walter (2010).

Do these findings translate to the Global South? First, unlike recent work indicating a backlash to globalization in the North (Norris and Inglehart 2019, Baker 2005), research points to broader support for globalization and trade in the South, especially in recent years (Stokes 2018). Baker (2003), for example, explains this widespread support through the consumption effects of trade. Others, following the classic factor endowment model, would point to the labor benefits (and corresponding support by low-skilled workers) of trade in the Global South (see Stolper and Samuelson 1941, Mayda and Rodrik 2005). Nooruddin and Rudra (2014) examine how developing countries use public employment as an embedded liberalism strategy to maintain support for trade. One conclusion of this work is that while compensation for domestic actors vulnerable to globalization manifests differently in the Global South, the ultimate result mirrors the findings from embedded liberalism work in the North.

Yet, much remains underexplored or without consensus. First, a debate is emerging on the relevance of the Heckscher–Ohlin model in the developing world. Dolan and Milner (2019) find evidence of it in Africa, while Beaulieu et al. (2005) do not in Latin America. Regional differences, limited data, differing skill categorizations could all contribute to these mixed findings. Research on attitudes towards trade-related welfare issues also presents mixed findings. On one hand, Bastiaens and Postnikov (2019) employ a survey experiment to show that labor and environmental provisions in PTAs do not increase support for freer trade in the Global South (while they do in the Global North) because the public in the Global South views such provisions as disguised protectionism (see also Kolben 2006). While Bernauer and Nyugen (2015) and Spilker et al. (2018) indicate labor and environmental concerns alongside trade liberalization in the Global South. Spilker et al.'s (2018) experiment also points out that the economic implications of trade liberalization are less salient than "antipathy toward particular countries" in explaining trade preferences in Costa Rica, Nicaragua, and Vietnam. Better understanding such public preferences as well as potential perceived trade-offs in the developing world, for example, between liberalizing and protecting the environment, will advance understanding of how the tide of globalization may turn in the future, and what types of disputes will emerge in trade negotiations and implementation.

It is certainly important for future work to analyze the relevance to the South of arguments from the research on the North. For example, it is important to establish the salience of individual trade attitudes when participating in politics and voting for a particular issue or candidate. Yet, much other scholarship on the decision to act in the political arena or voting preferences relies on data from the Global North (see Marshall and Fisher 2014, Jensen et al. 2016). Urbatsch (2013), who compares attitudes on globalization to voting patterns in Costa Rica, is an exception.

Two areas within this field of work on globalization and participation need further investigation. First, scholars must investigate non-material determinants of trade preferences in the South. Identity politics, for one, is grossly underexplored in IPE: we know little about how race and ethnicity affect trade preferences and policies. Guisinger (2017), for instance, explores race and trade preferences, but only in the Global North. Focusing more on the Global South, Singh (2020) points to the role of racism within the values and institutions of trade policymaking. More work on such topics is undoubtedly appropriate and needed reflecting the broader post-colonial reorientation of IPE scholarship. Second, the role of civil society and firms in shaping preferences is little understood in the developing world. Data gathering on lobbying activity in the developing world is critical (see, for example, Baccini 2019, Kim and Osgood 2019).

Thus, arguments and analyses on the relationship between trade attitudes and political behavior in the Global South are quite underdeveloped. It is critical to understand how preferences are mediated through institutions and translated into developing countries' policies. It would be helpful to have both new surveys and to employ data from existing polls in the Global South. To date, much of the work on the Global South focuses only on Latin America or a few countries, such as Vietnam, so a more systematic perspective is needed. In this way scholars may be able to signal how states of the Global South will lead and challenge liberal policies into the future.

The second agenda for future research: the rise of South–South PTAs and developing countries in the multilateral trade system

There is extensive scholarship examining the role of the Global South, particularly some of its key economies, within the multilateral trading system (Hopewell 2016). Collectively, Brazil, India and China are playing a more assertive role within the WTO, disrupting the US-led liberal institutional order. However, the global trade system nowadays consists of the two major and equally important pillars, the WTO and a plethora of PTAs that emerged largely as a response to the Doha round impasse (Baldwin 2016). We focus on the latter first, then the former.

While North–South PTAs have been a feature of the global trade system for a long time, South–South PTAs have proliferated since the 2000s. Agreements formed among developing nations, often excluding China, constitute the biggest proportion of new PTAs (Donno and Rudra 2019). Extensive literature has emerged to explore the causes and effects of North–South agreements (see Baccini 2019). Scholars have mapped out the design of PTAs and have amassed a large amount of data on their various provisions (see Dür et al. 2014, Raess and Sari 2018, Morin et al. 2018). Various studies explore the rationale behind the inclusion of such provisions, particularly focusing on trade-plus/non-trade issues, such as social and environmental standards, intellectual property rights, and other regulatory issues (e.g., Lechner 2016, Postnikov 2020, Bastiaens and Postnikov 2019). There is a robust consensus that developing countries act as policy-takers in these agreements as the Global North tries to externalize its own regulations (Young 2015). Yet, the political drivers and institutional variation of South–South trade is substantially underexplored by existing scholarship.

Nascent literature investigates the causes of South–South PTA formation. Donno and Rudra (2019) attribute this trend to the growing influence of China and a desire by smaller developing nations to offset it. Yet, few studies examine the design of South–South PTAs, leaving a large empirical gap (e.g., Blümer et al. 2020). Gamso and Postnikov (2021) build on the DESTA dataset

(Dür et al. 2014) to map the growing depth of South–South PTAs. They show that it is increasing over time, as agreements cover new regulatory issues, and they attribute this trend to the socialization of Southern trade executives within North–South agreement networks. However, disentangling the design of South–South agreements remains a critical task, given the multiplicity of their provisions, the variation in the PTA depth across the Global South, and the complexity of diffusion processes happening within the trade agreement network. Similarly, the historical and political nature of South–South trade cooperation and resistance from the Global North needs to be taken into account in such empirical work (Scott 2016). Future research should also critically analyze the effects of South–South PTAs on various economic and social outcomes in the developing world. Studies of the welfare effects of such agreements remain limited (e.g., Bloomfield 2020).

Importantly, understanding the design and drivers of the South–South trade cooperation needs to move beyond the highly descriptive material on agreement texts of PTAs (Allee and Elsig 2019). The key next step is to explore political variables. This necessitates a closer focus on trade policymaking institutions in the developing world. While the analysis of trade policymaking institutions across the Global North abounds, the paucity of data has blocked all but a few scholars from exploring the domestic politics of trade in the Global South (e.g., Hankla and Kuthy 2013).

A more extensive focus on the institutional dynamics of trade policy in the South will allow scholars to test the generalizability of some popular models, including the Open Economy Politics (Lake 2009), to non-traditional institutional contexts and probe the role of societal preferences over trade policy outcomes across the heterogenous Global South. Taylor (2005), for example, explains that the domestic outcomes of globalization in Africa, South Asia, the Pacific region, and Central Asia are largely neglected in IPE studies (see also Deciancio and Quiliconi 2020). Future work needs to compare and contrast the trade policies of various developing nations, moving beyond the tendency to focus on only the BRICS and their institutions. More comparisons could also be drawn between the role of societal preferences and political institutions in the North and South. For example, Helleiner's (2021) comparison of economic nationalism in the US and China shows the distinctiveness of economic policymaking in the South. The role of Southern policy elites and their views on global trade should not be underestimated (Scott 2015). Exploring how factors like geo-economic competition, socialization, and domestic preferences interact and shape various forms of South–South trade cooperation is a crucial task for future scholarship on the IPE of trade.

Finally, in regard to the Global South and the global trade regime, future work should undoubtedly explore the role of developing countries in the WTO. As the new, and first African, Director-General of the WTO Ngozi Okonjo-Iweala takes on prominent challenges in the WTO, the Global South members are urgently seeking attention to the Appellate Body's lack of judges, e-commerce, and agriculture (see Bartmann 2021). More generally, defining "special and differential treatment" (SDT) in the WTO is hotly contested by the members, and a burgeoning area of research ripe for further investigation. SDTs are provisions in the WTO that give developing countries special rights, such as extended time to implement WTO rules, technical support from the Global North, and preferential tariff schemes (Ornelas 2016). While in principle SDTs help the Global South meet WTO obligations, Bacchus and Manak (2021) assert that SDTs do not support the integration of developing nations into the global trade regime. Instead, SDTs lead to exemptions from WTO obligations, which does not effectively promote development or full integration into the global trade regime (see Bacchus and Manak 2021). Further exploration of SDTs in the WTO would help explain how multilateral institutions can better address the needs and preferences of the Global South, while ameliorating the North–South conflict within the trade system (see Ornelas 2016).

Conclusion

In this chapter, we argue that more scholarly attention in IPE needs to be devoted to the trade politics of the Global South. We have suggested several avenues for future research focusing on understanding trade preferences in the Global South, the drivers, design, and effects of South–South PTAs, developing countries' role in the WTO, and examining the variation in trade policymaking institutions in the developing world. What does this mean in practice? First, scholars should prioritize the collection of further data on issues related to trade in the Global South. Surveys on public attitudes and political participation on trade issues as well as lobbying efforts by firms and non-governmental organizations are especially apt. Second, analyzing the role of non-economic inputs and outputs of trade practices, including ideational and geo-economic factors, is critical for future IPE scholarship. Understanding trade policymaking, public preferences on it, and the welfare effects of it in the Global South requires a more rigorous focus on factors such as race and ethnicity, as well state power and domestic institutions.

Ultimately, shifting away from the exclusive focus on the trade politics and policymaking in the Global North will advance the understanding of various forms of South–South trade cooperation against the backdrop of the current crisis of liberal international order. Such future research is an important step to globalize IPE, ensuring that the voices, histories, and events of the Global South are better centered within our understanding of the causes and consequences of trade. Perhaps this will also help introduce the currently neglected issues of race, colonialism, and the challenges of neoliberalism to the forefront of *mainstream* IPE scholarship.

References

Allee, T. and Elsig, M. 2019. "Are the Contents of International Treaties Copied and Pasted? Evidence from Preferential Trade Agreements." *International Studies Quarterly* 63(3): 603–613.

Bacchus, James and Inu Manak. 2021. *The Development Dimension: Special and Differential Treatment in Trade.* Routledge.

Baccini, Leonardo. 2019. "The Economics and Politics of Preferential Trade Agreements." *Annual Review of Political Science* 22: 75–92.

Baccini, Leonardo and Johannes Urpelainen. 2014. *Cutting the Gordian Knot of Economic Reform: When and How International Institutions Help.* Oxford: Oxford University Press.

Baker, Andy. 2003. "Why is Trade Reform so Popular in Latin America? A Consumption-Based Theory of Trade Policy Preferences." *World Politics* 55: 423–455.

Baker, Andy. 2005. "Who Wants to Globalize? Consumer Tastes and Labor Markets in a Theory of Trade Policy Beliefs." *American Journal of Political Science* 49(4): 924–938.

Baldwin, Richard. 2016. "The World Trade Organization and the Future of Multilateralism." *Journal of Economic Perspectives* 30(1): 95–116.

Bartmann, Yvonne. "A New Era for the WTO?" *IPS.* February 3, 2021. https://www.ips -journal.eu/topics/foreign-and-security-policy/a-new-era-for-the-wto-5015/

Bastiaens, Ida and Evgeny Postnikov. 2019. "Social Standards in Trade Agreements of Free Trade Preferences: An Empirical Investigation." *Review of International Organizations* 15(4): 793–816.

Bastiaens, Ida and Nita Rudra. 2018. *Democracies in Peril: Taxation and Redistribution in Globalizing Economies.* Cambridge: Cambridge University Press.

Beaulieu, Eugene, Ravindra A. Yatawara, and Wei Guo Wang. 2005. "Who Supports Free Trade in Latin America?" *World Economy* 28(7): 941–958.

Bernauer, Thomas and Quynh Nyugen. 2015. "Free Trade and/or Environmental Protection?" *Global Environmental Politics* 15(4): 105–129.

Bloomfield, Michael. 2020. "South–South Trade and Sustainable Development: The Case of Ceylon Tea." *Ecological Economics* 167.

Blümer, Dominique, Jean-Frédéric Morin, Clara Brandi, and Axel Berger. 2020. "Environmental Provisions in Trade Agreements: Defending Regulatory Space or Pursuing Offensive Interests?" *Environmental Politics* 29(5): 866–889.

Bouët, Antoine, Jean-Christophe Bureau, Yvan Decreux, and Sébastien Jean. 2005. "Multilateral Agricultural Trade Liberalisation: The Constrasting Fortunes of Developing Countries in the Doha Round." *World Economy* 28(9): 1329–1354.

Bown, Chad. 2005. "Participation in WTO Dispute Settlement: Complainants, Interested Parties, and Free Riders." *World Bank Economic Review* 19(2): 287–310.

Brandi, Clara, Jakob Schwab, Axel Berger, and Jean-Frédéric Morin. 2020. "Do Environmental Provisions in Trade Agreements Make Exports From Developing Countries Greener?" *World Development* 129.

Busch, Marc L. and Eric Reinhardt. 2006. "Three's a Crowd: Third Parties and WTO Dispute Settlement." *World Politics* 58: 446–477.

Cao, Xun and Aseem Prakash. 2012. "Trade Competition and Environmental Regulations: Domestic Political Constraints and Issue Visibility." *Journal of Politics* 74(1): 66–82.

Cohen, Benjamin J. 2014. *Advanced International Political Economy*. Cheltenham, UK and Northampton, MA, USA: Edward Elgar Publishing.

Davis, Christina L. and Sarah Blodgett Bermeo. 2009. "Who Files? Developing Country Participation in WTO Adjudication." *Journal of Politics* 71(3): 1033–1049.

Deciancio, Melisa and Cintia Quiliconi. 2020. "Widening the Global Conversation: Highlighting the Voices of IPE in the Global South." *All Azimuth*. doi:10.20991/allazimuth.7226271

Desai, Raj M. and Nita Rudra. 2019. "Trade, Poverty, and Social Protection in Developing Countries." *European Journal of Political Economy* 60.

Dolan, Lindsay and Helen Milner. 2019. "Low-Skill Liberalizers: Support for Globalization in Africa." Working Paper.

Donno, D. and N. Rudra. 2019. "David and Goliath? Small Developing Countries, Large Emerging Markets, and South–South Preferential Trade Agreements." *International Studies Quarterly* 63(3): 574–588.

Dür, A., L. Baccini, and M. Elsig. 2014. "The Design of International Trade Agreements: Introducing a New Dataset." *Review of International Organizations* 9(3): 353–375.

Ehrlich, Sean D. 2018. *The Politics of Fair Trade*. Oxford: Oxford University Press.

Eichengreen, Barry and David Leblang 2008. "Democracy and Globalization." *Economics and Politics* 20(3): 289–334.

Gamso, Jonas. 2017. "South–South Trade and Collective Labour Laws: Do Developing Countries Race to the Top when they Trade with the South?" *Journal of International Relations and Development* 22: 954–982.

Gamso, Jonas and Evgeny Postnikov. 2021. "Leveling-up: Explaining the Depth of South–South Trade Agreements." *Review of International Political Economy*. doi:10.1080/09692290.2021.1939762

Goldberg, Pinelopi K. and Nina Pavcnik. 2004. "Trade, Inequality, and Poverty: What Do We Know? Evidence from Recent Trade Liberalization Episodes in Developing Countries." NBER Working Paper No. 10593.

Goldstein, Judith. 2017. "Trading in the Twenty-First Century: Is There a Role for the World Trade Organization?" *Annual Review of Political Science* 20: 545–564.

Goldstein, Judith, Douglas Rivers, and Michael Tomz. 2007. "Institutions in International Relations: Understanding the Effects of the GATT and the WTO on World Trade." *International Organization* 61: 37–67.

Gourdon, Julien. 2007. "Trade and Wage Inequality in Developing Countries: South–South Trade Matters." MPRA Paper 4824.

Greenaway, David and Chris Milner. 1990. "South–South Trade: Theory, Evidence, and Policy." *World Bank Research Observer* 5(1): 47–68.

Greenhill, Brian, Layna Mosley, and Aseem Prakash. 2009. "Trade-based Diffusion of Labor Rights: A Panel Study, 1986–2002." *American Political Science Review* 103(4): 669–690.

Guisinger, Alexandra. 2017. *American Opinion on Trade: Preferences without Politics.* Oxford: Oxford University Press.

Hainmueller, Jens and Michael J. Hiscox. 2006. "Learning to Love Globalization: Education and Individual Attitudes Toward International Trade." *International Organization* 60(2): 469–498.

Hankla, Charles R. and Daniel Kuthy. 2013. "Economic Liberalism in Illiberal Regimes: Authoritarian Variation and the Political Economy of Trade." *International Studies Quarterly* 57(3): 492–504.

Hays, Jude, Sean Ehrlich, and Clint Peinhardt. 2005. "Government Spending and Public Support for Trade in the OECD: An Empirical Test of the Embedded Liberalism Compromise Thesis." *International Organization* 59(2): 473–494.

Helleiner, Eric. 2021. "The Diversity of Economic Nationalism." *New Political Economy* 26(2): 229–238.

Helleiner, Eric and Antulio Rosales. 2017. "Toward Global IPE: The Overlooked Significance of the Haya-Mariátegui Debate." *International Studies Review* 19: 667–691.

Hiscox, Michael J. 2002. "Commerce, Coalitions, and Factor Mobility: Evidence from Congressional Votes on Trade Legislation." *American Political Science Review* 96(3): 593–608.

Hopewell, K. 2016. *Breaking the WTO: How Emerging Powers Disrupted the Neoliberal Project.* Stanford, CA: Stanford University Press.

Hopewell, Kristen. 2021. "Trump & Trade: The Crisis in the Multilateral Trading System." *New Political Economy* 26(2): 271–282.

Horner, Rory. 2016. "A New Economic Geography of Trade and Development? Governing South–South Trade, Value Chains and Production Networks." *Territory, Politics, Governance* 4(4): 400–420.

Jensen, J. Bradford, Dennis P. Quinn, and Stephen Weymouth. 2016. "Winners and Losers in International Trade: The Effects on U.S. Presidential Voting." NBER Working Paper No. 21899.

Kim, In Song and Iain Osgood. 2019. "Firms in Trade and Trade Politics." *Annual Review of Political Science* 22: 399–417.

Kim, Moonhawk. 2008. "Costly Procedures: Divergent Effects of Legalization in the GATT/WTO Dispute Settlement Procedures." *International Studies Quarterly* 52(3): 657–686.

Kim, Moonhawk. 2012. "Ex Ante Due Diligence: Formation of PTAs and Protection of Labor Rights." *International Studies Quarterly* 56(4): 704–719.

Kolben, K. 2006. "The New Politics of Linkage: India's Opposition to the Worker's Rights Clause." *Indiana Journal of Global Legal Studies* 13(1): 225–259.

Kowalski, Przemyslaw and Ben Shepherd. 2008. "South–South Trade in Goods." OECD Trade Policy Papers No. 40.

Lake, David A. 2009. "Open Economy Politics: A Critical Review." *Review of International Organizations* 4: 219–244.

Lechner, L. 2016. "The Domestic Battle Over the Design of Non-trade Issues in Preferential Trade Agreements." *Review of International Political Economy* 23(5): 840–871.

Mansfield, Edward D. and Diana C. Mutz. 2009. "Support for Free Trade: Self-Interest, Sociotropic Politics, and Out-Group Anxiety." *International Organization* 63(3): 425–457.

Mansfield, Edward D. and Diana C. Mutz. 2013. "Us Versus Them: Mass Attitudes Toward Offshore Outsourcing." *World Politics* 65(4): 571–608.

Mansfield, Edward D. and Eric Reinhardt. 2015. "International Institutions and the Volatility of International Trade," in *The Political Economy of International Trade*, pp. 65–96. World Scientific.

Mantz, Felix. 2019. "Decolonizing the IPE syllabus: Eurocentrism and the coloniality of knowledge in International Political Economy." *Review of International Political Economy* 26(6): 1361–1378.

Margalit, Yotam. 2012. "Lost in Globalization: International Economic Integration and the Sources of Popular Discontent." *International Studies Quarterly* 56(3): 484–500.

Marshall, John and Stephen D. Fisher. 2014. "Compensation or Constraint? How Different Dimensions of Economic Globalization Affect Government Spending and Electoral Turnout." *British Journal of Political Science* 45: 353–389.

Mayda, Anna Maria and Dani Rodrik. 2005. "Why Are Some People and Countries More Protectionist Than Others?" *European Economic Review* 49(6): 1393–1430.

Milner, Helen. 1999. "The Political Economy of International Trade." *Annual Review of Political Science* 2: 91–114.

Milner, Helen and Keiko Kubota. 2005. "Why the Move to Free Trade? Democracy and Trade Policy in the Developing Countries." *International Organization* 59(1): 107–143.

Moncarz, Pedro E. and Marcel Vaillant. 2010. "Who Wins in South–South Trade Agreements? New Evidence for Mercosur." *Journal of Applied Economics* 13(2): 305–334.

Morin, J.F., A. Dür, and L. Lechner. 2018. "Mapping the Trade and Environment Nexus: Insights from a New Dataset." Global Environmental Politics 18(1).

Mosley, Layna and Saika Uno. 2007. "Racing to the Bottom or Climbing to the Top? Economic Globalization and Collective Labor Rights." *Comparative Political Studies* 40: 923.

Neumayer, Eric and Indra DeSoysa. 2011. "Globalization and the Empowerment of Women: An Analysis of Spatial Dependence via Trade and Foreign Direct Investment." *World Development* 39(7): 1065–1074.

Nielson, Daniel. 2003. "Supplying Trade Reform: Political Institutions and Liberalization in Middle-Income Presidential Democracies." *American Journal of Political Science* 47(3): 470–491.

Nooruddin, Irfan and Nita Rudra. 2014. "Are Developing Countries Really Defying the Embedded Liberalism Compact?" *World Politics* 66(4): 603–640.

Norris, Pippa and Ronald Inglehart. 2019. *Cultural Backlash: Trump, Brexit, and Authoritarian Populism.* Cambridge: Cambridge University Press.

Ornelas, E. 2016. "Special and Differential Treatment for Developing Countries." *Handbook of Commercial Policy* 1(B): 369–432.

Peinhardt, Clint, Alisha A. Kim, and Viveca Pavon-Harr. 2019. "Deforestation and the United States–Peru Trade Promotion Agreement." *Global Environmental Politics* 19(1): 53–76.

Postnikov, E. 2020. *Social Standards in EU and US Trade Agreements.* London: Routledge.

Raess, Damian and Dora Sari. 2018. "Labor Provisions in Trade Agreements (LABPTA): Introducing a New Dataset." *Global Policy*. https://onlinelibrary.wiley.com/doi/full/ 10.1111/1758-5899.12577

Rho, Sungmin and Michael Tomz. 2017. "Why Don't Trade Preferences Reflect Economic Self-Interest." *International Organization* 71: S85–S108.

Rogowski, Ronald. 1987. "Political Cleavages and Changing Exposure to Trade." *American Political Science Review* 81: 1121–1137.

Rudra, Nita. 2002. "Globalization and the Decline of the Welfare States in Less-Developed Countries." *International Organizations* 56(2): 411–445.

Rudra, Nita. 2008. *Globalization and the Race to the Bottom in Developing Countries.* Cambridge: Cambridge University Press.

Scott, J. 2015. "The Role of Southern Intellectuals in Contemporary Trade Governance." *New Political Economy* 20(5): 633–652.

Scott, J. 2016. "The International Politics of South–South Trade." *Global Governance* 22(3): 427–445.

Simmons, Beth A. and Zachary Elkins. 2004. "The Globalization of Liberalization: Policy Diffusion in the International Political Economy." *American Political Science Review* 98(1): 171–189.

Singh, J.P. 2020. "Race, Culture, and Economics: An Example from North–South Trade Relations." *Review of International Political Economy* 28(4): 1–13.

Spilker, Gabriele, Thomas Bernauer, and Victor Umaña. 2018. "What Kinds of Trade Liberalization Agreements Do People in Developing Countries Want?" *International Interactions* 44(3): 510–536.

Stokes, Bruce. 2018. "Americans, Like Many in Other Advanced Economies, Not Convinced of Trade's Benefits." PEW Research. https:// www .pewresearch .org/ global/ 2018/ 09/ 26/ americans -like -many -in -other -advanced -economies -not -convinced-of-trades-benefits/

Stolper, Wolfgang and Paul Samuelson. 1941. "Protection and Real Wages." *Review of Economic Studies* 9(2): 58–73.

Taylor, Ian. 2005. "Globalisation Studies and the Developing World: Making International Political Economy Truly Global." *Third World Quarterly* 26(7): 1025–1042.

Urbatsch, Robert. 2013. "A Referendum on Trade Theory: Voting on Free Trade in Costa Rica." *International Organization* 67: 197–214.

Walter, Stefanie. 2010. "Globalization and the Welfare State: Testing the Microfoundations of the Compensation Hypothesis." *International Studies Quarterly* 54(2): 403–426.

Walter, Stefanie. 2021. "The Backlash Against Globalization." *Annual Review of Political Science* 24(1): 421–442.

Young, Alasdair R. 2015. "Liberalizing Trade, Not Exporting Rules: The Limits to Regulatory Co-ordination in the EU's 'New Generation' Preferential Trade Agreements." *Journal of European Public Policy* 22(9): 1253–1275.

3. Turning out or turning away: international political economy effects on political participation

Celeste Beesley and Ida Bastiaens

The winning vote for "Leave" in the Brexit referendum of 2016 took many people, including experts, by surprise. Much scholarly attention has focused on understanding why individual citizens in the United Kingdom (UK) supported leaving the European Union (EU). However, understanding the outcome of the national referendum requires an examination of both citizens' preferences *and* which segments of the electorate actually voted in the referendum. Notably, 2.9 million more voters turned out in the Brexit vote than in the previous general election, and the referendum recorded the highest turnout in England since 1992 (Cowling 2017). While political science provides various theories of political participation, less research explores how the international economy affects the decision to participate. For example, why did a referendum on the UK's economic integration in the EU spur significantly greater political participation? Were all potential voters similarly mobilized or did voters with certain demographics or ideologies respond differently to get-out-the-vote efforts for Brexit?

In international political economy (IPE) much research focuses on explaining preferences for globalization, and trade in particular.[1] IPE scholars examine both material (i.e., economic insecurity) and non-material (i.e., cultural threats) determinants of public opinion on globalization.[2] A smaller body of work in the discipline reviews how public opinion on globalization affects partisanship or vote choice.[3] However, the link between globalization and the *decision to participate* in the political arena remains understudied in IPE.

An examination of the effects of trade, foreign investment, immigration, and other globalization-related economic flows on different forms of political action is fertile ground for theorizing and empirical investigation. Understanding the connection between globalization and participation is absolutely essential

53

for assessing the overall political impact of globalization. Participation is the means by which public grievances, demands, and policy attitudes (all of which have been shown to be affected by globalization) are actually reflected in government decisions and policymaking. It is unlikely that elected officials or political parties are responsive to grievances or attitudes of citizens if they do not turn out to vote or otherwise express their voice politically. Conversely, if people are moved to vote, make political donations, or even protest in response to globalization, the economic and social effects of globalization are more likely to be reflected in the political arena.[4] Given the rising political salience of globalization in recent years, understanding how winners and losers from globalization become mobilized or quiescent in politics is vital to understanding 21st-century politics in many countries, such as in the Brexit referendum in the UK.

In this chapter, we review the existing literature on globalization and participation, highlighting unresolved debates and as-yet unexplored questions. We then propose pathways for future research about how international economic interdependence might spur or depress political participation.

Existing research

The existing literature in IPE primarily considers how globalization affects political participation by (1) influencing the structural importance of participation or (2) by creating grievances that increase incentives for political action. We briefly review each in turn.

First, scholars have found mixed evidence on whether and by what means globalization affects the structural importance of political participation. One strain of this literature focuses on the insight that voters have fewer incentives to vote when the policies proposed by different parties and candidates do not strongly differ. In such cases, the outcome of elections is relatively unimportant because, regardless of who wins, similar policies will be implemented. Global market forces and international financial institutions are often assumed to limit the kinds of taxation and spending policies that are countries can viably pursue without incurring dramatic economic costs (such as loss of capital and production to other, lower-cost locations) (see Bastiaens and Rudra 2018, Friedman 1999, Garrett 1995, Rodrik 1997, and Swank 1998 for examples). If globalization constrains governments' ability to set economic policy, globalization may then reduce incentives for the public to participate in politics because of limited policy differences across parties or candidates.

This is known as the room to maneuver (RTM) hypothesis. If globalization reduces the ability of government officials to manage their economies or respond to public demands and voters are aware of it, the public logically will have fewer incentives to turn out to vote. Scholars such as Marshall and Fisher (2015) and Steiner (2010) find evidence of lower voter turnout in globalized economies and ascribe it to limited RTM. Steiner and Martin (2012) present evidence for the RTM mechanism by demonstrating that economic integration leads political parties to be less polarized on economic dimensions. This lower polarization is, in turn, correlated with lower turnout. This effect is especially marked during an economic crisis because voters become disillusioned with the political system (Karp and Milazzo 2016).[5] These studies tend to focus on national-level measures of political participation.

In contrast, other work, which tends to rely on micro-level data, asks whether globalization influences individual-level voting behavior and/or beliefs that governments face policy limitations. Steiner (2016) shows lower reported retrospective voting for UK citizens who believe the government has limited RTM. However, the link from globalization to perceptions of RTM in this study could be stronger. The analysis does not consider objective measures of exposure to globalization (i.e., sector of employment or regional economic conditions) or attitudes towards globalization (i.e., support for protectionism). Rather, the measure of RTM perceptions simply asks about the government's influence on the economy in "today's worldwide economy." In fact, Kosmidis (2018) primes international constraints or RTM in a survey experiment and finds no effect on respondents' electoral decisions. Hellwig et al.'s (2008) survey also fails to find evidence that public perceptions of government RTM are affected by globalization.

In sum, the micro-level data on how globalization affects political participation is not consistently supportive of the assumptions the macro-level literature makes on why globalization is linked to lower voter turnout. Thus, moving forward, future work could examine how globalization affects the receptivity of government to voters and further disentangle how RTM affect citizens' decisions to participate under various economic and institutional contexts. Given the mixed findings to date, it is quite possible that RTM perceptions are conditional on electoral rules, party structure, level of globalization, or other factors.

Another strand of research on globalization and participation in IPE focuses on how globalization can create grievances and thereby change incentives to participate in the political arena. Globalization has been associated with a host of potential grievances including economic distributional consequences and inequality, governance concerns, social dislocations, and environmental problems (examples include Castles 2006, Choucri and Mistree 2009, Dreher and Gaston 2008, Doytch and Uctum 2016). Much of this research explores protest as the dependent variable (see Dodson 2015, Palmtag et al. 2020, Robertson and Teitelbaum 2011) and finds that economic or social grievances from globalization affect the incentives or ability to engage in protest activity, especially in non-democracies. Other work explores how globalization-induced grievances affect incentives to vote. Che et al. (2016), for example, find that in districts harmed by Chinese imports voter turnout is lower. Beesley and Bastiaens (2020) use survey data to highlight that voting depends on the intersection of personal and national perceptions of globalization. Individuals who feel personally harmed by globalization report lower voting intention. But, if those personally harmed believe that globalization is broadly perceived as harmful in their country,[6] their intended voting behavior is indistinguishable from those who view globalization more positively.

Building on these studies, future IPE scholarship should address the role of mediating factors such as inequality, job insecurity, and public compensation policies in the globalization-participation relationship. Globalization affects these factors (Garrett and Mitchell 2001, Hicks and Zorn 2005, Scheve and Slaughter 2004, Walter 2010), which in turn may then influence political participation (see Rosenstone 1982, Schlozman and Verba 1979, Kurer et al. 2019, Bernburg 2015). Solt (2008), for instance, finds that inequality depresses political interest, discussion, and voting, thereby producing a vicious cycle of economic and political inequality. Linking Solt's (2008) work to globalization-induced inequality would add further nuance to how and why globalization affects political participation. Mughan, Bean, and McAllister (2003), for example, highlight how economic insecurity is associated with anti-globalization, pro-populist attitudes in Australia. Yet, not only is it crucial to investigate these globalization-induced economic issues but also how they are politicized and publicized. Current scholarship debates whether economic hardship motivates greater participation when others are not experiencing hardships (Killian, Schoen, and Dusso 2008) or when others are also seen as hurting (Beesley and Bastiaens 2020). Further research is thus essential to better understand how individual and social costs and contexts affect these important political behaviors.

Future directions: scope, measures, and refining theory

Moving beyond the refining of theory, measures, and tests for the mechanisms that are already represented in existing research, there are many other avenues to explore to better understand the connection between globalization and political participation. In this section, we present various potential hypotheses about the link from globalization to participation that may be fruitful directions for future research. To better understand how globalization affects political participation, further research needs to expand our knowledge by examining (1) globalization beyond trade and FDI; (2) participation beyond voting and protesting; and (3) the scope of the current findings beyond the context of the advanced, industrialized countries. In addition, we explain how future research on globalization and participation should explore important nuances such as mediating variables, what the public actually know about the effects of globalization, and how they gain that knowledge.

Hypothesis 1: various aspects of globalization affect political participation differently

Globalization (even when focusing exclusively on international economic flows) has multiple facets. Thus, it is not accurate to think of globalization as a monolithic force uniformly affecting citizen grievances or the structural importance of participation. Different dimensions of globalization such as trade, foreign direct investment, portfolio capital flows, immigration, may be politicized or interpreted differently by citizens as they make decisions about their political behavior. Indeed, much of the existing research tends to focus on only one form of globalization at a time. Robertson and Teitelbaum (2011), for example, focus exclusively on FDI's effects on protest. Marshall and Fisher (2015), on the other hand, examine both trade and FDI separately for their impact on political behavior and find that they have differential effects on participation. They argue that trade patterns, based disproportionately in intra-industry and intra-firm flows, are slow to change, while capital flows are quite mobile and quick to react to changing circumstances. Governments are thus more constrained by capital flows than trade. Voter perceptions on limited room to maneuver are thus strongest under conditions of high capital flows (Marshall and Fisher 2015). Accordingly, they find that FDI lowers voter turnout in OECD countries, while trade measures have no effect. This finding provides strong evidence that understanding how globalization affects participation requires a serious consideration of potentially differing effects across the various dimensions of economic globalization. Other features of globalization, such as financial capital and immigration, are both growing forms of global exchange and salient features of current political and media debates. However, the potential impact that they have on political participation has not been considered. It may well be that immigration, for example, is perceived as far less constraining on a government's room to maneuver than

FDI or trade. This, in turn, is less likely to reduce participation (assuming RTM considerations dominate).

Other key dimensions of global exchange, such as outsourcing and exchange rate shocks, impact political attitudes and vote choice, and therefore are also likely to affect decisions to participate in the political arena (Rickard 2021, Ahlquist et al. 2020). These dimensions differ in the breadth of their positive and negative impacts of globalization. It is unclear whether broader or narrower globalization-induced grievances are more likely to increase (or decrease) political participation. It may be that being left behind when the rest of the country is prospering is more likely to produce a participation-enhancing grievance (Killian, Schoen, and Dusso 2008), or it may be that grievances are only seen as political and participation-inducing if they are believed to be widely experienced (Beesley and Bastiaens 2020).

Additionally, these globalization-induced redistributions may well affect participation broadly, or much more narrowly. Outsourcing may affect the participation of only certain classes, occupations, or industries of workers. Or it may cause more widespread insecurity among workers and thereby induce broad based effects on participation. Despite the paucity of research on how these flows affect participation, these questions are well worth exploring. Indeed, different effects on political mobilization have important implication for electoral outcomes, public demands for policy, and the size and content of social movements.

Hypothesis 2: globalization affects more than voting and protest, especially in democracies

Much of the research to date focuses on explaining globalization's impact on patterns of voting or protest. Yet, the public engages in other forms of political expression such as donations, petitions, and civil society activism. These other forms of political participation are more common in democracies, but also often impact politics even in less democratic systems. How might globalization affect such political behaviors? Robertson and Teitelbaum (2011), for example, claim that foreign direct investment-induced grievances, such as social dislocations due to labor migration or relatively low wages compared to similar workers in other locations, are not associated with increased protest in democracies (even though FDI does lead to protest in non-democracies). They argue that, in democracies, political parties address grievances through policy and thus avoid protest. This raises a question as to the mechanism by which globalization-induced grievances become part of candidate and party platforms. Politicians must be responding to demands that are articulated through participation in the political process. But what kind of participation? Voting, of course, is one possible answer. But what pre-electoral forms of participation may be effective in informing and influencing candidates and officeholders to be responsive to globalization-induced grievances? How can we better understand when voters feel that candidate platforms sufficiently address their grievances? Political activity such as petitions, labor movement participation, political donations, civil society activism, and campaigning are all forms of participation to explore to understand this communication between the public and government.[7] Thus, an important avenue for future research is to examine how globalization (and attitudes towards it) affects these forms of political participation. Focusing on non-voting political participation also allows us to explore globalization's effects on participation even in less democratic regimes, where voting is less influential. These promising lines of investigation into pre-electoral participation may also help to answer questions about when and why globalization becomes a salient issue in electoral competition.

Hypothesis 3: mechanisms and relationships on the linkages between globalization and political participation in the Global North may differ in the Global South

The overwhelming majority of research on globalization and participation in IPE uses observational or survey data from the Global North. Although some studies examine participation across countries at varying degrees of development (for example, Karp and Milazzo 2016), most studies do not include data to compare the effects of globalization on participation in developing versus developed countries. Fundamental questions on how globalization affects voter turnout or other forms of participation in the Global South remain unanswered.

There is a wide range of reasons why the effects of globalization on participation in developing countries may not cleanly transfer from the wealthy countries. Reduced RTM may be a mechanism by which globalization depresses political participation in wealthy countries, but in poorer countries (and particularly the world's poorest countries), governments may be perceived as having low levels of RTM independent of globalization (for example, due to low state capacity or aid dependence). Thus, globalization pressures may not noticeably depress participation, at least via the RTM mechanism, in the Global South. The effects of grievances on participation may also vary by development levels because globalization exposes the population of developing countries to a race to the bottom in labor standards, welfare states, or other protections to a greater extent than in developed countries (Davies and Valamannati 2013,

Mosley and Uno 2007, Rudra 2005, Rudra and Haggard 2005, Wibbels and Arce 2003).

Additionally, according to the widely used Heckscher–Ohlin and Stopler–Samuelson theorems of trade, in wealthy countries globalization-induced grievances are generally born by less educated and poorer people, who already have a lower baseline of conventional political participation. Yet, in the Global South the beneficiaries of globalization are expected to be individuals with less education and lower socio-economic statuses (Dutt and Mitra 2002, Mayda and Rodrik 2005, Milner and Kubota 2005). Thus, in these less developed countries, the social classes more likely to be harmed by globalization have greater socio-economic and political resources, which enables higher participation (Verba, Schlozman, and Brady 1995). This means that it is critical to investigate whether differing abilities to participate politically produces different patterns of political mobilization across national income levels. Additionally, these differences are likely to mediate how globalization shapes inequality, which has known impacts on participation, as discussed in this chapter. Analyses must look more deeply into these questions and the underlying relationship between globalization and political action in developing countries.

Hypothesis 4: factors such as institutions, race, and partisanship mediate the globalization-participation relationship

The sections above discuss productive pathways to expand the scope and conceptual operationalization of globalization-participation research in IPE. It is equally urgent to understand how institutional and social contexts shape the interaction of globalization and participation. A few of the key mediating variables might include institutional infrastructures, race and ethnicity, racism, and partisanship or polarization. These factors may make globalization-induced economic losses or gains more politically salient (leading to greater mobilization) or less so (leading to less mobilization) depending on whether the winner–loser divide cross-cuts or reinforces existing political cleavages. For example, whether individual economic losses from globalization spur or depress political activity may vary across different electoral or democratic systems. For example, voting patterns following trade shocks may differ in the majoritarian United States (see Autor et al. 2017) in comparison to those in proportional representation systems.

Race and ethnicity are egregiously understudied, underutilized factors in IPE. One of the few scholars studying race and culture in globalization interactions is Singh (2020), who presents evidence of racialized values and interactions in North–South trade relationships. Guisinger (2017) also explores race and trade preferences in the United States. A next step would be to link this work to local political attitudes and behaviors. For example, political behavior scholars outside of IPE point to race and culture as a critical link between participation and preferences (Hutchings and Valentino 2004, Leighley and Vedlitz 1999, Fraga 2018). Finally, motivated by Brexit and the 2016 election of Trump, recent work has started to unravel the effect of partisanship and polarization on attitudes towards globalization and corresponding political participation. This important research is just emerging, and much remains unknown (Autor et al. 2017).

Hypothesis 5: what voters know and how they know it is critical to understanding when and why they participate under various economic contexts

What do voters actually know and understand about the economy under globalization? Where do voters get their information on the economy? People are frequently uninformed, misinformed, or have attitudes about globalization that do not comport with its actual redistributive impacts on them. This means that public attitudes about globalization may come from sources other than objective exposure to globalization or ascribed interests based on trade theory, i.e., attitudes cannot always be deduced from individuals' skill level or industry of employment. Some existing research examines where attitudes towards economic issues come from. Alhquist, Clayton, and Levi (2014), for example, provide evidence that objective winners of trade—such as unionized dockworkers at major trade ports—can and do express anti-trade attitudes because of the networks in which they are embedded.[8] Whether objective losers—such as blue-collar manufacturing workers in import-competing industries—can express pro-globalization attitudes is less understood. Kayser and Peress (2020) look at the role of the media in affecting voter information and economic voting. Rho and Tomz (2017) find that an individual's level of knowledge changes how closely their views of globalization comport with how globalization affects their economic status. Flynn et al. (2020) show that many Americans are factually misinformed about the international economy, but that trade policy preferences are relatively stable to that misinformation. However, these studies consider stated policy preferences, rather than examining the effects of globalization and information on participation.

Research is limited on how such attitudes (either alone or in combination with objective economic impacts) might affect the link between globalization and participation. For example, the RTM mechanism, discussed above, requires that potential voters have knowledge on economic conditions and beliefs about government responsiveness. However, as Kayser and Peress (2020) point out, this RTM logic is difficult "to square with other findings in the literature that suggest that voters are ill informed ... myopic ...driven by emotions ... and apt to vote against their own interests" (p. 2).

Additionally, other research in IPE explores the role of majority opinion or bandwagon-ing on decisions to participate. For example, populist rhetoric relies on invoking the majority (the people) versus the elite (Mudde 2007: 22–23). This rhetoric frequently invokes globalization, and may convince a subset of otherwise marginalized citizens (who are currently non-voters) that they are part of a larger body of citizens and thus motivate them to vote.[9] The political and media messaging surrounding globalization could influence beliefs about the societal context (i.e., community welfare, mass support for globalization, etc.), which could politicize personal economic or cultural grievances and induce higher levels of participation (see Beesley and Bastiaens 2020).

Thus, it is important to examine other variables that influence attitudes about globalization, or to specifically account for self-reported attitudes (with some understanding of why people hold them) when theorizing about globalization's impact on participation. For example, there may be differing effects on political behavior for those directly exposed to globalization versus those who are not directly affected (workers in non-tradeable sectors, for example) if the former is influenced by economic impacts and the latter by media or partisan discussion of globalization. Better understanding of the role of the media, community effects, and political rhetoric in affecting the public's knowledge of globalization and the likelihood of participating is critical. This, in turn, will enable scholars to explain both the well-established and the new mechanisms of political behavior under various economic conditions.

Conclusion

In recent years, the salience of globalization in electoral politics has increased in a number of democracies (Meunier and Czesana 2019). This shift means that patterns of participation in response to globalization are likely changing. A few of the most notable examples in the Global North include the protests against the 1999 World Trade Organization's ministerial meeting in Seattle or the Transatlantic Trade and Investment Partnership in Europe in 2016, as well as the Brexit vote of 2016. While some prior research posits mechanisms for understanding the linkages between globalization and protest, these recent examples point to how far we are from truly understanding when and how globalization influences people's decision to stay home or show up in the political arena. In this chapter, we present promising avenues that future research may take to enhance our knowledge of these relationships across the globe. First, we encourage researchers to expand their conceptualizations of both globalization and participation. We also assert that it is crucial to understand this globalization-participation relationship in various institutional, racial, and economic contexts. A final, highly promising, and understudied direction for future research is exploring public knowledge generation and acquisition. In this way, we will learn when and how individuals choose to engage or disengage in politics in globalizing economies.

Notes

1. See, for example, Mayda and Rodrik (2005).
2. See, for example, Margalit (2012), Mansfield and Mutz (2013), Rho and Tomz (2017), Hainmueller and Hiscox (2006), and Rogowski (1987). Inglehart and Norris (2019) recently provided evidence that a cultural backlash as opposed to economic insecurity is influencing political preferences in Europe.
3. See, for example, Jensen et al. (2017), Margalit (2011), and Becker et al. (2017).
4. Of course, there is an alternate view that trade policy, for example, has a low salience among voters (Guisinger 2009). However, this is likely to vary over time and space.
5. The RTM logic also appears in work on voter preferences: Duch and Stevenson (2008) find that survey respondents in Europe have greater intentions to vote for the incumbent when they believe the politician can influence the macroeconomy; Hellwig and Samuels (2007) and Kayser (2007) explore how incumbents are not punished nor rewarded for national economic performance under globalization.
6. This echoes studies such as Colantone and Stanig (2018) who show that district-level, trade-induced harms affect political preferences.
7. While some discussion on these topics exists in activist or policy spheres (for example, Weinberg n.d.), published academic work on these topics is either largely absent or focuses on aggregate political movements, rather than individual-level participation, as in the case of labor movements (see Mosley and Uno 2007, Ross 2000) or campaign finance (Grossman and Helpman 1994).
8. Alhquist et al.'s (2014) work also begs the question of how perceptions of globalization may be influenced by certain forms of political activity, in this case unionization. This endogenous relationship is due to be further understood and rigorously tested.
9. See endnote 2 and the in-text discussion previously for references to the debate on why people support populist parties and whether they are voting in their own material self-interest.

References

Ahlquist, J.S., M. Copelovitch, and S. Walter. 2020. "The Political Consequences from External Economic Shocks: Evidence from Poland." *American Journal of Political Science.*

Alhquist, John S., Amanda B. Clayton, and Margaret Levi. 2014. "Provoking Preferences: Unionization, Trade Policy, and the ILWU Puzzle." *International Organization* 68(1): 33–75.

Autor, David, David Dorn, Gordon Hanson, and Kaveh Majlesi. 2017. "Importing Political Polarization? The Electoral Consequences of Rising Trade Exposure." NBER Working Paper No. 22637.

Bastiaens, Ida and Nita Rudra. 2018. *Democracies in Peril: Taxation and Redistribution in Globalizing Economies.* Cambridge: Cambridge University Press.

Becker, Sascha O., Thiemo Fetzer, and Dennis Novy. 2017. "Who Voted for Brexit? A Comprehensive District-Level Analysis." *Economic Policy*: 601–651.

Beesley, Celeste and Ida Bastiaens. 2020. "Globalization and Intention to Vote: The Interactive Role of Personal Welfare and Societal Context." *Review of International Political Economy* 29(2): 646–668.

Bernburg, Jon Gunnar. 2015. "Economic Crisis and Popular Protest in Iceland, January 2009: The Role of Perceived Economic Loss and Political Attitudes in Protest Participation and Support." *Mobilization: An International Quarterly* 20(2): 231–252.

Castles, S. 2006. "Guestworkers in Europe: A Resurrection?" *International Migration Review* 40(4): 741–766.

Che, Yi, Yi Lu, Justin R. Pierce, Peter K. Schott, and Zhigang Tao. 2016. "Does Trade Liberalization with China Influence U.S. Elections?" NBER Working Paper No. 22178.

Choucri, N. and D. Mistree. 2009." Globalization, Migration, and New Challenges to Governance." *Current History* 108: 173–179.

Colantone, I. and P. Stanig. 2018. "Global Competition and Brexit." *American Political Science Review* 112(2): 201–218.

Cowling, David. 2017. "General Election 2017: The Mystery of the Three Million 'Extra' Voters." BBC, May 17. Accessed February 12, 2019 at https://www.bbc.com/news/election-2017-39922798

Davies, R.A. and K.C. Valamannati. 2013. "A Race to the Bottom in Labor Standards?: An Empirical Investigation." *Journal of Development Economics* 103: 1–14.

Dodson, Kyle. 2015. "Globalization and Protest Expansion." *Social Problems* 62(1): 15–39.

Doytch, N. and M. Uctum. 2016. "Globalization and the Environmental Impact of Sectoral FDI." *Economic Systems* 40(4): 582–594.

Dreher, A. and N. Gaston. 2008. "Has Globalization Increased Inequality?" *Review of International Economics* 16: 516–536.

Duch, Raymond M. and Randolph T. Stevenson. 2008. *The Economic Vote: How Political and Economic Institutions Condition Election Results.* Cambridge: Cambridge University Press.

Dutt, Pushan and Devashish Mitra. 2002. "Endogenous Trade Policy Through Majority Voting: An Empirical Investigation." *Journal of International Economics* 58(1): 107–133.

Flynn, D.J., Yusaku Horiuchi, and Dong Zhang. 2020. "Misinformation, Economic Threat and Public Support for International Trade." *Review of International Political Economy*.

Fraga, B.L. 2018. *The Turnout Gap: Race, Ethnicity, and Political Inequality in a Diversifying America*. Cambridge: Cambridge University Press.

Friedman, Thomas L. 1999. *The Lexus and the Olive Tree*. Picador.

Garrett, Geoffrey. 1995. "Capital Mobility, Trade, and the Domestic Politics of Economic Policy." *International Organization* 49(4): 657–687.

Garrett, Geoffrey and Deborah Mitchell. 2001. "Globalization and the Welfare State: Income Transfers in the Advanced Industrialised Democracies, 1965–1990." *European Journal of Political Research* 39(2): 145–177.

Grossman, G.M. and E. Helpman. 1994. "Protection for Sale." *American Economic Review* 84(4): 833–850.

Guisinger, A. 2009. "Determining Trade Policy: Do Voters Hold Politicians Accountable?" *International Organization* 63(3): 533–557.

Guisinger, Alexandra. 2017. *American Opinion on Trade: Preferences without Politics*. Oxford: Oxford University Press.

Hainmueller, Jens and Michael Hiscox. 2006. "Learning to Love Globalization: Education and Individual Attitudes Toward International Trade." *International Organization* 60(2): 469–498.

Hellwig, T. and D. Samuels. 2007. "Voting in Open Economies: The Electoral Consequences of Globalization." *Comparative Political Studies* 40(3): 283–306.

Hellwig, Timothy T., Eve M. Ringsmuth, and John R. Freeman. 2008. "The American Public and the Room to Maneuver: Responsibility Attributions and Policy Efficacy in an Era of Globalization." *International Studies Quarterly* 52: 855–880.

Hicks, Alexander and Christopher Zorn. 2005. "Economic Globalization, the Macro Economy, and Reversals of Welfare: Expansion in Affluent Democracies, 1978–94." *International Organization* 59(3): 631–662.

Hutchings, Vincent L. and Nicholas A. Valentino. 2004. "The Centrality of Race in American Politics." *Annual Review of Political Science* 7: 383–408.

Inglehart, Ronald and Pippa Norris. 2019. Cultural Backlash: Trump, Brexit and Authoritarian Populism. Cambridge University Press.

Jensen, J.B., D.P. Quinn, and S. Weymouth. 2017. "Winners and Losers in International Trade: The Effects on US Presidential Voting." *International Organization*, 71(3): 423–457.

Karp, Jeffrey A. and Caitlin Milazzo. 2016. "Globalization and Voter Turnout in Times of Crisis," in Jack Vowles and Georgios Xezonakis (eds.), *Globalization and Domestic Politics: Parties, Elections, and Public Opinion*. Oxford: Oxford University Press, p. 190.

Kayser, M.A. 2007. "How Domestic is Domestic Politics?" *Annual Review of Political Science* 10: 341–362.

Kayser, Mark A and Michael Peress. 2020. "Do Voters Respond to the Economy or to News Reporting on the Economy? Media Effects in the Economic Vote." Presented at GRIPE in August 2020.

Killian, M., R. Schoen, and A. Dusso. 2008. "Keeping Up With the Joneses: The Interplay of Personal and Collective Evaluations in Voter Turnout." *Political Behavior* 30: 323–340.

Kosmidis, Spyros. 2018. "International Constraints and Electoral Decisions: Does the Room to Maneuver Attenuate Economic Voting?" *American Journal of Political Science* 62(3): 519–534.

Kurer, T., S. Hausermann, B. Wuest, and M. Enggist. 2019. "Economic Grievances and Political Protest." *European Journal of Political Research* 58(3): 866–892.

Leighley, Jan E. and Arnold Vedlitz. 1999. "Race, Ethnicity, and Political Participation: Competing Models and Contrasting Explanations." *Journal of Politics* 61(4): 1092–1114.

Mansfield, E.D. and D.C. Mutz. 2013. "US Versus Them: Mass Attitudes Toward Offshore Outsourcing." *World Politics* 65(4): 571–608.

Margalit, Yotam. 2011. "Costly Jobs: Trade-Related Layoffs, Government Compensation, and Voting in U.S. Elections." *American Political Science Review* 105(1): 166–188.

Margalit, Y. 2012. "Lost in Globalization: International Economic Integration and the Sources of Popular Discontent." *International Studies Quarterly* 56(3): 484–500.

Marshall, John and Stephen D. Fisher. 2015. "Compensation or Constraint? How Different Dimensions of Economic Globalization Affect Government Spending and Electoral Turnout." *British Journal of Political Science* 45: 353–389.

Mayda, Anna Maria and Dani Rodrik. 2005. "Why are Some People (and Countries) More Protectionist than Others?" *European Economic Review* 49(6): 1393–1430.

Meunier, Sophie and Rozalie Czesana. 2019. "From Back Rooms to the Street? A Research Agenda for Explaining Variation in the Public Salience of Trade Policy-Making in Europe." *Journal of European Public Policy* 26(12): 1847–1865.

Milner, H.V. and K. Kubota. 2005. "Why the Move to Free Trade? Democracy and Trade Policy in the Developing Countries." *International Organization* 59(1): 107–143.

Mosley, L. and S. Uno. 2007. "Racing to the Bottom or Climbing to the Top? Economic Globalization and Collective Labor Rights." *Comparative Political Studies* 40(8): 923–948.

Mudde, C. 2007. *Populist Radical Right Parties in Europe*. Cambridge: Cambridge University Press.

Mughan, A., C. Bean, and I. McAllister. 2003. "Economic Globalization, Job Insecurity, and the Populist Reaction." *Electoral Studies* 22(4): 617–633.

Palmtag, Tabea, Tobias Rommel, and Stefanie Walter. 2020. "International Trade and Public Protest: Evidence from Russian Regions." *International Studies Quarterly* 64(4): 939–955.

Rho, S. and M. Tomz. 2017. "Why Don't Trade Preferences Reflect Economic Self-interest?" *International Organization* 71: S85–S108.

Rickard, S. 2021. "Incumbents Beware: The Impact of Offshoring on Elections." *British Journal of Political Science* 52(2): 1–23.

Robertson, Graeme B. and Emmanuel Teitelbaum. 2011. "Foreign Direct Investment, Regime Type, and Labor Protest in Developing Countries." *American Journal of Political Science* 55(3): 665–677.

Rodrik, Dani. 1997. *Has Globalization Gone Too Far?* Washington, DC: Institute for International Economics.

Rogowski, Ronald. 1987. "Political Cleavages and Changing Exposure to Trade." *American Political Science Review* 81(4): 1121–1137.

Rosenstone, S.J. 1982. "Economic Adversity and Voter Turnout." *American Journal of Political Science* 26(1): 25–46.

Ross, G. 2000. "Labor Versus Globalization." *ANNALS of the American Academy of Political and Social Science*, 570(1): 78–91. https:// doi .org/ 10 .1177/ 000271620057000106

Rudra, N. 2005. "Are Workers in the Developing World Winners or Losers in the Current Era of Globalization?" *Studies in Comparative and International Development* 40: 29–64.

Rudra, N. and S. Haggard. 2005. "Globalization, Democracy, and Effective Welfare Spending in the Developing World." *Comparative Political Studies* 38(9): 1015–1049.

Scheve, K. and M.J. Slaughter. 2004. "Economic Insecurity and the Globalization of Production." *American Journal of Political Science* 48: 662–674.

Schlozman, K.L. and S. Verba. 1979. *Injury to Insult: Unemployment, Class, and Political Response.* Cambridge, MA: Harvard University Press.

Singh, J.P. 2020. "Race, Culture, and Economics: An Example from North–South Trade Relations." *Review of International Political Economy* 28(4): 1–13.

Solt, Frederick. 2008. "Economic Inequality and Democratic Political Engagement." *American Journal of Political Science* 52(1): 48–60.

Steiner, Nils D. 2010. "Economic Globalization and Voter Turnout in Established Democracies." *Electoral Studies* 29: 444–459.

Steiner, Nils D. 2016. "Economic Globalization, the Perceived Room to Maneuver of National Governments, and Electoral Participation: Evidence from the 2001 British General Election." *Electoral Studies*, 41: 118–128.

Steiner, Nils D. and Christian W. Martin. 2012. "Economic Integration, Party Polarisation and Electoral Turnout." *West European Politics* 35(2): 238–265.

Swank, Duane. 1998. "Funding the Welfare State: Globalization and the Taxation of Business in Advanced Market Economies." *Political Studies* 46: 671–692.

Verba, S., K.L. Schlozman, and H.E. Brady. 1995. *Voice and Equality: Civic Voluntarism in American Politics.* Cambridge, MA: Harvard University Press.

Walter, S. 2010. "Globalization and the Welfare State: Testing the Microfoundations of the Compensation Hypothesis." *International Studies Quarterly* 54(2): 403–426.

Weinberg, Adam. n.d. "Globalization of Campaign Funding: The Problem of Private Money in Politics." Democracy Matters. http:// www .democracymatters .org/ what -you -need -to -know -about -money -in -politics -2/ overview/ globalization -of -campaign-funding-the-problem-of-private-money-in-politics/

Wibbels, E. and M. Arce. 2003. "Globalization, Taxation, and Burden-Shifting in Latin America." *International Organization* 57(1): 111–136.

PART III

IPE in a crisis-driven world: mitigating and managing externally induced crises

4. International political economy and the study of financial crises

Puspa D. Amri[1]

Introduction

Financial crises are costly and traumatic events with negative output and employment consequences that can last for years. Yet episodes of banking, currency, and sovereign debt crises have become a common feature of our international financial system, especially since cross-border capital movements were made more free beginning in the 1970s. While financial globalization helps countries gain access to capital for investment spending – an important booster to economic growth, it inevitably exposes states to the volatile nature of global capital flows. In some cases, the volatility costs outweigh the growth-enhancing feature of access to capital (Carney 2019).[2]

Indeed, severe crisis episodes[3] such as the Global Financial Crisis of 2008–2009 or the 1997–1999 Asian Financial Crisis remind us that financial globalization is a double-edged sword, although in many cases financial globalization serves more as a catalyst for an already precarious domestic situation. According to one estimate, extreme crisis episodes that have a global reach may entail losses up to 3% to 4.5 % of world GDP (Kapp and Vega 2014). The GFC in particular has provoked some public reflection among economists, criticizing not only the discipline's failure to foresee the 2007 crisis, but also to have incorrectly ruled out the possibility of a financial crisis in an advanced economy like the United States (Krugman 2009, Joyce 2012).[4] Misunderstanding what financial crises are and why they occur, Gorton (2012) considers this blindness an "intellectual failure."

Due to the global spread of this event to various corners of the world, understandably international and comparative political economy scholars also engaged in some public soul-searching of their own, noting in particular the paucity of IPE work on financial crises (e.g., Helleiner 2011, Drezner and

McNamara 2013, Johnson et al. 2013) or the lack of attention to the substantial cross-country variations in the exposure to financial crises (Johnston 2017). Since then, there has been tremendous growth in the scholarly work that fills the gap, and, accordingly, the main purpose of this chapter is to map out the areas of inquiry that have been tackled by political economists studying causes of financial crises. A political economy approach to analyzing financial crises is not entirely new, so I will highlight existing work prior to the GFC, as well as more recent research that have furthered our understanding of the government behavior, political institutions, and economic policies that contributed to financial crises. It would not be possible to cover the universe of the work on this topic, thus I will concentrate on the issues I found most important and questions that I think have not been as extensively addressed.

While economic analysis has developed important tools to understand factors that lead to or even predict financial crises (see, e.g., Sufi and Taylor 2021), as previously argued in Amri and Willett (2017, p. 2), we need to "devote more attention to the political economy considerations that generate prolonged inconsistencies that end in financial crises." Given the substantial costs of financial crises, it is curious why governments do not more frequently step in to handle crises before they occur, despite having the knowledge about the most common precursors to financial crises,[5] and the ability to prevent capital flow surges from causing unwanted credit booms and financial crises, at least to some degree (Amri et al. 2016, Walter 2013). However, uncertainty characterizes the history of financial crises. Although we have considerable knowledge about the risk factors that precede a financial crisis, there is no consensus about the certainty with which these factors would lead to a financial crisis. For example, many countries experience things like very high credit growth and sharp increases in home or equity prices, without metastasizing into a financial crisis (Gerber 2019, Goetzmann 2015). There is even less of a consensus among academic and policy-oriented economists about whether early policy interventions to deflate a credit boom would be effective (e.g., Brunnermeier and Schnabel 2015), nor is there a firm agreement that stringent regulatory and supervisory policies reduce the likelihood of banking instability (Barth et al. 2008, Amri and Kocher 2012).

While these uncertainties provide a partial account, it is also important to investigate the political underpinnings of the policy choices that lead to the build-up of these risk factors. For example, to better understand why regulatory authorities repeatedly failed to restrain a build-up of bad loans in the financial system, we need to dig deeper on the role of interest groups in shaping lax regulatory policies (Pagliari and Young 2016, Shuknecht and Siegerink 2020) or the cognitive biases and faulty mental models that led to such regulatory inattention (Willett 2012). Social conventions concerning central bank practices that contributed to risk and uncertainty in a financial crisis should also be taken into account (Nelson and Katzenstein 2014). Both economic and political factors interact, and there is a good amount of work that is already addressing this.

This chapter proceeds as follows. It first discusses some of the most important risk factors that precede the three main types of financial crises – banking, currency, and sovereign debt, largely drawing from the economics literature. This section also highlights integrative research on credit booms, which are a major cause of banking crises and the political influences on credit booms. I then outline current debates on political economy research on the causes of financial crises. Following a section on government behavior and currency crisis, the final section concludes with some areas of political economy studies of financial crises that remain under-explored.

Financial crises: common types of crises and common risk factors[6]

Financial crises can be explained by a variety of factors, depending on the type of crisis. Excessive credit growth is widely considered to be the most important contributor to banking crises, a pattern documented by several scholars in the early 2000s (e.g., Kaminsky and Reinhart 1999, Borio and Lowe 2002, Gourinchas et al. 2001), and confirmed also by research that included the 2008–2009 crisis countries (e.g., Hume and Sentence 2009, Reinhart and Rogoff 2009, Schularick and Taylor 2012, Dell'Ariccia et al. 2012, Gennaioli and Shleifer 2018, Sufi and Taylor 2021).

For currency crises, common explanations involve sizeable and prolonged inconsistencies[7] between domestic macroeconomic and exchange rate policies (Amri and Willett 2017), which is reflected in a build-up of over-valued exchange rates (Steinberg 2017, Chiu and Willett 2009). In the context of (quasi-) fixed or managed floating exchange rate regimes, these inconsistencies are then spotted by currency speculators, but whether traders will sell off the currency is largely dependent on the perceived government commitment to the exchange rate peg, determined by such factors as the timing of elections, the state of the domestic economy, and the size of foreign exchange reserves. Higher degrees of capital mobility amplify the speculative pressures on the currency, as they generate a faster depletion of forex reserves to defend the currency. However, the extent to which international capital flows are an independent cause of crises or rather reflect poor underlying fundamentals is a matter of dispute.

For sovereign debt crises, where government borrowers fail to pay interest or principal within the specified grace period on either domestic or external debt, the precursors are relatively under-theorized compared to banking and currency crises, although this is slowly changing due to more availability of public sovereign debt data (Tomz and Wright 2013). Defaults have happened at relatively high and low levels of debt/GDP (Van Rijckeghem and Weder 2009), which means the role of the size of debt and past fiscal spending that contributed to the debt levels must be combined with other important factors such as the maturity of the debt, or whether the debt is primarily external versus domestic (Gerber 2019).[8] Also important are the political incentives that influence whether governments decide to default, as the international costs of defaulting (e.g., reputational damage) are sometimes less than the domestic political costs of adopting the policies necessary to continue to service the debt. Of course, there are also instances where one type of crisis spills over to another – banking turned sovereign debt, and/or banking turned currency crises (Kaminsky and Reinhart 1999) – in which cases factors that initially explained banking crises became important factors in the occurrence of debt or currency crises, for example.

Economic research on financial crisis has made substantive strides in identifying the fragility and sources of vulnerability to financial crises even before the 2007 crisis, as suggested by the references cited in the introduction. A major contribution has been efforts to document and make publicly available cross-country quantitative data sets on the occurrences of financial crises, from early ones such as Caprio and Klingebiel (1997) that enabled econometric tools to detect the probability of financial crises. Such efforts took a more serious turn after the 2008 crisis, producing more comprehensive data sets such as Reinhart and Rogoff (2009), Laeven and Valencia (2013), Schularick and Taylor (2012) – which focus on historical data in several advanced economies. Baron, Verner, and Xiong (2021) have augmented these crises data sets with more fine-grained bank equity data. However, to better understand how societies can minimize future crisis occurrences, we also need to look at the political sources of such instability. To illustrate this point, it is worthwhile to further explain credit growth as a main culprit in generating banking crises.

The insights of economic historians as pioneers in identifying risk factors stemming from the pro-cyclicality of credit supply[9] should be appreciated (Minsky 1977, Kindleberger and Aliber 2011). During economic upturns, euphoria and optimism characterize the investment climate. Credit expands rapidly to the private sector, leading to investment in low-productivity projects and a household consumption spree. Lending standards are lowered (Dell'Ariccia, Igan, and Laeven 2012, Quinn and Turner 2020), and more projects – both good and bad ones – get funded. Banks' longer-term financial soundness tends to deteriorate when credit is expanding, as banks increasingly make use of non-deposit borrowings, which is a more fragile source of funds compared to traditional deposits (Elekdag and Wu 2011). In many cases, the build-up of the boom was financed in part by borrowing from abroad, for both advanced and emerging market countries (Kauko 2014). When the euphoria resides and the economy slows down, the process is reversed, banks are forced to write down the value of their assets, and a banking crisis becomes inevitable. The larger and more prolonged the boom, the higher the likelihood of it being followed by a financial crisis (Borio and Drehman 2009, Castro and Martins 2020).

The rise in the supply of credit by itself is arguably not the main culprit, rather the build-up of risk and the overall vulnerability of the economy during the credit boom are the more pressing issues. When heavily indebted societies experience negative shocks such as a sudden fall in income, the economy is afforded less flexibility to respond, as resources are tied to servicing the existing stock of debt, which suddenly becomes much more difficult (Gerber 2019). Credit-driven consumption slumps in the aftermath of the crisis often cause severe contractions in economic growth (Mian and Sufi 2014).

Of course excessive credit growth is not the only factor that causes banking crisis. Scholars also attribute blame to financial liberalization, surges in capital inflows, asset price booms, loose fiscal policy, moral hazard resulting from explicit or implicit protection of banks' creditors (such as deposit insurance systems), and weak banking regulation and supervision.[10] This list is far from exhaustive and these sources of financial fragility are not always independent of each other.[11] Neither is it the case that all credit booms are dangerous, although credit booms may be the most robust predictor of banking crises (see Sufi and Taylor 2021 for a comprehensive review). As aptly summed up by Copelovitch and Singer (2020) "we need a more nuanced analysis and less outright acceptance of prevailing wisdom that crises are always caused by credit booms and booms are always caused by capital surges."

It is encouraging that recent economic and financial research has begun to address these nuances and heterogeneity. For example, research has identified that it is household, rather than business, debt that carries the greater risk of a credit boom to escalate into a full-blown banking crisis (Büyükkarabacak and Valev 2010, Mian, Sufi, and Verner 2017). Similarly, credit booms that end in busts tend to be directed towards final goods consumption, rather than towards the productive sectors of the economy (Gorton and Ordonez 2020), which underscores the importance of misallocation of credit. This body of work should be more tightly connected to the growing amount of scholarship on the political economy causes of credit booms, including the electoral incentives to "prime the credit pump" (e.g., Antoniades and Calomiris 2020, Kern and Amri 2021) and the use of fiscal policy such as mortgage subsidies in explaining private credit growth (Fuller 2015, Lepers 2021). Comparative politics as well as sociology research has further highlighted why policies to boost household credit such as mortgage subsidies are more popular with some countries than with others (Ahlquist and Ansell 2017, Johnston et al. 2021, Krippner 2012, Quinn 2019, Reisenbichler 2021, Schwartz and Seabrooke 2008).

In short, while economists have identified factors that make a country more vulnerable to financial crises, political economy research strengthens our understanding of what causes financial crises by probing the political sources of certain financial vulnerabilities, such as credit booms.

The political underpinnings of financial crises

The Global Financial Crisis generated extensive conversations about how international relations and political economy scholarship should address financial booms and busts that characterize the global economy (Drezner and McNamara 2013, Helleiner 2011, Johnson et al. 2013, Oatley 2011, to name a few). While these early papers lamented the paucity of IPE research on financial crises, political economy research addressing this very question has advanced since. Broadly speaking the work can be divided into those that primarily fault "system-level" factors for the generation of financial crises (e.g., global economic imbalances and the power structure that explain these imbalances) and those that emphasize 'domestic attributes' such as excessive risk-taking and regulatory failures – mainstays of the so-called open economy politics[12] framework. Both are summarized in the paragraphs below.

To an extent, these varying perspectives reflect ongoing debates about approaches in the IPE discipline more broadly. One particularly provocative reflection by Thomas Oatley was that the predominant IPE open economy politics scholarship has overly emphasized domestic relative to systemic considerations. Oatley (2011) encourages scholars to look at structural factors behind global financial orders that lead to financial crises. Drezner and McNamara (2013) delivered a similar critique, noting that open economy politics have performed well in identifying domestic political factors that contribute to currency crises, such as cabinet termination (Bernhard and Leblang 2008) and government ideology (Leblang and Bernhard 2000), but have not sufficiently accounted for the role of contagion of crises.

However, these critiques are not meant to discount the usefulness of studying the domestic causes[13] of financial instability (Bauerle Danzman, Winecoff, and Oatley 2017). In fact, a domestic-focused explanation seems natural: while many crisis episodes tend to bunch together (the 1980s debt crisis, the Asian financial crisis, the Scandinavian banking and currency twin crises in the early 1990s), in nearly all cases, the international shock would not have gained traction were it not for the precarious domestic political economy conditions in the crisis-hit countries (Indonesia in 1997 is a case in point). Most importantly, in the countries at the epicenter of a particular global or regional episode, it is often national economies' failure to manage the deleterious effects of capital flow surges that prove to be the culprit (Johnston 2017). This was the case for both the United States pre-2007 and Thailand pre-1997. Hence the domestic factors approach to studying financial crises indeed has its merits. The range of factors are impressively wide, including the levels of financial regulation and supervision (Amri and Kocher 2012, Garriga 2017), the independence of financial regulatory bodies and central banks (Fraccaroli et al. 2020, Jordana and Rosas 2014), and the degree to which banks compete with non-bank institutions in the market for loans (Copelovitch and Singer 2017, 2020). Other important yet relatively under-explored areas are the roles of interest group influence[14] (Steinberg 2017) and type of political regime (Steinberg et al. 2015, Lipscy 2018).

An important area for additional research is the issue of regulatory independence. Indeed, the existing literature has yet to reach a broad consensus on the salutary aspects of financial regulatory independence. For example, Fraccaroli et al. (2020) found that more independent regulatory agencies are associated with lower bank non-performing loans, which are correlated with a lower likelihood of banking crisis. Meanwhile, Jordana and Rosas (2014) found that independent banking regulators contribute to lowering the likelihood of a banking crisis, but only in institutional settings where regulators are unable to shirk on their mandate to secure banking stability.

As financial crises become less and less self-contained to one country, there is also value in looking more closely at the power structure behind global monetary orders, including the behavior of state and private actors in the financial center (Oatley 2015). Inevitably, this means examining the behavior of the center of the current power structure, the United States, although there is some disagreement about the relative influence of the US alone versus the collective group of advanced economies. In this regard, Rey's (2015) work has been especially influential. US monetary policy is a central influence in a (global) pattern of interactive gross capital flows, of leverage of the banking sector, and credit booms and risky assets (Rey 2015). Recent political economy scholarship investigates how the United States contributes to these global boom-and-bust cycles, both in causing a domestic crisis (Oatley 2015) and catalyzing crises in countries worldwide (Aklin and Kern 2019, Ba 2018, Bauerle Danzman et al. 2017).

I highlight two quite provocative contributions to this debate. Examining three postwar US financial crises – the dollar crisis of 1968–1970 that led to the breakdown of the Bretton Woods international monetary system, the Savings and Loan Crisis of 1988, and the 2007 subprime mortgage meltdown – Oatley (2015) identifies a common factor behind all three: large preceding jumps in American military spending.[15] Specifically, each time the US government engaged in a military build-up financed by increased borrowing, it sowed the seeds of an unsustainable credit boom that eventually turned into a financial crash. Meanwhile, Aklin and Kern (2019) investigate American commitment and support to other states (as proxied by the presence of US troops) as a factor that leads to moral hazard, which then contributes to systemic financial crises. They argue that American military support provides a cover for both the governments that host the US troops and to the financial market participants who take bigger risks that contribute to the generation of systemic financial crises. For governments, the implicit support from the US enables them to adopt risky expansionary financial policies that might have electoral pay-offs such as credit booms. For financial market actors, the American seal of approval short-circuits market discipline. This means that private capital inflows no longer discriminate between governments that preside over good economic housekeeping (e.g., balanced budget, stable current account balances), and those that do not.

By identifying US military build-ups and the presence of US military troops in third countries as key elements behind boom-and-bust cycles, the larger message conveyed by Oatley, and Aklin and Kern, seems to be that America's military power unintentionally makes the world more financially unstable. While both of these works inspire new questions, to accept their conclusions one must test the reliability of how they assess each link in the causal chain. However, many of these causal links, (e.g., the roles of moral hazard and budget deficits in financial crises) are also the subject of much debate in the literature. For example, credit booms are probably at most a necessary, but not sufficient, condition for banking crises, while the correlation between strong capital inflows and credit booms is also weaker than often thought (Amri et al. 2016).

In sum, IPE scholars present varying perspectives and debates about approaches in the discipline more broadly and also about their discipline's take on financial crises. Yet neither side calls for a "uniquely global" (or solely domestic) approach. Rather, each advocates for a more balanced view, recognizing that both factors interact in important ways. Johnston (2017) aptly emphasizes the need to combine IPE and CPE in order to more fully appreciate the causes and consequences of global financial crises. This integrated approach would help explain why governments have, or have not, intervened to adjust their economic policies. The next section explores this question with regards to currency crises.

Application: government behavior and currency crises

One question that continues to puzzle scholars of financial crises is why governments do not do more to head off crises before they occur. An example is the lack of action taken by governments to correct large imbalances in their balance of payments that led to over-valuations of their currencies. Examples include the cases of Thailand, Mexico, and Argentina (Ito 2007, Walter 2013). This is puzzling as delaying actions only heightens the likelihood of a more severe crisis once it occurs. In brief, how is government behavior most likely to influence currency crises?[16]

Most prominently, governments may either create the shock that triggers the crisis, or delay the adjustments required to prevent the cascade into crisis (Amri and Willett 2017). The extent to which governments engage in these different types of behavior will depend on key factors, such as their ideologies (Leblang and Bernhard 2000), institutional constraints on their behavior, and distributional and electoral considerations (Walter 2013).

In the first instance, weak governments may initiate shocks when facing a tough election by overspending and generating high budget deficits, with little consideration for the impact on balance of payments disequilibrium (Amri and Willett 2017). In the second case, the so-called "second generation" economic models of currency crisis showed that certain factors make an economy vulnerable to speculative attacks that lead to a currency crisis, especially over-valued exchange rates and capital inflows that lead to maturity and currency mismatches. They also indicated that countries can stay in the vulnerable zone for a while without tipping over into a crisis (see Amri and Willett 2017). Sudden shifts in agents' expectations can translate these vulnerable zones into a crisis. While these shifts could be due to arbitrary factors they are usually generated by economic and political developments. Political economy research shows that governments can exacerbate these vulnerabilities by delaying economic adjustments.

One interesting explanation lies in the combination of electoral concerns and distributional considerations, combined with the short time-horizons in the political process. There are two types of adjustments to balance of payments disequilibrium: internal and external. The former involves contractionary macroeconomic policies that raise interest rates and cut spending, in order to bring down spending (on imports) and to slow down inflation that leads to real exchange rate appreciation. The latter involves a devaluation of the exchange rate, which should boost exports but raise the cost of imports.

Both types of adjustments are painful for many voters in the short run, but the choice of external or internal adjustments has different distributional consequences (Frieden 1991). According to Walter (2013), how governments perceive these different types of exposures to adjustment strategies affects the actions taken. Walter (2013) finds that governments are more likely to delay devaluation and other economic adjustments when the majority of voters are vulnerable to both internal adjustment (e.g., voters who work in sectors vulnerable to government spending cuts) and external adjustment (e.g., importers and citizens who borrow in foreign currency). Interest groups that are disproportionately exposed to these adjustments also contribute to delayed actions on the part of the government. An upcoming election timed in the midst of rising vulnerability explains the crucial delays in necessary adjustments that were observed before 1997 in Korea and Thailand. It also does not help that while the possibility of a looming crisis is uncertain, the domestic political costs of enacting adjustment policies are quite certain. Instead, a temporary fix was instituted in both countries – selling forex reserves through sterilized interventions, which in retrospect further prolonged the vulnerability that made them ripe for speculative attacks.

Concluding remarks

To understand why financial crises continue to occur with troubling frequency despite the substantial costs to society, we need to not only combine standard economic models with political economy, but also explore system- and domestic-level policies, institutions, and government behavior that interactively generated exposure to financial crises in the first place. The imperative to study financial crises from a political economy perspective arises from the observation that even when governments have capability to mitigate problems in advance, many times they fail to take the necessary adjustments to their economic policies in order to avert the crises.

In sum, there are several important avenues for future research on financial crises. Clearly, from a domestic policy perspective, electoral considerations and interest group influence play important roles in affecting the policy choices that governments take, including those policies that contribute to credit booms that often turn into banking crises. The political incentive to slow down credit growth is weak nearly everywhere, as many benefit from the pursuit of the easy credit policies that increase the risk of generating crises. In fact, governments have long used fiscal and financial policy instruments to boost credit demand and credit supply for various goals including income redistribution, improving financial inclusion, and also for maximizing their chances of staying in office. In this regard, it is important to emphasize the emerging work identifying sources of variations in government credit policy (e.g., Fuller 2015, Lepers 2021). We also need a better understanding of the conditions under which these credit policies increase financial risks.

This chapter also highlighted the increase in research explaining how the global power structure, including the United States' financial and military power contributes, perhaps unintentionally, to financial instability. As the structure of the global economy undergoes substantial changes with the rise of China and other emerging market powers (see Wei Liang's chapter on China's rise, this volume), it is important to push deeper into this line of work. Moreover, this raises the question of how China's autocratic regime, with much less institutional constraints on her economic policymaking ability, behaves and responds to an impending financial instability. Indeed, IPE research should investigate the roles of political regime types in contributing to financial crises and affecting whether countries adopt better economic policies after a financial crisis. A closer examination on the interactions between system-level and domestic sources of financial fragility is equally important. While this chapter highlights selected key advances and gaps in IPE research, there are many other interesting and promising areas for work on the political economy causes and consequences of financial crises.

Notes

1. This chapter draws on and extends some of my past research on financial crises, co-written with Eric Chiu, Andreas Kern, Brett Kocher, Jake Meyer, Greg Richey, and Tom Willett. I thank them for their perspectives. All errors are my own.
2. Carney (2019) found that a typical financially open emerging market with higher capital inflows will grow 0.3 percentage points faster compared to those that do not liberalize their capital account. However, the same research found that emerging markets with more volatile capital flows will grow 0.7 percentage points slower.
3. For the US alone, the 2007 crisis translated to a cut of US$70,000 of annual income for every American in terms of present value (Barnichon et al. 2018).
4. Such strong views are encapsulated in the so-called efficient markets hypothesis. While there were a few economists who did sound the alarm bell, such as former IMF Chief Economist Raghuram Rajan, the majority missed it, partly because economists tend to adopt narrow specializations and not take broader views, although recent developments in behavioral economics and finance have been important in challenging this position (see e.g., Willett 2021).
5. There are hundreds of papers on financial crises (Gorton 2012). Examples include the combination credit booms and asset price bubbles, and over-valued exchange rates. As discussed by Ito (2007) and Walter (2013), both the Thai and Mexican governments have been warned about the misalignments of their real exchange rates prior to the crises, but chose not to adjust their macroeconomic policies.
6. The use of the term "risk" in lieu of "causal" factors follows Gerber (2019). Economists have yet to generate a strong theory about causes of banking crises, yet there are extensive studies on the common factors that precede a crisis.
7. For example, large fiscal deficits that are inconsistent with the maintenance of a pegged exchange rate and governments that do not take actions to reduce these deficits (Krugman 1979). For more detailed insights on formal currency crisis models see, for example, Pilbeam (2013) or other texts in international money and finance.
8. For examples of political economy causes of sovereign debt crises, see, e.g., Van Rijckeghem and Weder (2009) for a cross-country and time-series study, and Johnston et al. (2014) and also Copelovitch, Frieden, and Walter (2016) for the specific case of the European Debt Crisis.
9. Relatedly, for an interpretation on how Veblen's theory of credit demand can lead to economic crises and recessions see Davanzati and Pacella (2014).
10. For political economy sources of banking crises along similar lines, see, e.g., Aklin and Kern (2019), Amri and Kocher (2012), Bauerle Danzman et al. (2017), Copelovitch and Singer (2020), Garriga (2017), Oatley (2015), and the contributions to the volume edited by Oatley and Winecoff (2014).
11. For example, capital flow surges can by themselves lead to a banking crisis (Caballero 2016), and indirectly cause a banking crisis through credit demand and credit supply channels. See, e.g., Amri et al. (2016).
12. Open economy politics maps out the economic policy preferences of different actors and then aggregated through domestic institutions (electoral systems, regime types, regulatory agencies) to explain international outcomes (Drezner and McNamara 2013). See, e.g., Lake (2009) for an explanation of open economy politics.

13. While outside the scope of this chapter, there is also a very large literature on the political consequences (incumbents tend to get ousted) and policy responses to financial crises. See, e.g., Pepinsky (2012) and Chwieroth and Walter (2022) for a review.

14. There has, however, been growing work on the various ways in which the financial sector influences regulators (Pagliari and Young 2016), just as there have been several papers that look at international and domestic political forces shaping financial regulations (Wilf 2016).

15. The chain begins with military build-ups, which need to be financed through borrowing given the gridlock-prone nature of America's political institutions. Military build-ups are the "single most important cause of America's large and persistent budget deficits." Then, large budget deficits lead to large current account deficits. Large current account deficits produce large capital inflows, which then lead to credit booms.

16. While outside the scope of this chapter, government policy choices such as type of exchange rate regime and level of exchange rate (under- or over-valuation) and their respective roles in currency crises are also an interesting topic.

References

Ahlquist, John. S., and Ben Ansell. 2017. "Taking credit: Redistribution and borrowing in an age of economic polarization." *World Politics* 69:4: 640–675.

Aklin, Michaël, and Andreas Kern. 2019. "Moral hazard and financial crises: Evidence from American troop deployments." *International Studies Quarterly* 63:1: 15–29.

Amri, Puspa, and Brett Matthew Kocher. 2012. "The political economy of financial sector supervision and banking crises: A cross-country analysis." *European Law Journal* 18:1: 24–43.

Amri, Puspa D., and Thomas D. Willett. 2017. "Policy inconsistencies and the political economy of currency crises." *Journal of International Commerce, Economics and Policy* 8:1: 1750004.

Amri, Puspa, Greg Richey, and Thomas D Willett. 2016. "Capital surges and credit booms: How tight is the relationship?" *Open Economies Review* 27:4: 637–670.

Antoniades, Alexis, and Charles W. Calomiris. 2020. "Mortgage market credit conditions and US Presidential elections." *European Journal of Political Economy* 64: 101909.

Ba, Heather. 2018. "The systemic causes of financial crises in the long nineteenth century." *Business and Politics* 20:2: 208–238.

Barnichon, Regis, Christian Matthes, and Alexander Ziegenbein. 2018. "The financial crisis at 10: Will we ever recover." *FRBSF Economic Letter* 19.

Baron, Matthew, Emil Verner, and Wei Xiong. 2021. "Banking crises without panics." *The Quarterly Journal of Economics* 136:1: 51–113.

Barth, James R., Gerard Caprio, and Ross Levine. 2008. *Rethinking bank regulation: Till angels govern.* New York: Cambridge University Press.

Bauerle Danzman, Sarah, W. Kindred Winecoff, and Thomas Oatley. 2017. "All crises are global: Capital cycles in an imbalanced international political economy." *International Studies Quarterly* 61:4: 907–923.

Bernhard, William, and David Leblang. 2008. "Cabinet collapses and currency crashes." *Political Research Quarterly* 61:3: 517–531.

Borio, Claudio E.V., and Mathias Drehmann. 2009."Assessing the risk of banking crises – revisited." *BIS Quarterly Review*, March.

Borio, Claudio, and Philip Lowe. 2002. "Assessing the risk of banking crises." *BIS Quarterly Review* 7:1: 43–54.

Brunnermeier, Markus Konrad, and Isabel Schnabel. 2015. "Bubbles and central banks: Historical perspectives." Available at SSRN: https://ssrn.com/abstract=2592370

Büyükkarabacak, Berrak, and Neven T. Valev. 2010. "The role of household and business credit in banking crises." *Journal of Banking & Finance* 34:6: 1247–1256.

Caballero, Julián A. 2016. "Do surges in international capital inflows influence the likelihood of banking crises?" *The Economic Journal* 126:591: 281–316.

Caprio, Gerard, and Daniela Klingebiel. 1997. "Bank insolvency: Bad luck, bad policy, or bad banking?" *World Bank Economic Review*, January.

Carney, Mark. 2019. *Pull, push, pipes: Sustainable capital flows for a new world order.* Group of Thirty.

Castro, Vítor, and Rodrigo Martins. 2020. "Riding the wave of credit: Are longer expansions really a bad omen?" *Open Economies Review* 31:4: 729–751.

Chiu, E.M., and T.D. Willett. 2009. "The interactions of strength of governments and alternative exchange rate regimes in avoiding currency crises." *International Studies Quarterly* 53: 1001–1025.

Chwieroth, Jeffrey M., and Andrew Walter. 2022. "Financialization, wealth and the changing political aftermaths of banking crises." *Socio-Economic Review* 21:1: 54–84.

Copelovitch, Mark, and David A. Singer. 2017. "Tipping the (im)balance: Capital inflows, financial market structure, and banking crises." *Economics & Politics* 29:3: 179–208.

Copelovitch, Mark, and David A. Singer. 2020. *Banks on the brink: Global capital, securities markets, and the political roots of financial crises.* New York: Cambridge University Press.

Copelovitch, M., J. Frieden, and S. Walter. 2016. "The political economy of the Euro crisis." *Comparative Political Studies* 49:7: 811–840.

Davanzati, Guglielmo Forges, and Andrea Pacella. 2014. "Thorstein Veblen on credit and economic crises." *Cambridge Journal of Economics* 38:5: 1043–1061.

Dell'Ariccia, Giovanni, Deniz Igan, and Luc U.C. Laeven. 2012. "Credit booms and lending standards: Evidence from the subprime mortgage market." *Journal of Money, Credit and Banking* 44:2–3: 367–384.

Drezner, Daniel W., and Kathleen R. McNamara. 2013. "International political economy, global financial orders and the 2008 financial crisis." *Perspectives on Politics* 11:1: 155–166.

Elekdag, Selim, and Yiqun Wu. 2011. "Rapid credit growth: Boon or boom–bust?" IMF Working Paper 11/241.

Fraccaroli, Nicolò, Rhiannon Sowerbutts, and Andrew Whitworth. 2020. "Does regulatory and supervisory independence affect financial stability?" Bank of England Working Paper No. 893.

Frieden, Jeffry A. 1991. "Invested interests: The politics of national economic policies in a world of global finance." *International Organization* 45: 425–451.

Fuller, Gregory. 2015. "Who's borrowing? Credit encouragement vs credit mitigation in national financial systems." *Politics & Society* 43:2: 241–268.

Garriga, Ana Carolina. 2017. "Regulatory lags, liberalization, and vulnerability to banking crises." *Regulation & Governance* 11:2: 143–165.

Gennaioli, Nicola, and Andrei Shleifer. 2018. *A crisis of beliefs*. Princeton, NJ: Princeton University Press.

Gerber, James. 2019. *A great deal of ruin: Financial crises since 1929*. New York: Cambridge University Press.

Goetzmann, William N. 2015. *Bubble investing: Learning from history*. National Bureau of Economic Research No. w21693.

Gorton, Gary. 2012. *Misunderstanding financial crises: Why we don't see them coming*. Oxford: Oxford University Press.

Gorton, Gary, and Guillermo Ordonez. 2020. "Good booms, bad booms." *Journal of the European Economic Association* 18:2: 618–665.

Gourinchas, Pierre-Olivier, Rodrigo Valdes, and Oscar Landerretche. 2001. "Lending booms: Latin America and the world." NBER Working Paper 8249.

Helleiner, Eric. 2011. "Understanding the 2007–2008 global financial crisis: Lessons for scholars of international political economy." *Annual Review of Political Science* 14: 67–87.

Hume, Michael, and Andrew Sentence. 2009. "The global credit boom: Challenges for macroeconomics and policy." *Journal of International Money and Finance* 28:8: 1426–1461.

Ito, Takatoshi. 2007. "Asian currency crisis and the International Monetary Fund, 10 years later: Overview." *Asian Economic Policy Review* 2:1: 16–49.

Johnson, Juliet et al. 2013. "The future of international political economy: Introduction to the 20th anniversary issue of RIPE." *Review of International Political Economy* 20:5: 1009–1023.

Johnston, Alison. 2017. "Comparative and international political economy and the global financial crisis." In *Oxford Research Encyclopedia of Politics*.

Johnston, A., B. Hancké, and S. Pant. 2014. "Comparative institutional advantage in Europe's sovereign debt crisis." *Comparative Political Studies* 47:13: 1771–1800.

Johnston, A., Gregory W. Fuller, and Aidan Regan. 2021. "It takes two to tango: Mortgage markets, labor markets and rising household debt in Europe." *Review of International Political Economy* 28:4: 843–873.

Jordana, Jacint, and Guillermo Rosas. 2014. "When do autonomous banking regulators promote stability?" *European Journal of Political Research* 53:4: 672–691.

Joyce, Joseph P. 2012. *The IMF and global financial crises: Phoenix rising?* New York: Cambridge University Press.

Kaminsky, Graciela L., and Carmen Reinhart. 1999. "The twin crises: The causes of banking and balance-of-payments problems." *American Economic Review* 89:3: 473–500.

Kapp, Daniel, and Marco Vega. 2014. "Real output costs of financial crises: A loss distribution approach." *Cuadernos de economía* 37:103: 13–28.

Kauko, Karlo. 2014. "How to foresee banking crises? A survey of the empirical literature." *Economic Systems* 38: 289–308.

Kern, Andreas and Puspa Amri. 2021. "Political credit cycles." *Economics & Politics* 33:1: 76–108.

Kindleberger, Charles P., and Robert Z. Aliber. 2011. *Manias, panics and crashes: A history of financial crises*. Palgrave Macmillan.

Krippner, G.R. 2012. *Capitalizing on crisis: The political origins of the rise of finance*. Boston, MA: Harvard University Press.

Krugman, Paul. 1979. "A model of balance-of-payments crises." *Journal of Money, Credit and Banking* 11:3: 311–325.

Krugman, Paul. 2009. "How did economists get it so wrong?" *New York Times Magazine*, September 2.

Laeven, Luc, and Fabian Valencia. 2013. Systemic banking crises database. *IMF Economic Review* 62: 225–270.

Lake, David. 2009 "Open economy politics: A critical review." *Review of International Organizations* 4:3: 19–44.

Leblang, D., and W. Bernhard (2000). "The politics of speculative attacks in industrial democracies." *International Organization* 54: 291–324.

Lepers, Etienne. 2021 "Fiscal policy as credit policy: Reassessing the fiscal spending vs. private debt trade-off." CITYPERC Working Paper No. 2021–04.

Lipscy, Phillip Y. 2018. "Democracy and financial crisis." *International Organization* 72:4: 937–968.

Mian, Atif, and Amir Sufi. 2014. "What explains the 2007–2009 drop in employment?" *Econometrica* 82:6: 2197–2223.

Mian, Atif, Amir Sufi, and Emil Verner. 2017. "Household debt and business cycles worldwide." *The Quarterly Journal of Economics* 132:4: 1755–1817.

Minsky, Hyman P. 1977. "The financial instability hypothesis: An interpretation of Keynes and an alternative to standard theory." *Challenge* 20: 20–27.

Nelson, Stephen C., and Peter J. Katzenstein. 2014. "Uncertainty, risk, and the financial crisis of 2008." *International Organization* 68:2: 361–392.

Oatley, Thomas. 2011. "The reductionist gamble: Open economy politics in the global economy." *International Organization* 65: 311–341.

Oatley, Thomas. 2015. *A political economy of American hegemony: Military booms, buildups, and busts*. New York: Cambridge University Press.

Oatley, T., and W.K. Winecoff (eds.). 2014. *Handbook of the international political economy of monetary relations*. Cheltenham, UK and Northampton, MA, USA: Edward Elgar Publishing.

Pagliari, Stefano, and Kevin Young. 2016. "The interest ecology of financial regulation: Interest group plurality in the design of financial regulatory policies." *Socio-Economic Review* 14:2: 309–337.

Pepinsky, Thomas B. 2012. "The global economic crisis and the politics of non-transitions." *Government & Opposition* 47:2: 135–161.

Pilbeam, K. 2013. *International finance*, 4th edition. New York: Palgrave.

Quinn, Sarah L. 2019. *American bonds: How credit markets shaped a nation*. Princeton, NJ: Princeton University Press.

Quinn, William, and John D. Turner. 2020. *Boom and bust: A global history of financial bubbles*. New York: Cambridge University Press.

Reinhart, Carmen, and Kenneth Rogoff. 2004. "A re-interpretation of exchange rate regimes." *Quarterly Journal of Economics* 119: 1–48.

Reinhart, Carmen M., and Kenneth S. Rogoff. 2009. *This time is different: Eight centuries of financial folly*. Princeton, NJ and Oxford: Princeton University Press.

Reisenbichler, Alexander. 2021. "Entrenchment or retrenchment: The political economy of mortgage debt subsidies in the United States and Germany." *Comparative Politics*. https://doi.org/10.5129/001041522X16314500561319

Rey, Helene. 2015. "Dilemma not trilemma: The global financial cycle and monetary policy independence." NBER Working Paper 21162.

Schuknecht, Ludger, and Vincent Siegerink. 2020. "The political economy of the G20 agenda on financial regulation." *European Journal of Political Economy* 65: 101941.

Schularick, Moritz, and Alan. M. Taylor. 2012. "Credit booms gone bust: Monetary policy, leverage cycles, and financial crises: 1870–2008." *American Economic Review* 102:2: 1029–1061.

Schwartz, Herman, and Leonard Seabrooke. 2008. "Varieties of residential capitalism in the international political economy: Old welfare states and the new politics of housing." *Comparative European Politics* 6: 237–261.

Steinberg, David A. 2017. "Interest group pressures and currency crises: Argentina in comparative perspective." *Comparative Politics* 50: 61–82.

Steinberg, D.A., K. Koesel, and N. Thompson. 2015. "Political regimes and currency crises." *Economics & Politics* 27: 337–361.

Sufi, Amir, and Alan Taylor. 2021. "Financial crises: A survey." NBER Working Paper 29155.

Tomz, Michael, and Mark L.J. Wright. 2013. "Empirical research on sovereign debt and default." *Annual Review of Economics* 5:1: 247–272.

Van Rijckeghem, Caroline, and Beatrice Weder. 2009. "Political institutions and debt crises." *Public Choice* 138:3: 387–408.

Walter, Stefanie. 2013. *Financial crises and the politics of macroeconomic adjustments.* Cambridge: Cambridge University Press.

Wilf, Meredith. 2016. "Credibility and distributional effects of international banking regulations: Evidence from US bank stock returns." *International Organization* 70:4: 763–796.

Willett, Thomas D. 2012. "The role of defective mental models in generating the global financial crisis." *Journal of Financial Economic Policy* 4:1: 41–57.

Willett, Thomas D. 2021. "New developments in financial economics." *Journal of Financial Economic Policy*, ahead-of-print. https:// doi .org/ 10 .1108/ JFEP -04–2021–0113

5. The political economy of One Health: implications for crisis governance research

John Connolly

Introduction

This past century has seen human dominance over the biosphere manifest in technological innovations, accelerated mobility, and converted ecosystems that characterise industrialisation, globalisation, and urbanisation (Amuasi et al., 2020). The evolution and sustainability of our planet, as we know it, hinges on a symbiotic relationship between humans, animals, and the environment that we share. This symbiotic relationship is captured, in health security governance terms, by a 'One Health' approach. One Health (from here denoted as OH) is a perspective on health security that has become synonymous with the need to tackle health threats on a multi-disciplinary, inter-sectorial, and integrated basis in order to understand the 'causes of the causes' of health threats, such as disease outbreaks (Connolly, 2017; Rüegg et al., 2017). OH depends on forging and sustaining strong links between human and animal health services, the environment and public policy (Vandersmissen and Wellburn, 2014, p. 421).

There is a lack of political economy-focused OH research (Galaz et al., 2015). The disciplinary insights required to embed an OH framing of societal problems can go beyond environmental, public health, and veterinary health perspectives to include social science solutions for dealing with chronic problems such as poor sanitation, poverty, and urbanisation. These can be viewed from economic, sociological, anthropological, and political science perspectives. From the OH worldview, addressing the complex determinants of health – be they commercially driven or socially driven – requires both a 'whole of society' approach and adaptive institutional learning to address vulnerabilities at multiple levels of governance systems (Addy et al., 2014).

The 21st century has shown how the spread of diseases is enabled by the assistance from human behaviours and structural factors in society. For example, the 2014 Ebola crisis in West Africa and the global COVID-19 pandemic that emerged in 2020 highlight how living conditions, urbanisation, global travel, and human interactions represent a melting pot of drivers for human and societal vulnerability. These crises have challenged policy-makers to rethink how society operates in light of epidemics and pandemics. OH discourse, such as ideas about public policies reflecting the 'whole of society', has been subject to criticism. These criticisms are less about the intentions around implementing such an agenda; rather, such ideas fall down when there are high ambitions when, at the same time, silo-working leads to a lack of cooperation between stakeholders, which undermines a whole of society approach.

The complexities associated with OH mean that it can be interpreted and reinterpreted based on the specific context which shapes the positions and agendas of actors within policy systems. Moreover, certain disciplinary perspectives can dominate framing within the OH space. For example, Kamenshchikova et al. (2021, p. 314) examined OH in the context of the global challenge to address the impact of antimicrobial resistance (AMR) and they argue that 'OH discourses have been predominated by anthropocentric ideals'. In other words, networks within the OH space, and the actors which make up networks, are not necessarily sitting on a level playing field due to the potential for coalitions of actors to frame solutions from certain disciplinary lenses. For instance, diseases that sit at the animal–human interface, such as avian flu, call into question which actors should take the lead in presenting policy solutions to government (e.g. veterinarians or public health experts). In addition, the forces of market interests from the healthcare sector, such as pharmaceuticals, mean that profit-making motives do not always align with the values of those seeking to tackle the causes of the causes of disease outbreaks.

Social scientists have considered OH, along with 'sustainability' or 'social inclusion', as a 'polysemic' or even 'chameleonic' idea, whereby such ideas can be useful for agenda setting yet they fall apart when it comes to executing timely interventions (Hannah and Baekkeskov, 2020, pp. 427, 439). From an implementation perspective, it would also be wrong, even naïve, to assume that OH's call to integration will eliminate pre-existing barriers to joined-up approaches to governance (Connolly, 2016). The word 'governance' itself is a slippery concept in many ways. It refers to the dispersal of power and decision-making across multiple horizontal and vertical levels of the state. It also leads to questions about whether decision-making is state-centric or whether it can be better characterised as a fluid and multi-directional process involving partnerships and networks of societal actors across sectors. From a crisis governance perspective, OH is problematic due to its conceptual fluidity, and therefore presents major challenges for its implementation.

This chapter discusses the fact that despite successive crises, including the COVID-19 pandemic, there is a long road needing to be travelled in order for global institutions and national governments to invest in OH as a governance approach.

A One Health perspective on health security governance

The World Organisation for Animal Health (OIE) estimates that 75 per cent of the infectious diseases in humans, including coronavirus, Ebola, HIV, and influenza, have an animal origin. Furthermore, on average there are five new human diseases that emerge annually and, of these, three are of animal origin. Major examples of contemporary health security crises, such as SARS in 2013, the 2009 flu pandemic in the UK, and the 2014 Ebola crisis in West Africa have originated in animal infections. Heymann and Dixon (2013) note that it was most likely that the SARS outbreak emerged from a civet, or 'toddy cat', that was the carrier of the coronavirus in a live animal market in a province in South China (Heymann and Dixon, 2013). The 2009 pandemic influenza outbreak, or 'swine flu', also had animal health origins as the virus was a new strain of H1N1 due to a combination of bird, swine, and human flu viruses, which was further compounded with a Eurasian pig flu virus.

Managing zoonotic diseases is one of the most pressing and complex challenges for modern risk governance, given they have severe social, environmental, political, and economic implications, but the degree of success in managing such risks depends heavily on political priorities and governance capacities. The 2019–2020 coronavirus (COVID-19), which emerged from China, has served to further highlight the need for global health security paradigms, which focus on the risks of diseases at the animal–human interface. The suspicion by health authorities was that there was a link to a large seafood and animal market, suggesting that the disease passed from animals to humans. Lowe et al. (2018) also highlight how the 2015 Zika virus outbreak in Brazil was found to be transferred to humans via Aedes mosquitoes. The 2014 Ebola outbreak in West Africa was most likely due to human exposure to bat roost. Ebola is contracted from forest animals, including monkeys and bats, and the severe outbreaks of Ebola in 2018–2019 in the Democratic Republic of Congo present a vivid reminder of the deadly nature of this disease.

The political economy of One Health

With such threats in mind, an OH approach to health security governance recognises the societal entanglements associated with capitalism, but the ordering of institutions in this light could be framed to be a feature of the risks to health security, such as through the forces of capitalism, the commercial determinants of health, and the implications of neo-liberalism for widening politico-economic inequalities between developed and less developed countries. For policy-makers the rise of monetarism and the rolling back of the frontiers of the state perpetuates the risk society due to the interdependencies that surround the capitalised system due to the increasing movements between people, goods, and technologies, which helps to facilitate the transmissibility of infectious diseases. Increasing urbanisation, ever shrinking habitations, and deteriorating living conditions are also heavily associated with economic development and commercial expansionism. Canali et al. (2018, pp. 204–205) summarise key pillars in the development of the economic thinking in their analysis of OH and conclude that systems thinking highlights the intrinsic complexity of economic phenomena through a systems approach, which has been applied in different economic levels from local, meso, and macro. Furthermore, Kock (2013) argues that unless knowledge is used to inform governments of the decline in ecosystems, which pose risks to human health, there is unlikely to be a 'new political economy'. Kock's argument that insufficient knowledge of the problem of the 'causes of the causes' of health threats will limit progress towards addressing OH is a convincing argument given the evidence about the relationship between political and economic structures and the impact on inequalities (Marmot, 2005; Mackenzie et al., 2017). In other words, understanding OH requires the need to understand how the outcomes of market forces increase probabilities for diseases to take hold.

The 2014 Ebola crisis showed how economic vulnerability in West Africa had implications for poor sanitation and poverty, which presented the disease with a breeding ground to spread rapidly. This, in turn, was exacerbated due to the poor quality of political decisions made during the management of the pandemic[1] (Maffioli, 2021). The interdependencies and complexities associated with how the political economy presents vulnerabilities for health security can be understood in the context of globalisation (Walt, 1998; Huynen et al., 2005; Amuasi et al., 2020). Economic growth and the liberalisation of markets has made the human population more vulnerable to a range of health threats, as shown by the COVID-19 pandemic, SARs, antimicrobial resistance, and non-communicable diseases. Moreover, climate change, migration, poverty, destabilised governance regimes, weak or distracted political leadership, and conflict further exacerbate health security threats.

The next section of the chapter considers the modern global health security policy regime and the governance challenges this brings for embedding a One Health approach.

The global health security policy regime

The extant global governance frameworks for health security recognise the forces of globalisation, and they are accounted for within the International Health Regulations (IHRs). The 1969 regulations were revised in 1995 in order to take account of emerging infectious diseases, but the over-reliance on national notifications created excessive risks, and they lacked specific mechanisms to prevent the spread of diseases. From the 1990s the health security debate was dominated by HIV/Aids, which helped to stimulate the Millennium Development Goals. The 2002–2004 SARs outbreak led to further revisions of the IHRs in 2005, which promoted new global norms on cooperation to override national sovereignty. The role of the World Health Organization (WHO) was also deepened and widened in relation to health security governance. The IHRs were expanded to cover not only a list of specific diseases but also any event that would be a public health concern. In other words, the IHRs became more flexible and future-oriented, requiring countries to consider the possible impact of all hazards, from the natural to the accidental or intentional. Overall, the IHRs obligate countries to detect, report, and respond to events on the basis of 'self-assessment', notify the WHO within 24 hours, and implement coordination measures.

Because the IHRs recognise the threat infectious diseases pose to public health and transnational security, they focus on public health emergencies of international concern as their core priority. However, there has been ambiguity as to how IHRs can be applied given the limited governance capacities of countries to fully implement them. This may, in part, contribute to the existing gaps in global preparedness for public health emergencies. Indeed, the Global Health Security Agenda (GHSA) of 2014 acknowledges the capacity gaps, often linked to the variations in the political economies of countries. The GHSA is a collaborative framework between countries, international organisations, and the private sector that aims to strengthen global capacity to prevent, detect, and respond to infectious disease threats worldwide. The GHSA provides the foundation needed to provide non-disease-specific resolutions. To achieve this, the

GHSA consists of 11 action packages that are split across three main categories: prevent, detect, and respond. It serves as a set of roadmaps to help countries build capacity to address infectious disease threats. The question remains as to why only 67 of the 196 WHO member states have signed up to the GHSA, particularly in light of the ease of spread of diseases (Toner et al., 2015).

Barriers to the adoption of the GHSA

The barriers to the adoption of the GHSA are generally threefold. First, the national security-centric approach of the GHSA may limit its appeal to countries that do not see the correlation between health and security (Bali and Taaffe, 2017). However, the experience of the COVID-19 pandemic – and the ensuing economic destabilisation, increased inequality, and social unrest (Galea and Abdalla, 2020) – emphasised the importance of health securitisation. This pandemic unambiguously identifies health security as a foundation of national security, and stresses the need to build core public health capacities that bridge the existing prevention, detection, and response gaps to infectious diseases. The second barrier to the global adoption of GHSA is its focus on physical health, and the omission of mental health. This is despite the intricate interlinkage between physical and mental health, and the precipitation of mental health conditions by health security triggering events (Ip and Cheung, 2020). Third, the limited economic incentives for GHSA implementation have been identified as another barrier to its implementation (see Bali and Taaffe, 2017). Funding to build national health security capacity is provided by member nations, international organisations, and the private sector; however, implementation costs needed to address national health security needs are largely met by the implementing countries. Therefore, there are few incentives to boost national preparedness and response capacity, as it pertains to GHS, and this limits the inclination to prioritise health security within national budgets. Consequently, financing and executing health security projects by national and subnational governments might not be prioritised.

In light of the health, economic, and social costs associated with the COVID-19 pandemic, leaders at all levels of government must understand that prioritising health security is a necessity. Therefore, funding for GHS matters should not be an afterthought, driven only in response to ravaging epidemics or pandemics. That said, countries should be supported in their financial capacity to adopt agendas that focus on pandemic preparedness and response, specifically the GHSA. Funding to bridge capacity gaps as it pertains to national health security will provide the added incentive to adopt the GHSA. When funding is tied to the achievement of targets within the chosen action package(s), then completion of proposed deliverables, and closure in preparedness gaps could be more attainable.

Governance capacities and challenges

Governmental commitment to overcoming these challenges to GHSA adoption is another key determinant in the realisation of this agenda; however, governance challenges, as they relate to the adoption of the GHSA, remain. For example, Bell et al. (2017) consider a fundamental issue with GHSA adoption which is linked to the capacities for implementation, i.e. the evaluation capacities for countries to demonstrate their contributions towards GHSA (Bell et al., 2017). This is partly about having skilled personnel in place to execute policy design at national, regional, and local levels. It is also about having the skills in place to undertake community engagement, on the basis that communities themselves are also important sources of data/information on the effectives of health systems and interventions, including evidencing the impacts of One Health initiatives (Armstrong-Mensah and Serigne, 2018). Indeed, Armstrong-Mensah and Ndiaye (2018) note that 'a country's ability to prevent a local disease outbreak from becoming an epidemic often rests with the level of knowledge about the situation and the actions taken at the community level'. Moreover, capacity development is also important in terms of workforce development within healthcare settings. Purva et al. (2019) investigated the 'core capacities' for antimicrobial stewardship within Indian hospitals. The authors conclude that in order to be better placed to accommodate the global health security on AMR, restricting the usage of high antibiotics and implementing education and training and leadership support would be a positive step forward (Purva et al., 2019).

At a systems level, Paranjape and Franz (2015) discuss lessons around the implementation of global health security programmes. They emphasise the need for systems to be adequately agile to allow for inter-agency working given that global health imperatives require the ability to work across boundaries and cross-sectoral agencies. This highlights the need for multi-level leadership within systems, while avoiding confused lines of accountability and overly complex arrangements, which reduces the incentives for actors to avoid taking responsibility for their performance (Connolly, 2020). In many senses, these issues point to structural barriers within systems for national legislation to accommodate the GHSA. For example, Meier et al. (2017, p. 268) suggest that 'international efforts to address global health security have long focused on public health science rather than on the enabling legislation and authorizing regulations that empower, mandate, and authorize governments to prevent, detect, and respond to public health emergencies'. The authors argue, with a specific focus on sub-Saharan Africa, that to achieve GHSA objectives and targets, new or supplemental legal authorities and powers are needed to strengthen existing frameworks and implement the IHR frameworks. In sum, there needs to be a new political economy for global health security, which essentially 'brings the state back', as it were, and where OH ideas underpin the regulatory governance of health security. Equally, bridges are needed between disciplinary areas to ensure synergistic thinking. This is where this chapter will now turn.

Knowledge integration

A key lesson from Ebola and other epidemics is that the policy frameworks for future threats need to be based on the integration of expertise and disciplines. As Galaz et al. (2015) show in their interviews with officials within international organisations such as the UN, breaking down knowledge silos is far easier to argue than to implement. The authors show that although OH ideas promote the dovetailing of professions and expertise, in practice there can be professional hierarchies and differences in language, professional legacies, and even disciplinary biases (e.g. veterinarians are keener on pushing for a One Health agenda than public health experts, with public health experts/medics regarding themselves as the superior epistemic group). From the public health side, Heymann (2014) recognised around the time of the Ebola crisis that tensions between sectors can be more about economic considerations:

> The areas of animal and human security policy, and their knowledge networks, are by no means joined up. Stakeholder interests are divergent and the areas suffer from asynchronous political visions ... The difficulty is that animal health is to keep animals healthy, but the ultimate goal is a profit, whereas human health is to keep people alive and healthy. So already there are tensions between the two groups and if you want to sell anything to the animal health community it has to be different to how you sell something to the human health community.

There is a sense, however, that knowledge integration efforts are more evident within specific One Health initiatives (Connolly, 2017). The need to embed evaluation within One Health initiatives, which are co-created across disciplines, requires investment by global and national research councils and organisations in order to incentivise collaboration.

Pre-COVID-19 research has highlighted that the integration of social science within infectious disease epidemic preparedness and response, as well as within other areas (such as antimicrobial resistance), has been peripheral and fragmentary (Bardosh et al., 2020; Cameron et al., 2022). Social scientists are fundamental for addressing health threats and global security from a One Health perspective, and this needs to be promoted further. Health threats cannot be addressed satisfactorily unless we place the understanding of societal, organisational, community, and individual behaviors at the forefront of research studies and public policy responses. Indeed, it has been argued, convincingly, that global health security strategies should be underpinned by the analysis of threat perceptions, social psychology, and behavioural analysis (Van Bavel, 2020). These perspectives can also serve the fundamental purpose of informing science communication strategies, including understanding the roots and implications of 'fake news'/conspiracy theories and evaluating the moral/ethical considerations of health security interventions within governance systems.

The 'value added' of social science is that it can direct where scientific research can, or should, take place. This might be about identifying where and how to co-create interventions with civil society stakeholders, which requires trust-building with communities. It is crucial to achieve buy-in from those parties who ultimately need to change their behaviours, ranging from industry, policy-makers, to communities, and that is a matter for social scientists. Nevertheless, a new political economy for One Health is not just about targeting investment and rebalancing towards the regulatory state. Rather, the renewed post-COVID agenda for global and national institutions is to reflect the aims of a One Health approach to health security governance. As Connolly (2017) argues, this requires strategic leadership by the WHO to shape its organisational identity and become a network builder and advocate for One Health that shapes global health security policy responses. This needs to be met with investment by national agencies and other international organisations to continually evaluate the progress towards One Health.

Conclusions and implications for health security research

Health crises present opportunities for policy/institutional reform, and there have been many for policy-makers to learn from in recent times. Political scientists have examined the dynamics of post-crisis change, including how to establish post-crisis successes and failures, as well as the factors that shape the identification of lessons from crises, e.g. blame games and framing contests

(Marsh and McConnell, 2010; McConnell, 2015; Connolly, 2016; Stark, 2019; Karyotis et al., 2021). Political economists, on the other hand, have tended to focus on the nature or character of institutional change, especially whether change has been gradual or systematic, or even whether reform can be incremental with transformative results (Streeck and Thelen, 2005; Streeck, 2009).

Institutionalist political economy research emphasises the extensive society-economy interactions in capitalised political systems (Streeck, 2011). This intertwining is a useful way of thinking about how health security is researched in the future in terms of a systems perspective. Indeed, viewing policy frameworks for planning for the management of future global health threats necessitates a systems-based view of how regulatory regimes can help break down organisational and knowledge silos to address health threats from an OH perspective. This requires top-down institutional change and a strengthening of global health institutions as a rejoinder to what has often been evident as bottom-up and fragmentary approaches. It is necessary to build capacities and promote evaluation and innovation with national health systems. Moreover, Canali et al. (2018, p. 205) note, rightly, that 'economic concepts and theories should evolve to face new situations. One Health initiatives create new situations and problems that require a methodological innovation that will adapt the existing tools (or create new ones) to perform evaluations in complex frameworks.' There are, therefore, a number of implications for crisis governance research based on the discussion within this chapter. There is a need to:

- Understand how to build capacities to implement and evaluate approaches from an OH perspective at global, national, and regional levels.
- Evaluate the scalability of local or regional OH initiatives and determine the barriers and enablers for doing this.
- Investigate how to facilitate joined-up thinking between disciplinary areas and understand how to manage, facilitate, and mitigate unequal power relationships and learned behaviours based on professional cultures between disciplinary groups.
- Determine whether the integration between organisational knowledge and policy action is sustained and what might make the difference to ensuring sustainability.
- Examine how, and to what extent, OH narratives are a feature of post-COVID pandemic recovery regulatory/policy paradigms.
- Determine how the IHRs and GHSA can play their part in mobilising action and resources to address the 'causes of the causes' of disease outbreaks.

Overall, this chapter could be read as a challenge to policy-makers to consider a renewed political economy for health security. Yet, the argument to deal with the root causes of threats, be they environmental, social, political, or economic, should not be seen as unrealistic or undesirable. Beyond regulatory regimes, however, adopting an OH approach is as much a question of recalibrating global governance and statecraft as it is a moral endeavour.

Note

1.   There is evidence that resources were misallocated towards electoral swing villages in Liberia.

References

Addy, N. A., Poirier, A., Blouin, C., Drager, N., & Dubé, L. (2014). Whole-of-society approach for public health policymaking: a case study of polycentric governance from Quebec, Canada. *Annals of the New York Academy of Sciences, 1331*(1), 216–229.

Amuasi, J. H., Lucas, T., Horton, R., & Winkler, A. S. (2020). Reconnecting for our future: the Lancet One Health Commission. *The Lancet, 395*(10235), 1469–1471.

Armstrong-Mensah, E., & Ndiaye, S. (2018). Global health security agenda implementation: a case for community engagement. *Mary Ann Liebert Inc. Publishers.* https://doi.org/10.1089/HS.2017.0097

Bali, S., & Taaffe, J. (2017). The Sustainable Development Goals and the global health security agenda: exploring synergies for a sustainable and resilient world. *Journal of Public Health Policy.* https://doi.org/10.1057/s41271–016–0058–4

Bardosh, K. L., de Vries, D. H., Abramowitz, S., Thorlie, A., Cremers, L., Kinsman, J., & Stellmach, D. (2020). Integrating the social sciences in epidemic preparedness and response: a strategic framework to strengthen capacities and improve global health security. *Globalization and Health, 16*(1), 1–18.

Bell, E., Tappero, J. W., Ijaz, K., Bartee, M., Fernandez, J., Burris, H., Sliter, K., Nikkari, S., Chungong, S., Rodier, G., Jafari, H., & Secretariat, the C. J. T. and W. G. J. (2017). Joint external evaluation—development and scale-up of global multisectoral health capacity evaluation process. *Emerging Infectious Diseases, 23*(Suppl 1), S33. https://doi.org/10.3201/EID2313.170949

Cameron, A., Esiovwa, R., Connolly, J., Hursthouse, A., & Hendriquez, F. (2022), Antimicrobial resistance as a global health threat: the need to learn lessons from the COVID-19 pandemic. *Global Policy* (forthcoming).

Canali, M., Aragrande, M., Cuevas, S., Cornelsen, L., Bruce, M., Rojo-Gimeno, C., & Haesler, B. (2018). The economic evaluation of one health. In S. R. Rüegg, B. Häsler, & J. Zinsstag (eds), *Integrated Approaches to Health*, pp. 170–216. Wageningen Academic Publishers.

Connolly, J. (2016). *The Politics and Crisis Management of Animal Health Security*. Routledge.

Connolly, J. (2017). Governing towards 'One Health': establishing knowledge integration in global health security governance. *Global Policy*, 8(4), 483–494.

Connolly, J. (2020). Global crisis leadership for disease-induced threats: One Health and urbanisation. *Global Policy*, 11(3), 283–292.

Galaz, V., Leach, M., Scoones, I., & Stein, C. (2015). The political economy of One Health research and policy. STEPS Working Paper Series.

Galea, S., & Abdalla, S. M. (2020). COVID-19 pandemic, unemployment, and civil unrest: underlying deep racial and socioeconomic divides. *Jama*, 324(3), 227–228.

Hannah, A., & Baekkeskov, E. (2020). The promises and pitfalls of polysemic ideas: 'One Health' and antimicrobial resistance policy in Australia and the UK. *Policy Sciences*, 53, 437–452.

Heymann, D. (2014) 'Interview with the author', 25 March, 2014.

Heymann, D. L., & Dixon, M. (2013). The value of the One Health approach: shifting from emergency response to prevention of zoonotic disease threats at their source. *Microbiology Spectrum* 1: OH-0011–2012.

Huynen, M. M., Martens, P., & Hilderink, H. B. (2005). The health impacts of globalisation: a conceptual framework. *Globalization and Health*, 1(1), 1–12.

Ip, E. C., & Cheung, D. (2020). global mental health security—time for action. *JAMA Health Forum*, 1(6), e200622–e200622. https:// doi .org/ 10 .1001/ JAMAHEALTHFORUM.2020.0622

Kamenshchikova, A., Wolffs, P. F., Hoebe, C. J. P. A., & Horstman, K. (2021). Anthropocentric framings of One Health: an analysis of international antimicrobial resistance policy documents. *Critical Public Health*, 31(3), 306–315.

Karyotis, G., Connolly, J., Collignon, S., Judge, A., Makropoulos, I., Rüdig, W., & Skleparis, D. (2021). What drives support for social distancing? Pandemic politics, securitization, and crisis management in Britain. *European Political Science Review*, 1–21.

Kock, R. A. (2013). Will the damage be done before we feel the heat? Infectious disease emergence and human response. *Animal Health Research Reviews*, 14(2), 127–132.

Lowe, R., Barcellos, C., Brasil, P., Cruz, O. G., Honório, N. A., Kuper, H., & Carvalho, M. S. (2018). The Zika virus epidemic in Brazil: from discovery to future implications. *International Journal of Environmental Research and Public Health*, 15(1), 96.

Mackenzie, M., Collins, C., Connolly, J., Doyle, M., & McCartney, G. (2017). Working-class discourses of politics, policy and health: 'I don't smoke; I don't drink. The only thing wrong with me is my health'. *Policy & Politics*, 45(2), 231–249.

Maffioli, E. M. (2021). The political economy of health epidemics: evidence from the Ebola outbreak. *Journal of Development Economics*, 151, 102651.

Marmot, M. (2005). Social determinants of health inequalities. *The Lancet*, 365(9464), 1099–1104.

Marsh, D., & McConnell, A. (2010). Towards a framework for establishing policy success. *Public Administration*, 88(2), 564–583.

McConnell, A. (2015). What is policy failure? A primer to help navigate the maze. *Public Policy and Administration*, 30(3–4), 221–242.

Meier, B. M., Tureski, K., Bockh, E., Carr, D., Ayala, A., Roberts, A., Cloud, L., Wilhelm, N., & Burris, S. (2017). Examining national public health law to realize the global health security agenda. *Medical Law Review*, 25(2), 240–269. https:// doi .org/ 10 .1093/MEDLAW/FWX020

Paranjape, S., & Franz, D. (2015). Implementing the global health security agenda: lessons from global health and security programs. *Mary Ann Liebert Inc. Publishers.* https://doi.org/10.1089/HS.2014.0047

Purva, M., Randeep, G., Rajesh, M., Misra Mahesh, C., Sunil, G., Subodh, K., Sushma, S., Naveet, W., Pramod, G., Arti, K., Surbhi, K., Omika, K., Sonal, K., Manoj, S., Arunaloke, C., Pallab, R., Manisha, B., Neelam, T., Priscilla, R., ... & Kamini, W. (2019). Assessment of core capacities for antimicrobial stewardship practices in indian hospitals: report from a multicentric initiative of global health security agenda. *Indian Journal of Medical Microbiology, 37*(3), 309–317. https://doi.org/10.4103/IJMM.IJMM_19_445

Rüegg, S. R., McMahon, B. J., Häsler, B., Esposito, R., Nielsen, L. R., Ifejika Speranza, C., ... & Lindberg, A. (2017). A blueprint to evaluate One Health. *Frontiers in Public Health, 5,* 20.

Stark, A. (2019). *Public inquiries, policy learning, and the threat of future crises.* New York: Oxford University Press, USA.

Streeck, W. (2009). *Re-forming capitalism: institutional change in the German political economy.* Oxford University Press on Demand.

Streeck, W. (2011). Taking capitalism seriously: towards an institutionalist approach to contemporary political economy. *Socio-Economic Review, 9*(1), 137–167.

Streeck, W., & Thelen, K. (2005). Introduction. In *Beyond continuity: institutional change in advanced political economies* (pp. 1–39). Oxford University Press.

Toner, E., Adalja, A., Gronvall, G. K., Cicero, A., & Inglesby, T. v. (2015). Antimicrobial resistance is a global health emergency. *Health Security, 13*(3), 153. https://doi.org/10.1089/HS.2014.0088

Van Bavel, J. J., Baicker, K., Boggio, P. S., Capraro, V., Cichocka, A., Cikara, M., ... & Willer, R. (2020). Using social and behavioural science to support COVID-19 pandemic response. *Nature Human Behaviour, 4*(5), 460–471.

Vandersmissen, A., & Welburn, S. C. (2014). Current initiatives in One Health: consolidating the One Health global network. *Revue scientifique et technique (International Office of Epizootics), 33*(2), 421–432.

Walt, G. (1998). Globalisation of international health. *The Lancet, 351*(9100), 434–437.

6. Migration management and international political economy

Nicholas R. Micinski

Introduction

Migration management is an increasingly important policy issue within political science, as well as an emerging research area within international political economy (IPE). States and international organizations (IOs) prioritize the regulation and control of migration because migration is viewed both as a valuable resource and a strategic tool within geopolitical relations. Migrants and refugees are also valuable economic resources as temporary workers, remittances, and development aid. Migration management consists of a constellation of actors, responsibilities, and funding working to control who comes or goes in different countries. This is particularly relevant within IPE because the international migration regime has been a place for states and IOs to experiment with new forms of governance, to pursue state interests, and to avoid accountability. New forms of migration governance also introduce non-state actors, like private border guards and detention centers, and intergovernmental organizations like the International Organization for Migration and European Asylum Support Office. Incorporating these new actors into migration management has resulted in increasingly complicated financial arrangements that delegate, subcontract, externalize, and outsource responsibility for migrants. This raises important questions about power and funding within the international migration regime.

In this chapter, I focus on the financing of the international migration regime, shifting away from the typical IPE approach to migration that looks narrowly at the contribution of labor migration to trade and globalization. A rich literature within the IPE tradition has developed on the role of labor migration, guestworker programs, the migration and development nexus, and remittances within international relations (Peters 2017; Phillips 2011; Ruhs 2015; Hollifield 1992). Others have studied the impact of immigrants on wages and labor markets, the economic push and pull factors that lead to migration, and the global shift toward more selective immigration policies (Abowd and Freeman 2007; Sassen 1990; Hear, Bakewell, and Long 2018; Boucher and Gest 2018). Instead, this chapter sets out a research agenda on the global politics of who pays for and benefits from the international migration regime. By following the money, I examine how states conceptualize migration as a strategic resource in power relations. Overall, states are experimenting with new forms of migration governance to pursue their national interests and to avoid accountability within increasingly complicated contexts.

Emergent issues in IPE and migration management

Migration management aid

The clearest look into the IPE of migration regimes is to examine who pays for what. Increasingly, donor countries in the Global North are using foreign aid to target migration with the hope of addressing the "root causes of migration." The aid often falls into two camps: (1) development aid hoping to decrease emigration by improving local economies and (2) aid to national migration institutions hoping to decrease emigration by making it harder for people to leave. In total, some US$130.5 billion in official development aid went to migration-related activities from 2002–2018. Regionally, more than €4.7 billion was promised in 2015 through the EU Trust Fund for Africa to "address the root causes of destabilisation, forced displacement and irregular migration" (European Commission 2015, p. 6). In 2021, President Biden also proposed a US$4 billion aid package to address the root causes of migration in Guatemala, El Salvador, and Honduras (White House 2021). Norman and Micinski (2021) identify how migration management aid is different from other forms of aid, specifically that migration aid funds the state capacity of migration agencies, targets root causes of migration, and is often conditionally linked to restrictive migration policies. Donor countries funnel the aid through multiple pathways, such as increasing state capacity, improving economic development, supporting civil society, or engaging a diaspora (Norman and Micinski 2021). While migration management aid is often framed as "good governance" and lumped together with democratic governance reforms, it is not necessarily clear that stronger borders and more surveillance of citizens makes for stronger democracies. Lanati and Thiele (2018a, 2018b) found that foreign aid decreases emigration when the aid is used to improve public services and the social sector for the poorest individuals. Gamso and Yuldashev (2018) showed that governance-specific aid could reduce emigration but economic and social-specific aid could increase emigration. However, both studies look at total aid or other general categories of aid and do not account specifically for migration management aid. Little is known about the impact of aid targeting migration management, particularly its impact on human rights, democratic governance, and the economy of recipient countries. How does migration management aid change democratic institutions or the rule of law? How does migration management aid intersect with the securitization of migration policies? What are the negative externalities of these kinds of interventions on the rights of both migrants and citizens? Finally, who are the economic winners and losers with migration management aid, both inside and outside of state institutions? Future research should examine both the intended and unintended effects of migration management aid on power relationships at the national, regional, and global level.

Earmarked funding

A second key area of finance within migration management is the overwhelming role of earmarked funding within international organizations. In contrast to mandatory assessed contributions (i.e. United Nations dues), earmarked funding is any voluntary contribution to an international organization with restrictions on its use. These donations typically have strings attached: states dictate to IOs how and where to spend the money, while restricting who qualifies as beneficiaries. Since the 1990s, earmarked funding has increased in prevalence throughout the UN system, reaching a new high in 2017 with 79 percent of UN humanitarian funding and 73 percent of UN development funding that was earmarked (Jenks 2014; Baumann and Weinlich 2021, p. 154). In 2016, earmarked funding was a key part of UN migration agencies, including IOM (90.5%), UNHCR (80.7%), UNRWA (47.1%), and ILO (37.7%) (Chief Executives Board for Coordination 2018).

But the increasing reliance on voluntary, earmarked funding raises important questions about the politics of global migration governances. Graham argues that earmarked funding undermines multilateralism because it bypasses the UN's traditional democratic decision-making structures (Graham 2017; Goetz and Patz 2017). Others suggest that earmarking is a form of "selective multilateralism" that allows smaller groups of states to cooperate on controversial issues like migration because they do not need buy-in from all member states (Seitz and Martens 2017, p. 46). But earmarked funding can also lead to states boycotting or withdrawing their funding from UN agencies with which they disagree. For example, Bayram and Graham (2017) found that the US earmarked more funding to UN bodies from 1945–1980 when they disagreed with the governing bodies of those UN agencies—evidentially circumventing the executive boards to directly fund their priorities. Earmarked funding can also have other distorted effects on UN bodies: another study found a correlation between the amount of earmarked funding from a donor country and the number of staff from that country (Thorvaldsdottir 2016).

Within migration management, IOM stands out for its history of being influenced by major donor countries and its unique reliance on earmarked funding. IOM was created in 1951 in part because the United States objected to plans for the International Labour Organization (ILO) to coordinate the transfer of migrants in post-war Europe. The United States was concerned about Soviet influence within the ILO, instead preferring to funnel US funding to a new organization, the Provisional Intergovernmental Committee for the Movement of Migrants from Europe (PICMME), which was later renamed the International Organization for Migration (IOM) (Perruchoud 1989). The United States has remained the largest donor and, as a result, IOM's top priorities reflect those of the United States, particularly refugee resettlement. The European Union is also a significant donor to IOM, funding IOM projects on irregular migration and return. In the 1990s, IOM embraced its reputation and underwent the "projectization" of its activities; projectization is the practice of accounting for the full cost of each project (including staff, HQ, and infrastructure), freeing IOM from relying on core contributions for overhead costs. IOM often boasts of being the most efficient UN agency with the lowest rate of administrative support at only 7 percent (IOM 2014). Importantly, because the refugee regime is more rigid, member states relied on IOM and its flexible funding structure to provide support to vulnerable migrants who do not necessarily qualify as refugees under the 1951 convention (Lebon-McGregor and Micinski 2021, p. 31).

The significant dependence of earmarked funding within migration governance raises other important questions: how does earmarked funding impact the priorities of UNHCR and other normative actors within global migration governance? How do small donor countries use earmarked funding differently than large donors to influence migration management? How do international norms and human rights shape the way IOs use earmarked funding when implementing projects related to migration? And finally, in what ways can IOM and other actors within migration management be held accountable when the largest donors are also the most powerful members of their governing bodies?

Delegation to international organizations

A third trend is the delegation of key aspects of migration management to international organizations. Delegation is defined as the transfer of a task from a principle to an agent and can lead to greater efficiency because it develops expertise, consolidates tasks, and removes overlapping structures. Delegation can also be a strategy for ensuring states are credibly committed to policies over the long term because it removes the policy from short-term electoral pressures (Majone 2001). Delegation is not a new phenomenon: states delegate all sorts of tasks to committees or agencies. However, states are more hesitant to delegate sensitive tasks, like border control or asylum adjudication, that might infringe on their sovereign authority. States worry that international organizations might overstep their authority, make decisions that are not in their interest, or redirect resources to alternative projects. States experiment with new forms of delegation, such as subcontracting or privatization, as ways of overcoming challenges to their sovereignty and agency slack. Subcontracting is defined as the temporary transfer of authority to an external organization (outside of the national bureaucracies) (Micinski 2022, pp. 37–40). States are more likely to subcontract some aspects of migration management because subcontracting is a temporary rather than permanent transfer of authority. Subcontracts include additional control mechanisms like mandatory reporting and audits, partial disbursement of funds, and supervision by courts or ombudsmen. If a state is unhappy with the performance of the IO, they can choose to cancel or not renew the subcontract.

States are more likely to subcontract to IOs when migration state capacity is low and there are no credible partners on the ground. For example, during the 2015–2017 refugee crisis in Europe, the EU chose to subcontract much of the response in Greece to UNHCR because the Greek government had such low migration state capacity and the EU did not trust that the Greek government would implement EU policies (Micinski 2022, chapter 5). Instead of relying on Greek institutions, the EU delegated responsibility by directing 73 percent of the €772 million for refugees to IOs. As a result, delegation was a strategic workaround of the sovereignty of an intransigent EU member state that was not reliably implementing migration policies on the EU's external border.

Alternatively, states may delegate to IOs through indifference. Norman (2020) shows how Egypt, Morocco, and Turkey used strategic indifference to refugees and migrants in their territory in order to shift responsibility to IOs like UNHCR and IOM. This sort of delegation through indifference or lack of policy actions can have economic or political benefits because host states do not need to allocate their own resources to support refugees and are not necessarily held responsible by their domestic constituents for any negative impacts. In fact, states may prefer to delegate to IOs or a private contractor in order to create a buffer from accountability: private companies do not require the same level of transparency, are not subject to Freedom of Information requests, and the details of subcontracts are sometimes shielded by trade secrets protections. All of this means that delegation can be a strategy to obscure responsibility for migration policies in order to avoid accountability.

Why have delegation and subcontracting become so prominent within the international migration regime? In some ways, the structure of the regime itself incentivizes delegation in order to rely on the expertise of UNHCR and IOM, to shift politically difficult decisions to IOs, to credibly commit over the long term, and to avoid accountability for human rights violations. States do not necessarily want to abdicate their sovereign authority over migration management, but they also do not want to be held accountable for their many failings in migration policy. Delegation to IOs offers some strategic incentives for states. However, as funding and responsibilities shift within migration management, so do the power structures and influential actors. It remains to be seen what the impact will be for UNHCR and IOM as their budgets grow and they take on larger roles within global migration governance.

Externalization

The fourth trend in migration management funding is that of externalization. States in the Global North, particularly EU member states and the United States, seek to prevent migrants and asylum seekers from reaching their borders by "externalizing" or transferring border control policies to neighboring transit states. The European Council began in the early 2000s devising its "external dimension" of cooperation with third countries, including the exportation of more strict border controls and anti-trafficking policies (Boswell 2003). Externalization often occurred through bilateral agreements related to specific migration policies, labor migration, readmission of irregular migrants, cooperation between police and border agencies, international dialogues, and official development aid (Jaulin et al. 2021). The EU and US have built walls and fences, established carrier sanctions that fine airlines, and visa restrictions, all to prevent asylum seekers from ever arriving in their territory (FitzGerald 2020). FitzGerald (2019, p. 10) argues that this kind of externalization is a catch-22 because European governments agreed to "not kick you out if you come here. But we will not let you come here."

Perhaps the most infamous externalization agreement was the EU–Turkey deal in 2015 in which the EU committed to €3 billion in aid for refugees in

Turkey in exchange for strict enforcement of border controls and the readmission of all irregular migrants attempting to cross the Mediterranean Sea to Greece. European governments also promised to reopen EU accession negotiations with Turkey and to liberalize visa requirements for Turkish citizens. The deal represents a blatant example of externalization of migration management, particularly as the EU rushed to block the large number of arrivals during the 2015–2017 crisis. Human rights groups criticized the deal as undermining the EU's commitments to asylum seekers and for legitimizing illegal pushbacks that violate the principle of non-refoulement. Over the last 20 years, the EU has increasingly applied conditionality whereby development aid was linked to readmission agreements to facilitate the deportation of irregular migrants or refused asylum seekers from Europe to their country of origin. For example, EU member states had 96 readmission agreements in 2002, which increased to 514 by 2018 (Jaulin et al. 2021, p. 19). Jaulin et al. (2021) show that readmission agreements have some negative effect on the number of irregular border crossings in the EU, while also resulting in stranded asylum seekers in transit and a "rerouting" of migrants to alternative migration paths. More generally, the EU used "mobility partnerships" to link aid, readmission agreements, and trade deals with at least nine countries (Reslow 2015; Reslow and Vink 2015; Maisenbacher 2015). Scholars describe this use of diplomatic tools to control migration, like readmission agreements or trade deals, as "migration diplomacy" (Adamson and Tsourapas 2019; Thiollet 2011; İçduygu and Aksel 2014; Oyen 2015; Tsourapas 2021).

Scholars have identified several goals of externalizations, primarily to offshore border controls and outsource the processing of asylum claims (van Dessel 2019). Lavenex and Schimmelfenig (2009) theorize that externalization occurs through hierarchical relationships where powerful states dictate migration rules to their weaker neighbors. States pursue this through networked relationships, where more equal states cooperate together on rules, or through market-based relationships in which states compete for migration rules that favor their interests. Other international organizations, like UNHCR or IOM, also play a role in the externalization of EU migration policies by providing a counterweight to EU policies, subcontracting policy implementation, and transmitting EU rules through international networks (Lavenex 2015). Lavenex suggests that IOs both provide genuine expertise to implement EU migration policies abroad and lend their legitimacy as "neutral" or "technocratic" actors (Lavenex 2015, p. 560).

States continue to innovate in the sphere of externalization—devising more absurd and far-flung ways of keeping migrants and asylum seekers away from their shores. For example, the United States invoked in 2020 an obscure rule, Title 42, to immediately expel migrants and asylum seekers back across the border (and shifting the burden to Mexico) because of fears of spreading COVID-19—despite the fact that virus transmission was higher within the United States than their home countries. Indeed, the Biden Administration continues to rely on Title 42 to expel migrants on the southern border to shift responsibility to Mexico in the absence of wider US immigration reform. Elsewhere, Denmark and the UK have proposed hosting asylum seekers in reception centers in Rwanda while their applications are processed (BBC 2021).

These practices raise questions about how the externalization of migration policies is strategically used by states to avoid their legal responsibilities to asylum seekers. Ever more complex financial and logistical arrangements continue to be proposed, suggesting that states are both innovating to find more efficient models and learning from others on how best to externalize policies. Future research should address how externalization avoids domestic and regional accountability mechanisms, in addition to how third countries resist the shifting, or dumping, of the responsibility that results from externalization.

Refugee commodification

A final related issue within IPE and migration management is fundraising strategies used by states that host significant numbers of refugees. Because the majority of the world's refugees flee to neighboring states in the Global South, host countries typically do not have enough resources in their domestic budgets to provide adequate support to refugees, forcing governments to appeal for help from the international community. This phenomenon of refugee commodification points to "the instrumental use of asylum seekers, refugees and other internationally displaced people for specific material or non-material payoffs by state and non-state actors at the international or domestic level" (Freier, Micinski, and Tsourapas 2021). Tsourapas (2017, 2019) described these countries as "refugee rentier states" that either blackmail (coerce) or back-scratch (cooperate with) the international community to receive more foreign aid. Countries that are migrant-sending, transit, or receiving states have different leverage within negotiations and, as such, can impact their fundraising strategies (Adamson and Tsourapas 2019). For example, Jordan and Lebanon pursued back-scratching strategies regarding aid for Syrian refugees in their territory, while Turkey blackmailed the EU. The differing strategies in part reflect their different geopolitical positions and status as transit or border states (Tsourapas 2019). Similarly, Greece leveraged the 2015–2017 refugee crisis to blackmail the rest of the EU during its debt bailout negotiations while deportations back to Greece were temporarily paused. However, Greece was forced to switch strategies to back-scratching when deportations resumed (Tsourapas and Zartaloudis 2022).

States expel, or threaten to expel, migrants and refugees as part of their wider foreign policy strategies (Greenhill 2010). Other scholars have incorporated how relatively weak refugee hosting states exploit their importance to regional stability and proxy relationships with superpowers to get more aid (Micinski 2021). In both Kenya and Pakistan, the governments used repeated threats and six-month or one-year delays in order to exploit the legal uncertainty and deportability of their refugee communities, and to extract foreign aid from the international community (Micinski 2021, p. 8). Similarly, the United States instrumentalized displaced people by resettling more refugees from their allies than their enemies that neighbor refugee-producing countries (Micinski 2018). These examples show how states leverage refugees within international relations, a practice that has diffused across the Global South through state-to-state learning, regional cooperation, and global emulation (Freier, Micinski, and Tsourapas 2021). In response, UNHCR announced it was "increasingly concerned by the instrumentalization of refugees and migrants by states apparently to achieve political ends ... People are not, and should never be, pawns in geopolitical games" (UNHCR 2021).

While economists have long argued that migrants and refugees are a net positive for the economy of host states, the phenomenon of refugee commodification points to other ways in which refugees are a metaphorical windfall and economic resource to host communities, particularly if states are willing to instrumentalize refugees as a strategic tool within their foreign policy. Scholars should continue to explore the mechanisms through which states instrumentalize refugees, e.g. threats to expel and one-year delays, and how these strategies are diffused across the Global North and Global South. Finally, scholars should investigate how commitments to refugees in international law influence state behavior regarding refugee commodification and financing migration management more generally.

Conclusion

This chapter has laid out an emerging research agenda on the IPE of migration management by exploring five key trends: migration management aid, earmarked funding, delegation to international organizations, externalization, and refugee commodification. Underlying each of these trends are powerful states using migration governance to pursue their economic and political interests. Studies have shown that funding impacts the priorities of international organizations, which in turn shape the policies implemented on the ground by key states. The IPE of migration management seeks to "follow the money" in order to reveal how power relations influence funding, which in turn influences migration policies and the lives of migrants. Much of the literature on migration aid, earmarked funding, and delegation frames these financial arrangements as apolitical, but this chapter has shown how money and migration governance are deeply political.

There is important and urgent work for scholars researching the intersection of IPE and migration management. At a base level, more should be done to collect and report financial data for migration institutions in accessible and reliable ways. Much of the data relied on in this chapter were scraped from PDFs hidden in a maze of bureaucratic and outdated websites. The UN and other institutions should publish global data on migration governance funding. The second urgent area for researchers is to incorporate a critical lens in our analyses of migration funding. Instead of reporting voluntary contributions and donations as altruistic, we must critically examine the motivations and impact of migration funding on relevant political institutions and state foreign policies. The third area for scholars is on the role of accountability in migration finance. Who along a chain of delegation is accountable for the impact of migration policies and accompanying human rights violations? How do international norms and laws impact the financial arrangements in the migration regime? In what innovative ways are non-state actors pushing back externalization or the shirking of responsibilities?

Ultimately, IPE and migration scholars should continue to interrogate who pays for, and benefits from, the current international migration regime and the system of finance that makes that regime possible.

References

Abowd, John M., and Richard B. Freeman. 2007. *Immigration, Trade, and the Labor Market*. University of Chicago Press.

Adamson, Fiona B., and Gerasimos Tsourapas. 2019. "Migration Diplomacy in World Politics." *International Studies Perspectives* 20 (2): 113–128.

Baumann, Max-Otto, and Silke Weinlich. 2021. "Funding the UN: Support or Constraint?" In *Routledge Handbook on the UN and Development*, edited by Stephen Browne and Thomas G. Weiss, 151–164. Routledge, Taylor & Francis Group.

Bayram, A. Burcu, and Erin R. Graham. 2017. "Financing the United Nations: Explaining Variation in How Donors Provide Funding to the UN." *Review of International Organizations* 12 (3): 421–59. https://doi.org/10.1007/s11558-016-9261-0

BBC. 2021. "Denmark Asylum: Law Passed to Allow Offshore Asylum Centres." *BBC News*, June 3, 2021, sec. Europe. https://www.bbc.com/news/world-europe-57343572.

Boswell, Christina. 2003. "The 'External Dimension' of EU Immigration and Asylum Policy." *International Affairs* 79 (3): 619–638.

Boucher, Anna K., and Justin Gest. 2018. *Crossroads of Migration: Comparative Immigration Regimes in a World of Demographic Change*. Cambridge University Press.

Chief Executives Board for Coordination (CEB). 2018. "Agency Revenue by Revenue Type | United Nations System Chief Executives Board for Coordination." https://www.unsystem.org/content/FS-A00-01

van Dessel, Julia. 2019. "International Delegation and Agency in the Externalization Process of EU Migration and Asylum Policy: The Role of the IOM and the UNHCR in Niger." *European Journal of Migration and Law* 21 (4): 435–458. https://doi.org/10.1163/15718166-12340060

European Commission. 2015. "Agreement Establishing the European Union Emergency Trust Fund for Stability and Addressing the Root Causes of Irregular Migration and Displaced Persons in Africa, and Its Internal Rules."

FitzGerald, David Scott. 2019. *Refuge Beyond Reach: How Rich Democracies Repel Asylum Seekers*. Oxford University Press.

FitzGerald, David Scott. 2020. "Remote Control of Migration: Theorising Territoriality, Shared Coercion, and Deterrence." *Journal of Ethnic and Migration Studies* 46 (1): 4–22. https://doi.org/10.1080/1369183X.2020.1680115

Freier, Luisa Feline, Nicholas R. Micinski, and Gerasimos Tsourapas. 2021. "Refugee Commodification: The Diffusion of Refugee Rent-Seeking in the Global South." *Third World Quarterly* 42 (1): 1–20.

Gamso, Jonas, and Farhod Yuldashev. 2018. "Targeted Foreign Aid and International Migration: Is Development-Promotion an Effective Immigration Policy?" *International Studies Quarterly* 62 (4): 809–20. https://doi.org/10.1093/isq/sqy029

Goetz, Klaus H., and Ronny Patz. 2017. "Resourcing International Organizations: Resource Diversification, Organizational Differentiation, and Administrative Governance." *Global Policy* 8 (August): 5–14. https://doi.org/10.1111/1758-5899.12468

Graham, Erin R. 2017. "Follow the Money: How Trends in Financing Are Changing Governance at International Organizations." *Global Policy* 8 (August): 15–25. https://doi.org/10.1111/1758-5899.12450

Greenhill, Kelly. 2010. *Weapons of Mass Migration: Forced Displacement, Coercion, and Foreign Policy*. Cornell University Press.

Hear, Nicholas Van, Oliver Bakewell, and Katy Long. 2018. "Push–Pull Plus: Reconsidering the Drivers of Migration." *Journal of Ethnic and Migration Studies* 44 (6): 927–944. https://doi.org/10.1080/1369183X.2017.1384135

Hollifield, James F. 1992. *Immigrants, Markets, and States: The Political Economy of Postwar Europe*. Harvard University Press.

İçduygu, Ahmet, and Damla B. Aksel. 2014. "Two-to-Tango in Migration Diplomacy: Negotiating Readmission Agreement between the EU and Turkey." *European Journal of Migration and Law* 16 (3): 337–363. https://doi.org/10.1163/15718166-12342060

IOM. 2014. "Organizational Structure." International Organization for Migration. September 30, 2014. https://www.iom.int/organizational-structure

Jaulin, Thibaut, Alice Mesnard, Filip Savatic, Jean-Noël Senne, and Hélène Thiollet. 2021. "Offshoring Control: Externalization Policies and Their Differential Impacts on Migrant and Refugee Flows to Europe during 'Crises.'" Conference Paper. APSA.

Jenks, Bruce. 2014. "Financing the UN Development System and the Future of Multilateralism." *Third World Quarterly* 35 (10): 1809–1828. https:// doi .org/ 10 .1080/01436597.2014.971597

Lanati, Mauro, and Rainer Thiele. 2018a. "The Impact of Foreign Aid on Migration Revisited." *World Development* 111 (November): 59–74. https:// doi .org/ 10 .1016/ j .worlddev.2018.06.021

Lanati, Mauro, and Rainer Thiele. 2018b. "Foreign Assistance and Migration Choices: Disentangling the Channels." *Economics Letters* 172 (November): 148–151. https:// doi.org/10.1016/j.econlet.2018.09.002

Lavenex, Sandra. 2015. "Multilevelling EU External Governance: The Role of International Organizations in the Diffusion of EU Migration Policies." *Journal of Ethnic and Migration Studies* 42 (4): 554–570.

Lavenex, Sandra, and Frank Schimmelfennig. 2009. "EU Rules beyond EU Borders: Theorizing External Governance in European Politics." *Journal of European Public Policy* 16 (6): 791–812.

Lebon-McGregor, Elaine, and Nicholas R. Micinski. 2021. "The Changing Landscape of Multilateral Financing and Global Migration Governance." In *Money Matters in Migration: Policy, Participation, and Citizenship*, edited by Tesseltje De Lange, Willem Maas, and Annette Schrauwen, 19–37. Cambridge University Press.

Maisenbacher, Julia. 2015. "The Political Economy of Mobility Partnerships – Structural Power in the EU's External Migration Policy." *New Political Economy* 20 (6): 871–893.

Majone, Giandomenico. 2001. "Two Logics of Delegation: Agency and Fiduciary Relations in EU Governance." *European Union Politics* 2 (1): 103–122.

Micinski, Nicholas R. 2018. "Refugee Policy as Foreign Policy: Iraqi and Afghan Refugee Resettlements to the United States." *Refugee Survey Quarterly* 37 (3): 253–278. https://doi.org/10.1093/rsq/hdy007

Micinski, Nicholas R. 2021. "Threats, Deportability, and Aid: The Politics of Refugee Rentier States and Regional Stability." *Security Dialogue*. https:// doi .org/ 10 .1177/ 09670106211027464

Micinski, Nicholas R. 2022. *Delegating Responsibility: International Cooperation on Migration in the European Union*. University of Michigan Press.

Norman, Kelsey P. 2020. *Reluctant Reception: Refugees, Migration and Governance in the Middle East and North Africa*. Cambridge University Press.

Norman, Kelsey P., and Nicholas R. Micinski. 2021. "Aid, Migration Management, and Authoritarianism." Working Paper.

Oyen, Meredith. 2015. *The Diplomacy of Migration: Transnational Lives and the Making of U.S.-Chinese Relations in the Cold War*. Cornell University Press.

Perruchoud, Richard. 1989. "From the Intergovernmental Committee for European Migration to the International Organization for Migration." *International Journal of Refugee Law* 1 (4): 501–517. https://doi.org/10.1093/ijrl/1.4.501

Peters, Margaret E. 2017. *Trading Barriers: Immigration and the Remaking of Globalization*. Princeton University Press.

Phillips, Nicola. 2011. *Migration in the Global Political Economy*. Lynne Rienner Publishers.

Reslow, Natasja. 2015. "EU 'Mobility' Partnerships: An Initial Assessment of Implementation Dynamics." *Politics and Governance* 3 (2): 117–128.

Reslow, Natasja, and Maarten Vink. 2015. "Three-Level Games in EU External Migration Policy: Negotiating Mobility Partnerships in West Africa." *Journal of Common Market Studies* 53 (4): 857–874.

Ruhs, Martin. 2015. *The Price of Rights: Regulating International Labor Migration.* Princeton University Press.

Sassen, Saskia. 1990. *The Mobility of Labor and Capital: A Study in International Investment and Labor Flow.* Cambridge University Press.

Seitz, Karolin, and Jens Martens. 2017. "Philanthrolateralism: Private Funding and Corporate Influence in the United Nations." *Global Policy* 8 (August): 46–50. https://doi.org/10.1111/1758–5899.12448

Thiollet, Helene. 2011. "Migration as Diplomacy: Labor Migrants, Refugees, and Arab Regional Politics in the Oil-Rich Countries." *International Labor and Working-Class History* 79 (1): 103–121.

Thorvaldsdottir, Svanhildur. 2016. "How to Win Friends and Influence the UN: Donor Influence on the United Nations' Bureaucracy." http://www.svanhildur.com/uploads/3/0/2/2/30227211/howtowinfriends.pdf

Tsourapas, Gerasimos. 2017. "Migration Diplomacy in the Global South: Cooperation, Coercion and Issue Linkage in Gaddafi's Libya." *Third World Quarterly* 38 (10): 2367–2385. https://doi.org/10.1080/01436597.2017.1350102

Tsourapas, Gerasimos. 2019. "The Syrian Refugee Crisis and Foreign Policy Decision-Making in Jordan, Lebanon, and Turkey." *Journal of Global Security Studies* 4 (4): 464–481.

Tsourapas, Gerasimos. 2021. *Migration Diplomacy in the Middle East and North Africa: Power, Mobility, and the State.* Manchester University Press.

Tsourapas, Gerasimos, and Sotirios Zartaloudis. 2022. "Leveraging the European Refugee Crisis: Forced Displacement and Bargaining in Greece's Bailout Negotiations." *JCMS: Journal of Common Market Studies* 60 (2): 245–263. Accessed June 21, 2021. https://doi.org/10.1111/jcms.13211

UNHCR. 2021. "UNHCR Urges States to Protect Refugees' Rights, Not to Instrumentalize Their Plight." UNHCR Nordic and Baltic Countries. July 27, 2021. https://www.unhcr.org/neu/64163-unhcr-urges-states-to-protect-refugees-rights-not-to-instrumentalize-their-plight.html

White House. 2021. "Fact Sheet: President Biden Sends Immigration Bill to Congress as Part of His Commitment to Modernize our Immigration System." 20 January. https://www.whitehouse.gov/briefing-room/statements-releases/2021/01/20/fact-sheet-president-biden-sends-immigration-bill-to-congress-as-part-of-his-commitment-to-modernize-our-immigration-system

PART IV

IPE in transition

7. Geotech: converging technology, markets, and politics in international political economy

Mark Abdollahian and Zining Yang

> Earth has entered an entirely new geological epoch: the Anthropocene, or the age of humans. It means that we are the first people to live in an age defined by human choice, in which the dominant risk to our survival is ourselves.
> –Achim Steiner, UNDP Director (Human Development Report 2020)

Introduction

In our transition to a new geologic era, technology advancements and trends seismically shift the fundamental fabric of IPE. Today over 3.5 billion people have smartphones which are computationally more powerful than all of what NASA had in 1969 to send a man to the moon (Kaku 2011, Statista 2021). Almost 60% of the world's population has access to the internet. Over 75% of people in the developed world have smartphones. Conversely 70% of people in the developing world do not (Statista 2021). Technology powers the fourth industrial revolution engine of the knowledge economy (WEF 2020a). It also drives the transmission belts of growth, inclusion, and sustainability across the planet.

The pervasiveness of technology in our daily lives and the explosion of computational power redistributes equities, which creates new 'haves and have nots'. Whether proliferation or democratization of sources, such innovations drive new growth. China now leads the US in global patents across many fields of research, development, and engineering (World Intellectual Property Organization), surprising many by emerging from the COVID-19 crisis with higher GDP growth recovery than the US or European industrialized economies (World Bank 2021). While aggregate distributions of global extreme poverty have improved, the divide between developed and developing continues to widen (Rosner and Ortiz-Ospina 2019). Geotech, the intersection of technology, markets, and politics, makes IPE significantly more connected, complex, and uncertain than ever (Abdollahian 2021).

IPE is more connected from several interdependence perspectives, encompassing individuals' daily lives and workplace culture to the global trade system (Keohane and Nye 1989). International trade has increased over 700% since the collapse of the Soviet Union (World Bank 2021) causing greater macroeconomic goods and service interdependence through globalization. Facebook's 2.89 billion or Twitter's 396 million monthly active users are only a few of the myriad of social media platforms with global reach and consequence. Free access to an open-source internet means many information asymmetry boundaries are broken via a simple Google or Wikipedia search, resulting in knowledge democratization and dissemination. Instead of limited or filtered media channel constraints, instant social connectivity and platforms further disintermediates previously trusted, traditional information sources yet accelerated misinformation.

Social media is not solely confined to crowdsourcing information or collective knowledge creation, but based on deep human needs, including self-affirmation and affective validation (Ekkekakis and Russell 2013, McDonald 2018). Obvious echo chambers and misinformation threat vectors seen throughout the COVID-19 pandemic capitalize on over 180 different human cognitive biases (Manoogian 2018). Less nefariously, many firms have also figured out a new consumer value proposition of 'form–function–feeling' technologies which self-reinforces both technology growth and ecosystem scaling of interconnected products, solutions, and services (Abdollahian 2021).

IPE is more complex for potential step changes for individual agency and human attainment. Our neurological cognitive capabilities are not that much more advanced than those of early Neolithic man 10,000 years ago. With the advent of written language and the printing press, however, human beings harnessed collective learning in big history (Christian 2018) – the ability to transfer information across time, space, culture, and each other, not condemned to reinventing or rediscovering knowledge individually each time. Open-source internet, social media, and crowdsourcing information drives 'wisdom of the crowd' collective learning that scales human knowledge (Page 2007, Yi et al. 2012). Individual knowledge proliferation leads to new behavior and orders through coordinated social organization. New knowledge and experiences expand individuals' spaces of possibilities (Pentland 2015) which human agency may or may not take advantage of. Today this provides new lives and livelihoods, arbitrage, and value creation opportunity sets, while simultaneously threatening job destruction for many.

IPE production functions are also more complex. Many mid and large corporates are shifting towards increasingly diversified and sophisticated products, solutions, and services. New digital markets provide enormous opportunities for asset componentization in large online ecosystems. Today such 'ecosystem companies' like Apple and Alphabet account for over 80% of the most valuable firms globally (McKinsey 2021a). These platforms leverage networked, hyperscale effects, horizontally connecting goods and services across sectors and vertically melding B2B and B2C value creation for an integrated and connected experience.

While large firms own the ecosystem platform, thousands of other smaller firms contribute individual assets as a component in the larger ecosystem. This is in marked contrast to traditional firms' value chains that operate in well-defined horizontal and vertical goods and service delivery spaces (Porter 1985). Hyperconnected ecosystems have already produced several sectoral transformations in the last decade, as seen in online advertising, travel aggregators, streaming media platforms, and retail investment. Complex, digital platforms will continue to create new value chains as well as disintermediate established firms and markets.

Unfortunately, more core uncertainty also exists today at the nexus of IPE than ever before. How will national leaders navigate the tradeoff between domestic demand for political, social, and cultural security balanced against a global knowledge economy's supply of sustainable and inclusive growth? And as we witness a refocusing of past US global leadership to more domestic priorities coupled with stagflationary pressures, what is the future multilateralism? With the rise of China marching ahead on the growth curve, globally dominating both inbound and outbound FDI flows for the first time in history (Statista 2021), what will be the future of IPE for the 21st century? What will be individuals, firms, economies, and nations' choices sets across the conflict–competition–cooperation spectrum?

Below we explore a few of these fundamental Geotech shifts in the fabric of IPE, starting with technology advancements and trends. Then we briefly outline key elements and components for adopting a more holistic, complex adaptive systems (CAS) framework that captures the evolving nature of individual, firm, market, and economy activities in key IPE areas. Finally, we modestly offer some insight into possible alternative global futures as we navigate the new Anthropocene era.

Technology advancements and emerging trends

Today Geotech enables and shapes human activities across almost every aspect in our lives, spanning personal, financial, social, political, and economic domains. More data have been generated in the last few years than all of previous human history combined (IBM 2018). Moore's law of miniaturization has increased a thousandfold in 40 years, while the Kurzweil curve of computational costs has plummeted accordingly (Kurzweil 2005). These feats were accomplished from accelerating returns from engineering advancements, efficient manufacturing processes, and economies of scale. We have also created enough bandwidth and data capabilities to facilitate real-time, device-to-device communication through 5G rollouts, the proliferation of cloud centers, and private sector upgrades to the internet backbone. Over 28 billion devices are currently connected to the internet (Statista 2021) with significantly more linked things than people on the planet. Each thing is a sensor, an object, a big data input for creating higher resolution and real-time maps of systems from the internet of things (IOT).

Each IOT thing can also be a control mechanism in a feedback loop, creating new economic, social, and political value. Subsequently engineers have reconfigured the internet addressing system to allow for 2^{128} unique IP addresses, which is equivalent to each atom on the surface of the earth having 100 internet addresses (Internet Assigned Numbers Authority 2021). Smartwatches, smart homes, smart TVs, smart cities and smart 'everythings', whether we need them or not, scale, shift, and expand the frontier of human activities with immense effects. These include the revolutionary advent of big data, AI, bots, IOT, blockchain, personal devices, as well as virtual reality, augmented reality, and burgeoning mediated reality among many others. Here we offer insights into how such emerging technologies impacts society in three key areas.

First, technological progress forces us to recalibrate our timescales, perspectives, mental models, and worldviews (Denzau and North 1994) of key IPE dynamics. Moving from farming technologies developed during the agricultural revolution to the Industrial Revolution took over 8,000 years of daily human progress. But from the Industrial Revolution to the invention of the light bulb only took 120 years. From there the moon landing took another 90 years, the internet took 22 years afterwards, and the sequencing of the entire human genome only took nine years from the birth of the internet (Kurzweil 2005, Grossman 2011). The global mRNA vaccine development against SARS-CoV-2 in 10 months compared to the usual decade timeframe is another testament to the compression of activity timescales.

Such acceleration spills over into the global political economy faster than we realize. Unfortunately, the length and breadth of peace dividends from American leadership with the end of the Cold War are already being curtailed. Neoliberal institutional frameworks, norms, and rules created over 75 years ago do not reflect the realities of today's economic geographies (Malecki 2015). Moreover, many are brittle and slow to adapt to underlying changing political power realities, economic dynamics, and exogenous shocks alike. The 2016 creation of a forward-looking Asian Infrastructure Investment Bank versus often retrospective IMF and World Bank 'lenders of last resort' only amplifies such disconnects. Currently we see the enabling of new, non-state actors with access to cheap technologies in new contexts and the re-emergence of Great Power Competition at global scales (Farhadi and Masys 2021). Thus, our views, theories, research, and policy prescriptions in the IPE landscape need to change accordingly, leaning into dynamic *new normals* instead of chasing evaporating and retrospective *status quos*.

Second, technology as an enabler defines the boundaries of what is economically possible. A few key enablers include 5G infrastructure networks, autonomous vehicles, smart cities, advanced healthcare, and new financial systems built on blockchain and crypto currency technologies. As individuals, we have more apps that facilitate daily work productivity and satisfaction in our lives. As organizations, we have enterprise-wide software to keep track of specialized information that fuses invaluable human know-how into precise scheduling processes to deliver on complex production functions. Given this new power, we are transitioning from brute force, elegant, or compact algorithms that solve simple tasks based upon restrictive assumptions, to more generalized, AI-based approaches on more complex tasks. This empowers individuals with new capabilities for human achievement, potentially equalizing and harnessing opportunity sets together for entrepreneurs in Silicon Valley and the Panjshir Valley alike.

Third, technology as a disruptor creates new sources of innovation through proliferation as well as challenging market makers and political leaders. A vast majority of technology is also now available to almost anyone with access to a computer and the internet. Most AI and machine learning algorithms are open source. Today innovation sources proliferate and scale, not confined to domestic elites, nation states, or MNCs of the 20th century. Whether Greta Thunberg and climate change or Mohamed Bouazizi and the Arab Spring, individuals are more empowered to bend the arc of history than ever before through communication, learning from each other via crowdsourcing and networked mobilization (Abdollahian 2021). Conversely, 21st-century Luddites enabled by social media technologies might result in a very different outcomes than their 19th-century progenitors.

These new sources of innovation challenge established value chains and economic networks across multiple sectors and national economies (Root 2015). From humble beginnings, social media has become its own self-reinforcing marketplace of human activities. Social media and peer-to-peer (P2P) information sharing platforms also threaten established media information oligopolies and governments. Second and higher order effects include misinformation, amplified by bots, intensifying domestic or international political polarization as recently witnessed in the last US election cycle or the Ukraine crisis. The development of micro-financing and (P2P) lending networks over the last decade obviate the need for banks as intermediaries in all but agrarian economies (Root, Jones, and Wild 2015). Yet financial MNCs continue to perform exceedingly well even in the turbulent wake of second and third order COVID-19 macroeconomic effects.

New sources of growth also redistribute equities across national economies and within domestic polities. Leveraging technology proliferation and competing on multi-factor productivity, part of China's economic development story starts with providing low-cost labor and intermediate goods for increasing global electronics demand. Western consumers, MNCs, and investors benefitted alike. With increased success, profits, and market share came added Chinese opportunities to move up the production value chain from intermediate to finished goods with access to new markets in vacuums of Western investment. With new Chinese wealth comes new consumer behavior and markets that MNCs profitably deliver on.

Today some IPE observers are preoccupied with a pedantic *laissez-faire* free market versus a government centric, state-owned enterprise debate. Even in the most capitalistic economies, no firm practices free-for-all or anyone-do-anything. Without capital and labor, organizational hierarchies, or strategy and management, corporate production functions would cease to exist. Yet framing such narratives resonates well and mobilizes winning domestic political coalitions on all sides (Riker 1962, Bueno de Mesquita et al. 2003). Even more troubling, many are either surprised or reticent to find that China is on course to surpass the US as the largest economy when IR and IPE scholars have been projecting the possibility of such for decades (Organski et al. 1995, Kugler and Lemke 1996, Tammen et al. 2000, Abdollahian and Kang 2008). So, what can we do for new directions and promising paths in IPE?

Complexity perspectives for IPE

In order to cope with the fundamental shifting of the IPE fabric, we need to broaden and sharpen our mental models. Complex adaptive systems (CAS) offer one such way forward, with a scientific framework for understanding common and universally connected, complex, and uncertain phenomena. Complexity science and its associated theories, tools, and techniques have been applied to diverse phenomena across most physical and biological systems for decades, winning the 2021 Nobel prize in Physics. However only recently have CAS frameworks gained popularity in the social sciences (Mitchell 2009). Figure 7.1 demonstrates some principal components of CAS relevant to IPE, across scales, systems, and behavior of human activities. Here complexity encompasses many elements, dynamically interacting, across several scales of human activities, which can change and self-organize into hierarchical orders that produce novel emergent behaviors across multiple domains (McKelvey 1999).

A first step in decoding complex systems is unit and behavioral classification across scales or levels of human of activity. Micro-level units are typically heterogenous individuals and groups, with the goal-directed, political, economic, and social behavior of human agency given multiple mental models. Meso-level units are often collectives of individuals and groups, with individuals acting, reacting, and interacting who can form social communities, institutions, or nation states through their networked relationships, activities, information, and interests. Macro-level units are typically the nexus of political economy structures and sub-systems that result from the previous sum of all individual human, group, organizational, and institutional actions.

However, each scale activity does not occur in a vacuum but in multiple system and nested sub-system contexts. There are often feedback loops both within and across multiple levels in CAS: as changing macro structures incentivize or constrain micro-level human behavioral choice sets and meso-networked institutions, while micro human agency and meso collective action ultimately define and shape our IPE environments (Abdollahian et al. 2010, Abdollahian 2021). Meaning and sensemaking can be made in both local and global system contexts, given various mental models, biases, limited information, and misperceptions. Unfortunately, both the COVID-19 crisis and climate change present CAS frameworks with which we all have personal, first-hand experience.

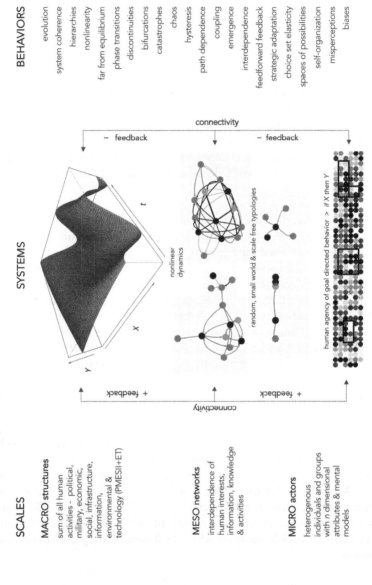

Figure 7.1 Characteristics of complex adaptive systems

As humans are dynamic, strategic, adaptive beings, behavior by design will change and evolve. Novel, emergent behavior or properties can appear when an individual or groups interact to form more complex behaviors with new actions, patterns, decisions, or structural orders. Emergent behavior is neither induced top-down nor forced into a system, but instead results from the interactions of system elements (Mitchell 2009).

Such new actions can provide benefits to some while imposing costs on others, with echo effects that reverberate up or down throughout CAS scales. Thus, new structures, hierarchies, orders, and coherence are created by interactivity and adaptive thinking (Nicolis and Prigogine 1989). Sometimes co-evolution occurs where individuals learn new behavior via mimicry or reciprocity and strategically adapt to each other and their environments (Ehrlich and Raven 1964).

CAS effects are often interactive, non-linear, and contingent (Holland 1998, Kauffman 2000). Those which might vary with the contextual state of each related individual and system at any particular time (Strogatz 2015). Understanding the current status of any individual unit, collective element, or a system includes its past history and future spaces of possibilities. Often prescribed by historical path dependence, unique final states of individuals, elements, and the system itself are achieved due to sensitivity to initial conditions, phase transitions, and accumulative endogenous momentum (Katz and Kahn 1978, Abdollahian 2021).

Agency, self-organization, emergence, path dependence, far from equilibrium behavior, co-evolution, and strategic adaptation are all critical concepts in CAS perspectives for IPE (Epstein and Axtel 1996, Axelrod and Cohen 2000, Mitleton-Kelly 2003). Random, small world and scale free network typologies, as well as their dynamics, can be instrumental for behavior. For example, activities by individual actors in a sparse, random network will not propagate locally or globally to other actors in the network. However, with preferential attachment typologies, this is not necessarily the case as one individual's actions can trigger several other reactions and interactions among other actors, often providing necessary conditions for contagion effects and tipping points (Abdollahian et al. 2006).

However, complexity theory does not argue for ever-increasing interconnectivity between related systems or entities. Dynamic cycles of cooperation and competition between individual units or system actors can change dramatically under differing orders (Abdollahian et al. 2010). In fragile states, increased government service delivery and rising market expectations can alter actors' conflict–competition–cooperation choice sets (Abdollahian et al. 2012, Kugler et al. 2015). Conversely, exogenous shocks such as COVID-19 and unexpected catastrophes such as climate change can propel coherence phase transitions from order to disorder and back again to a new order (Mitchell 2009). Such tipping points can force disorders and precipitate disintegration in systems with limited carry capacities or inelastic adaptation abilities given slow institutional response times (Gleick 1987, Waldrop 1992, Çambel 1993) as perhaps we are witnessing in multilateral institutional responses to today's IPE challenges.

CAS IPE frameworks encompass the past success of micro motivations of macro behavior (Shelling 1978), extending 'bottom-up' flows of individual, domestic institutional, and international levels of analysis in Open Economy Politics (OEP) (Katzenstein et al. 1998, Lake 2009, Oatley 2017). However, CAS approaches are neither exclusively bottom-up or top-down nor unidirectional, but holistic in how coupling, feedback, and bi-directional scale activities can change in systems and sub-systems. Figure 7.2 depicts such an interrelated macro system of contemporary growth, inclusion, sustainability, and governance interactions given broad findings across the IPE literature.

Although built on simple-to-understand, stand-alone bivariate relationships, phenomena coupling, balancing, and endogenous feedback loops create deep, rich, and nuanced insights for IPE integrating theory, evidence, and policy. While seemingly complicated, systems should be based upon the myriad of scientific theories and evidence, not constrained by our cognitive limits as human beings. Today's Anthropocene realities necessitate us to move from static, linear, and additive explanations to dynamic, non-linear, and interactive approaches both in theory and practice (Willett 2021).

However holistic from a macro perspective, cross-scale activities of micro-level individual agency and meso networked groups and communities are often absent. These induce far from equilibrium behavior that stress many macro models. Like tips of icebergs, these need to be disaggregated to understand the undercurrents that result in macro growth, societal stability, and inequality dynamics across all scales of human activities (Abdollahian et al. 2013, Yang 2016, Abdollahian et al. 2021).

Developing CAS perspectives throughout IPE can allow for behavioral, informational, and ideational context-centric approaches as well as new economic geography (Owen and Walter 2017, Rickard 2021). Such systems thinking, theory, science, and engineering (Parsons 1951, von Bertalanffy 1968) compliment IPE's innate transdisciplinary perspectives. Most recently, scholars

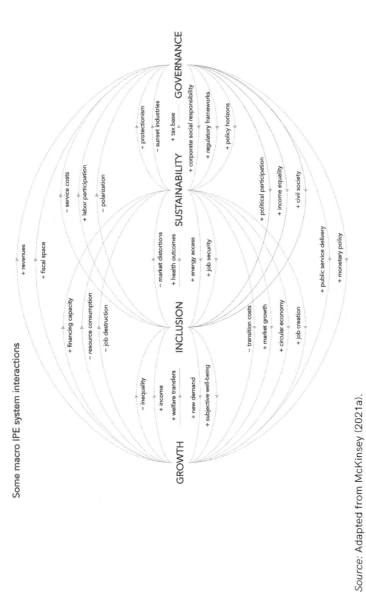

Source: Adapted from McKinsey (2021a).

Figure 7.2   Growth, inclusion, sustainability, and governance interactions

advocate the adoption of multiple partial analysis, contextually dependent with contingent hypotheses relevant to theories, narratives, or mental models of systems and sub-systems (Willett 2021).

Shifting the fabric of IPE

As Geotech accelerates, scales, and proliferates, the Anthropocene will continue to evolve. This in turn transforms individual incentives, firm production functions, national sustainable growth trajectories, and global economic complexity in step change. Increasing connectivity amplifies the coupling of micro-meso and macro-human activities. This generates new sources of innovation that leapfrog past market leaders, creating new winners and losers in economies and society (Arthur 1995). As seen in Figure 7.2, the macro IPE system of growth, inclusion, sustainability, and governance is as interrelated as ever.

Today, modern economies possess a wealth of knowledge. Specific pieces are distributed among various individuals and groups who functionally specialize. A new knowledge economy production function creates, identifies, and organizes know-how, know-what, know-who, and know-where together in new, unique ways. Know-how is key information and skills each individual holds from know-what expertise and experience. This can be dedicated to a single task or intermediate goods and services as part of a larger production function for greater value creation. Know-who creates, identifies, and organizes these key pieces of information. Know-where synchronizes all elements together to focus down on a particular production function (Hausmann et al. 2014, Balland et al. 2022).

Managerial economics harnesses specialized, individual know-how into more complex know-what for any organization, aggregating micro-level production functions into a greater synergistic whole (Felipe and Fisher 2001). An effective organization or firm can often quickly accomplish more and higher-quality outputs than the summed lifetime activities of any individual. This diversity of know-how can be recombined in different ways than any one individual ever imagined, addressing market needs or creating new markets altogether (Arthur 2021).

However, getting individuals to work together still presents a collective action problem, fusing an individual's private labor or goods into a larger, organized economic group output or social public good (Olson 1965). One obvious collection action challenge posits the convenience of individuals' hydrocarbon lifestyles against climate change negative externalities in the Anthropocene. Such social traps (Hardin 1968, Platt 1973) span not only ecology, but include key contemporary IPE themes such as poverty alleviation, inequality reduction, shared prosperity, as well as cultural diversity, equity, and inclusion.

As Geotech progresses, collective action coordination and managing the private versus public goods tradeoff will become even more difficult. This will likely occur due to diminishing relative contributions of individuals to more complex production functions and value chains. These trends will likely amplify tensions between individual human activities with perceived political, social, or cultural freedom and equality, compared to that of massively larger group collectives, institutions, governments, and MNCs promising economic growth (Feng 2005).

And if such amplifying friction between individuals and firms' collective production functions or even governments' public service delivery is not addressed, then higher real unemployment can cause lower labor force participation, disengaging social groups from the economy. Knock-on effects including stifling income growth with persistent, negative inclusion and sustainability effects. This presents regressive political populism opportunities as seen throughout many conflict trap economies (Collier and Hoeffler 2004, Hegre and Sambanis 2006). However, such cross-scale, interconnected ripple effects are not confined to the developing world anymore. Some observers even recently quipped that the greatest threat to global political economy is actually predicated on domestic US politics (Bremmer 2019).

As the knowledge economy becomes more complex, enterprise value chains and production functions must become even more sophisticated to continually provide relative value, often in new areas. Building infrastructure creates jobs and secondary markets and has multiplier effects across economies. However, innovative products, solutions, and services enabled by technology create novel, adjacent market spaces that did not exist previously (Kim and Mauborgne 2004). Blockchain technology led to new, blue ocean crypto currency markets with dramatic yet volatile returns.

Twentieth-century automotive and aerospace manufacturing asset componentization now pervades the digital economy. The tremendous valuation of online marketing, social media, and fintech firms results from delivering hyperconnected individual goods and services in a broader ecosystem of integrated verticals and markets. These sophisticated production functions and integrated value chains unlock more complex economic value realization.

A recent survey found that over 60% of jobs today did not exist a generation ago due to the evolutionary effects of technology in the labor markets (Autor et al. 2020). However, such aggregate upsides mask disaggregated downsides. Job destruction uncertainty varies by sectors, skill level, and ultimately value creation. While many believe that AI has the potential to disrupt a majority of jobs in some fashion (World Economic Forum 2020b), whether it results in net job destruction or net job gains remains to be seen. Lower skilled labor is at greater risk for job destruction, which would only exacerbate income inequalities in advanced knowledge economies. And these would only further drive existing structural gender, religious, and ethnic cleavages in societies.

Neither individuals' livelihoods nor firms' production functions are perfectly elastic. Each take time to transition to new market opportunities. Some can retrain and pivot while other disenfranchised groups and sunset industries lobby for government subsides, political protectionism, and trade barriers (Aggarwal 1985, Aggarwal and Newland 2014). Such transformations of value chain inputs naturally resonate throughout economies, facilitating the growing multiplexity of global supply chains. This exposes individuals, investors, markets, and governments to increasing complex accumulative risk as well as new systemic risk (Bonabeau 2007).

Regulatory reverberations from the 2008 global financial crisis strained many international financial institutions operating below their cost of capital. Recently this has forced both the adoption of new environmental, social, and governance (ESG) criteria to attract continued investment as well as leveraging technology advancements for efficiencies (Ruetschi 2022). And as lean, under-resourced healthcare systems and broken, just-in-time global supply chains from the pandemic remind us, we might need to reconsider our production function goals: optimizing efficiency and maximizing profits or delivering robust and resilient ESG growth.

In this context, political leaders must contend with the tradeoff between the supply of economic growth versus the domestic demand for political security (Abdollahian et al. 2012, 2013, Yang 2016). A post-WWII neoliberal milieu created peace through deterrent strength via alliance security organizations. Together with multilateral international institutions, they facilitated shared prosperity. Such macro environments and meso networks subsequently incentivized and constrained behavior to be aligned with increasing globalization, albeit with variegated results. 'Sustainable growth' was birthed as a key buzzword for leaders and politicians worldwide. If organizations and governments can deliver on the promise of things always getting better with expanding upside opportunities, who would want to change that vision of the *status quo*?

Domestically, such political security concerns also encompass social, cultural, and ethno-religious values. The pandemic's exogenous shock, higher order ripple effects create tipping points and *new normals* on how we work and live daily. Nearly 70 million Americans left their jobs in 2021 (McKinsey 2021b). The 'great resignation' in the US labor market centers on rebalancing work-life activities to be more in line with individuals' status, needs, and wants. Such refocusing offers improved human attainment, subjective well-being (Helliwell et al. 2021), transitions to post-materialistic values (Inglehart and Welzel 2003), and better societal outcomes (Sachs et al. 2021). However, new individual attitudes also challenge established social, cultural, economic, and political networks which will only beget new networks, rules, and social norms.

These will likely propel American cultural work and social values to be more post-materialistic and aligned with Europeans, albeit with much a more individualistic focus. Such a transition from traditional materialistic to more self-expressive and rational or secular values is a hallmark of advanced democracies but also a harbinger of lower economic growth due to diminishing marginal returns from previously realized productivity gains (Kostis et al. 2017). Yet this will not occur homogeneously within societies, further stressing polarization divides along urban and rural economic geographies.

However, the economic growth game may also fundamentally change, for better or worse. We already see heterogenous pandemic recoveries across different sectors and national economies with domestic political, social, and cultural polarization cycles: short, sharp *V* shaped, medium-to-longer-term *U* shaped, *L* shaped structural breaks in either supply or demand sides of markets, and *K* shaped divergent bifurcations where new political economy winners and losers are determined (Sheiner and Yilla 2020).

At the firm level, basic versus applied RDE investments in AI, quantum computing, and the internet of things for almost everything generate new sources of innovation. Basic RDE in quantum computing promises to revolutionize the pace and reach of the digital economy as *in silico* AI learning far outpaces human *in vivio* double loop learning. Cold fusion, looming sometime on the horizon this century, will certainly rewrite most of what we know about energy economics (Conrad and Rondeau 2020). However, most private sector investment is skewed towards less transformational, applied RDE for short-term ROI for shareholders.

As new digital markets are created in knowledge economies, this might provide the opportunity for innovative, highly specialized labor pools with increasing marginal productivity gains in advanced economies to capture new growth and escape the conditional convergence trap (Barro 1991, Levine and Renelt 1992, Barro and Sala-i-Martin 1992, Sperlich and Sperlich 2012, Abdollahian and Yang 2013, Yang and Abdollahian 2014). Some estimate that the value of a digital ecosystem economy will be over US$80 trillion, accounting for a third of the total global output by 2030 (McKinsey 2021b). Throughout all, Geotech advancements will continue to accelerate, enable, and disrupt the very fabric of IPE for individuals, firms, markets, and nations.

Alternative IPE futures

Finally, we explore some possible alternative IPE driven by the convergence of technology, markets, and politics through the lens of scenario analysis. Here we extend these new 21st-century political economy trends, processes, and insights spanning the conflict–competition–cooperation spectrum, including the rise of populism, decoupling, and unilateralism compared to the multilateral, global, and neoliberal norms of the past.

Given changing global power dynamics and economic trajectories, Figure 7.3 outlines the ranges of key IPE uncertainties across national policy and strategy dimensions. National policy spans nationalism, regionalism, and globalism outlooks often driven by domestic political-economy production functions while firm and government strategies span the conflict–competition–cooperation continuum given operational interests. Conflict strategies are usually zero sum with relative gains and based upon non-cooperative game theory while cooperation strategies are non-zero sum with absolute gains and based on cooperative game theory. In between, competition strategies employ mixed strategies but usually agree on the norms, rules, and frameworks for competition. By plotting the ranges of these key uncertainties, a mix of different global IPE scenarios emerges. While not assigning any probability or likelihood to one, it outlines the realm of possible scenarios and nine different plausible alternative futures with systemic consequences.

Shedding light on alternative futures for the remainder of this century starts with learning from the last century. In the Cold War era, global containment and conflict were the dominant strategies, resulting in a bifurcation of East and West. Due to an existential nuclear threat, this eventually morphed into more competitive strategies worldwide with spheres of influence between capitalist and communist worldviews and systems. After the collapse of the Soviet Union, partly due to the West's economic and democratic performance, a new *pax Americana* pushed national strategies towards the competition and

Nine different 21st-century scenarios given national policy stance and strategic interactions

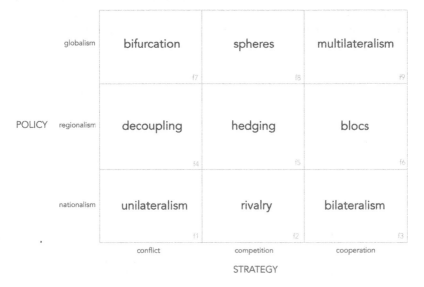

Figure 7.3   Scenario analysis of alternative IPE futures

cooperation end of the global policy spectrum, facilitating multilateralism and unprecedented global growth. However, global multilateralism did not benefit all equally.

In the last 20 years, changing US priorities from global economic leadership to the global war on terror, combined with China's meteoric development and value chain ascendency, set the stage for recent trends. Here we see calls for decoupling markets and institutions based on regional political and economic influence, weighted towards the conflict side of the strategy spectrum. Gone are coalitional alliance consultations, leveraging multilateral track 1 and track 2 frameworks with more unilateralism, decide-announce-defend rivalries from nationalistic focused policy perspectives. Today we are still hovering around weighted competition-conflict strategies, albeit with a more global outlook. Concurrently, a vast majority of both allies and adversaries on all sides are adopting hedging postures in a 'wait and see' approach on US–China power dynamics and how the fabric of IPE will likely evolve.

While the intersection of technology, markets, and politics has a new Geotech name, the dynamics are not completely novel. The same interplay of innovation, economic growth, population demography, market forces, and national political policy making that drove the US to pre-eminence in the 20th century also drove the UK and Germany in the 19th century, and France in the 18th century, as well as many other societies beforehand. However, Geotech convergence will only continue to accelerate, expand, and fundamentally transform the fabric of IPE through increased connectivity, complexity, and uncertainty.

As individuals, firms, and national leaders this forces us to lean ahead and reconsider new paths and directions for IPE. We cannot settle on retrospective lenses built on an eroding the *status quo* to navigate the future of IPE. Perhaps equally inspiring and terrifying, which scenario or mix of alternative futures we end up in the new Anthropocene era is still our very human choice.

References

Abdollahian, Mark. 2021. 'Surfing the Conflux: Technology, Information Environments and Great Power Competition Convergence,' in A. Farhadi et al. (eds.), *The Great Power Competition Volume 1*, Springer Nature Switzerland AG.

Abdollahian, Mark and Kyung-Kook Kang. 2008. 'In Search of Structure: The Nonlinear Dynamics of Power Transitions,' *International Interactions* 34: 333–357.

Abdollahian, Mark and Zining Yang. 2013. 'Towards Trade Equalization: A Network Perspective on Trade and Income Convergence Across the Twentieth Century,' *New Political Economy* 16: 3.

Abdollahian, Mark, Yi-Ling Chang and Yuan Yuan Lee. 2021. 'A Complex Adaptive System Approach for Anticipating Technology Diffusion, Income Inequality and Economic Recovery,' in O. Gervasi et al. (eds.), *Computational Science and Its Applications*. Springer International Publishing AG.

Abdollahian, Mark, Michael Baranick, Brian Efird and Jacek Kugler. 2006. 'Senturion: A Predictive Political Simulation Model,' *Defense & Technology*, National Defense University, Washington DC. Volume 32.

Abdollahian, Mark, Jacek Kugler, Brice Nicholson and Hana Oh. 2010. 'Politics and Power,' in A. Kott and G. Citrenbaum (eds.), *Estimating Impact: A Handbook of Computational Methods and Models for Anticipating Economic, Social, Political and Security Effects*. Springer Science and Business Media.

Abdollahian, Mark, Travis Coan, Hana Oh and Birol Yesilida. 2012. 'The Dynamics of Cultural Change: The Human Development Perspective,' *International Studies Quarterly* 56:3: 1–17.

Abdollahian, Mark, Zining Yang, Travis Coan and Birol Yesilada. 2013. 'Human Development Dynamics: an Agent Based Simulation of Macro Social Systems and Individual Heterogeneous Evolutionary Games' *Complex Adaptive Systems Modeling* 1:18.

Aggarwal, Vinod. 1985. *Liberal Protectionism: The International Politics of Organized Textile Trade*. University of California Press.

Aggarwal, Vinod and Sara Newland. 2014. *Responding to China's Rise: US and EU Strategies*. Springer.

Arthur, Brian W. 1995. *Increasing Returns and Path Dependence in the Economy.* University of Michigan Press.

Arthur, Brian W. 2021. 'Foundations of Complexity Economics,' *Nature* 3, February.

Autor, David, David Mindell and Elisabeth Reynolds. 2020. *The Work of the Future: Building Better Jobs in an Age of Intelligent Machines.* MIT Press.

Axelrod, Robert and Michael D. Cohen. 2000. *Harnessing Complexity: Organisational Implications of a Scientific Frontier.* Free Press.

Balland, Pierre-Alexandre, Tom Broekel, Dario Diodato, Elisa Giuliani, Ricardo Hausmann, Neave O'Clery and David Rigby. 2022. 'The new paradigm of economic complexity,' *Research Policy*, 51:3.

Barro, Robert. 1991. 'Economic Growth in a Cross-Section of Countries,' *Quarterly Journal of Economics*, 106.

Barro, Robert and Xavier Sala-i-Martin. 1992. 'Convergence,' *Journal of Political Economy*, 223–51.

Bonabeau, Eric. 2007. 'Understanding and managing complexity risk,' *MIT Sloan Management Review*, 48:4.

Bremmer, Ian. 2019. *The End of the American Order.* 2019 GZERO Summit.

Bueno de Mesquita, Bruce, Alastair Smith, Randolph M. Sieverson and James D. Morrow. 2003. *The Logic of Political Survival.* The MIT Press.

Çambel, Ali Bulent. 1993. *Applied Chaos Theory: A Paradigm for Complexity.* Academic Press.

Christian, David. 2018. *Origin Story: A Big History of Everything.* Little, Brown and Company.

Collier, Paul and Anke Hoeffler. 2004. 'Greed and Grievance in Civil War,' *Oxford Economic Papers* 56: 563–595.

Conrad, Jon and Daniel Rondeau. 2020. *Natural Resource Economics: Analysis, Theory, and Applications.* Cambridge University Press.

Denzau, Arthur T. and Douglass C. North. 1994. 'Shared Mental Models: Ideologies and Institutions,' *Kyklos* 47: 94.

Ehrlich, Paul R. and Peter H. Raven. 1964. 'Butterflies and Plants: A Study in Co-evolution,' *Evolution* 18: 586–608.

Ekkekakis, P. and J. Russell. 2013. 'The Measurement of Affect, Mood, and Emotion: A Guide for Health-Behavioral Research,' *Psychology* February 28.

Epstein, Joshua M. and Robert Axtel. 1996. *Growing Artificial Societies: Social Science from the Bottom Up.* Brookings Institution Press.

Farhadi, Adib and Anthony Masys (eds.). 2021. *The Great Power Competition Volume 1: Regional Perspectives on Peace and Security.* Springer Nature, Switzerland AG.

Felipe, Jesus and Franklin M. Fisher. 2001. 'Aggregation in Production Functions: What Applied Economists Should Know,' MIT monograph.

Feng, Yi. 2005. *Democracy, Governance, and Economic Performance Theory and Evidence.* The MIT Press.

Gleick, James. 1987. *Chaos: Making a New Science.* Vintage.

Grossman, Lev. 2011. '2045: The Year Man Becomes Immortal,' *Time Magazine*, February 10.

Hardin, Garrett. 1968. 'The Tragedy of the Commons,' *Science* 162:3859: 1243–1248.

Hausmann, Ricardo, César Hidalgo, Sebastián Bustos, Michele Coscia, Alexander Simoes and Muhammed A. Yildirim. 2014. *The Atlas of Economic Complexity.* MIT Press.

Hegre, Håvard and Nicholas Sambanis. 2006. 'Sensitivity Analysis of the Empirical Literature on Civil War Onset,' *Journal of Conflict Resolution* 50:4: 508–535.

Helliwell, John F., Richard Layard, Jeffrey D. Sachs, Jan-Emmanuel De Neve, Lara B. Aknin, and Shun Wang. 2021. *World Happiness Report 2021*. Accessed at https:// worldhappiness.report/ed/2021/

Holland, John. 1998. *Emergence: From Chaos to Order*. Addison-Wesley.

Inglehart, Ronald F. and Christian Welzel. 2003. 'The Theory of Human Development: A Cross-Cultural Analysis,' *European Journal of Political Research* 42:3: 341–379.

International Business Machines. 2018. https://www.ibm.com/analytics/data-science

Internet Assigned Numbers Authority. 2021. 'Number Resources'. https://www.iana .org/numbers

Kaku, Michio. 2011. In Alexis C. Madrigal, 'Your Smart Toaster Can't Hold a Candle to the Apollo Computer,' *The Atlantic*. https://www.theatlantic.com/science/archive/ 2019/07/underappreciated-power-apollo-computer/594121/

Katz, Daniel and Robert Kahn. 1978. *The social psychology of organizations*. Wiley.

Katzenstein, Peter J., Robert O. Keohane and Stephen D. Krasner. 1998. 'International Organization and the Study of World Politics,' *International Organization* 52:4: 645–685.

Kauffman, Stuart. 2000. *Investigations*. Oxford University Press.

Keohane, Robert O. and Joseph S. Nye. 1989. *Power and Interdependence*. HarperCollins.

Kim, W. Chan and Renee Mauborgne. 2004. 'Blue Ocean Strategy,' *Harvard Business Review* October: 76–84.

Kostis, Pantelis C., Kyriaki I. Kafka and Panagiotis E. Petrakis. 2017. 'Cultural change and innovation performance,' *Journal of Business Research* 88:2017, 306–313.

Kugler, Jacek and Douglas Lemke. 1996. *Parity and War*. University of Michigan Press.

Kugler, Jacek, Amir Bagherpour, Mark Abdollahian and Ashraf Singer. 2015. 'Pathways to Stability for Transition Governments in the Middle East and North Africa,' *Asian Politics & Policy*, 7, 5–38.

Kurzweil, Ray. 2005. *The Singularity is Near: When Humans Transcend Biology*. Penguin.

Lake, David A. 2009. 'Open Economy Politics: A Critical Review,' *Review of International Organizations* 4:3: 219–244.

Levine, Ross and David Renelt. 1992. 'A Sensitivity Analysis of Cross-Country Growth Regressions,' *American Economic Review*, 82.

Malecki, E. J. 2015. 'Connecting Local Entrepreneurial Ecosystems to Global Innovation Networks: Open Innovation, Double Networks and Knowledge Integration,' *International Journal of Entrepreneurship and Innovation Management* 14:1: 36–59.

Manoogian, John III. 2018. 'The Cognitive Bias Codex.' https://commons.wikimedia .org/wiki/File:Cognitive_bias_codex_en.svg

McDonald, Hal. 2018. 'Social Media Affirmation Goes Both Ways,' *Psychology Today*. https://www.psychologytoday.com/intl/blog/time-travelling-apollo/201809/social -media-affirmation-goes-both-ways

McKelvey, Bill. 1999. 'Self-organization, Complexity Catastrophe, and Microstate Models at the Edge of Chaos,' in J. A. C. Baum and B. McKelvey (eds.), *Variations in Organization Science: In Honor of Donald T. Campbell*. Sage.

McKinsey. 2021a. 'Our Future Lives and Livelihoods: Sustainable *and* Inclusive *and* Growing,' October 26, 2021. https://www.mckinsey.com/featured-insights/ sustainable-inclusive-growth/our-future-lives-and-livelihoods-sustainable-and -inclusive-and-growing

McKinsey. 2021b. 'America 2022 in charts: An economic opportunity snapshot,' December 13, 2021. https://www.mckinsey.com/featured-insights/sustainable -inclusive-growth/america-2022-in-charts-an-economic-opportunity-snapshot

Mitchell, Melanie. 2009. *Complexity: A Guided Tour*. Oxford University Press.
Mitleton-Kelly, Eve. 2003. 'Ten Principles of Complexity & Enabling Infrastructures,' in *Complex Systems and Evolutionary Perspectives on Organizations: The Application of Complexity Theory to Organizations*. Elsevier.
Nicolis, Gregorie and Ilya Prigogine. 1989. *Exploring Complexity*. W. H. Freeman.
Olson, Mancur. 1965. *The Logic of Collective Action: Public Goods and the Theory of Groups*. Harvard University Press.
Oatley, Thomas. 2017. 'Open Economy Politics and Trade Policy,' *Review of International Political Economy*, 24:4, 699–717.
Organski, A. F. K., Jacek Kugler and Mark Abdollahian. 1995. 'The Mosaic of International Power,' in Bouda Etemad et al. (eds.), *Towards an International Economic & Social History*. Editions Passé Present.
Owen, Erica and Stefanie Walter. 2017. 'Open Economy Politics and Brexit: Insights, Puzzles and Ways Forward,' *Review of International Political Economy* 24:2: 179–202.
Page, Scott E. 2007. *The Difference: How the Power of Diversity Creates Better Groups, Firms, Schools, and Societies*. Princeton University Press.
Parsons, Talcott. 1951. *The Social System*. Free Press.
Pentland, Alex. 2015. *Social Physics: How Social Networks Can Make Us Smarter*. Penguin Random House.
Platt, John. 1973. 'Social Traps,' *American Psychologist* 28, 641–51.
Porter, Michael. 1985. *Competitive Advantage. Creating and Sustaining Superior Performance*. Free Press, New York.
Rickard, Stephanie J. 2021. 'Economy Politics Revisited,' in Jon C. W. Pevehouse and Leonard Seabrooke (eds.), *The Oxford Handbook of International Political Economy*. Oxford University Press.
Riker, William H. 1962. *The Theory of Political Coalitions*. Yale University Press.
Root, Hilton. 2015. *Dynamics among Nations: The Evolution of Legitimacy and Development in Modern States*. The MIT Press.
Root, Hilton, Harry Jones and Leni Wild. 2015. *Managing Complexity and Uncertainty in Development Policy and Practice*. Overseas Development Institute.
Rosner, Max and Estaban Ortiz-Ospina. 2019. 'Global Extreme Poverty,' *Our World in Data*. https://icrc.icourban.com/crypto-https-ourworldindata.org/extreme-poverty
Ruetschi, Joerg. 2022. *Transforming Financial Institutions: Value Creation through Technology Innovation and Operational Change*. Wiley & Sons
Sachs, Jeffrey D., Christian Kroll, Guillame Lafortune, Grayson Fuller and Finn Woelm. 2021. *Sustainable Development Report 2021*. Accessed at https://www.sdgindex.org/reports/sustainable-development-report-2021/.
Sheiner, Louise and Kadija Yilla. 2020. 'The ABCs of the Post-COVID Economic Recovery,' *Brookings*. Accessed at https://www.brookings.edu/blog/up-front/2020/05/04/the-abcs-of-the-post-covid-economic-recovery/.
Shelling, Thomas. 1978. *Micromotives and Macrobehavior*. Norton.
Sperlich, Yvonne and Stefan Sperlich. 2012. 'Growth and Convergence in South–South Integration Areas: Empirical Evidence,' *SSRN*. Available at SSRN: https://ssrn.com/abstract=2001542.
Statista. 2021. https://www.statista.com/statistics/274774/forecast-of-mobile-phone-users-worldwide/ and https://www.statista.com/statistics/471264/iot-number-of-connected-devices-worldwide/
Strogatz, Steven H. 2015. *Nonlinear Dynamics and Chaos*. Perseus Books.Tammen, Ronald, Jacek Kugler, Douglas Lemke, Allan Stam, Carole Alsharabati, Mark

Abdollahian, Brian Efird and A. F. K. Organski, 2000. *Power Transitions: Strategies for the 21st Century*. Chatham House Publishers.

von Bertalanffy, Ludwig. 1968. *General System Theory: Foundations, Development, Applications*. Braziller.

Waldrop, Mitchell. 1992. *Complexity: The Emerging Science at the Edge of Order and Chaos*. Simon & Schuster.

Willett, Thomas D. 2021. 'New Developments in Financial Economics,' *Journal of Financial Economic Policy* 13:3.

World Bank. 2021. *Global Economic Prospects*. June 2021. Washington DC.

World Economic Forum. 2020a. 'The Global Risks Report,' 15th edition, January.

World Economic Forum. 2020b. 'The Future of Jobs Report,' October.

Yang, Zining. 2016. 'An Agent-Based Dynamic Model of Politics, Fertility and Economic Development,' *Journal of Systemics, Cybernetics and Informatics*, 14:4.

Yang, Zining and Mark Abdollahian. 2014. 'Trade, Income Convergence and Sustainable Development,' in David A. Deese (ed.), *Handbook of the International Political Economy of Trade*, Cheltenham, UK and Northampton, MA, USA: Edward Elgar Publishing.

Yi, Sheng Kung Michael, Mark Steyvers, Michael D. Lee and Matthew J. Dry. 2012. 'The Wisdom of the Crowd in Combinatorial Problems,' *Cognitive Science* 36:3: 452–470.

8. From Chimerica to decoupling: US–China trade war and failed neoliberalism

Wei Liang

Introduction

Robert Jervis thinks that Trump's presidency offered a good opportunity to test the relevancy of International Relations theory (Jervis 2018), as we are in fact currently witnessing major changes in global politics and international political economy that are good tests for the theoretical models. In this chapter, I aim to use the ongoing US–China trade and economic tension as a test for neoliberal theory; particularly the validity of the key constraining domestic and international factors that have been identified by the theory to facilitate cooperation and prevent drastic policy change. Joseph Nye described US–China relations over the past few years as being at "their lowest point in 50 years" (Nye 2020). This pessimistic view has been widely shared by IR scholars and policy observers around the world and embarked a new era in global politics.

What all this amounts to is a major deterioration in US–China relations since Trump became president in 2017 and the emergence of what some China hands described as a "new Cold War" (Brands and Gaddis 2021), a "tech war" (Segal 2020), and "decoupling" (Segal and Reynolds 2021). Against this backdrop, the flip side of the reality is that these two countries have established unprecedented levels of economic interdependence and technological collaboration over the past two decades despite their ideological and regime differences. With US support and endorsement, China's accession into the WTO in 2001 led to the direct connection of these two very different economies which had previously enjoyed limited economic exchange. In the two decades thereafter, US goods and services trade with China totaled an estimated $634.8 billion in 2019 (exports were $163.0 billion; imports were $471.8 billion). The US goods and services trade deficit with China was $308.8 billion in 2019. China was the United States' largest supplier of goods imports and China was the United States' third largest export market in 2019. In 2020, China remained the top trading partner of the United States based on import value despite the existence of tariffs on more than $300 billion in imports from China (Statista 2020). Besides trade, a large number of US companies have invested in China. For instance, MNCs such as Apple, GM, and Nike are all dependent on their sales in China to stay profitable. In addition, China holds about $1 trillion of US government bonds. In other words, the "thick interdependence" developed over the past two decades did not dissolve as a result of the US–China trade war, deteriorating political relationship, and relocation decisions of some foreign MNCs from China to other developing countries during the COVID-19 pandemic.

By January 2022, average US tariff levels on Chinese exports had increased more than sixfold since 2018. By dragging the world's two largest economies into a costly battle of tariffs, the US–China trade war seemed to contradict the widely held neoliberal belief about how economic interdependence should place constraints on strategic confrontation. Economic conflict of this scale would have been unthinkable a decade ago as US investors led a new gold rush into China. This trade war also seems to contradict established theories that predict that economic interdependence and rule-based neoliberal institution together will mitigate bilateral political tensions, de-escalate trade conflict, and induce cooperation. The purpose of this chapter is to analyze the worsening of US–China ties with an eye towards how they might shed light on our understanding of the effectiveness and relevance of neoliberal IPE theories. I ask three main questions in this chapter. First, what are the factors that have driven US–China relations from close economic cooperation (Chimerica) to today's decoupling? Second, why in fact does the US domestic consensus remain hostile to China and defy neoliberal theory? Why did the WTO fail to settle the long-standing disputes between the two countries as suggested by the neoliberal institutionalism? Third, in what ways and to what extent can neoliberalism cope with and accommodate increasing variety in economic systems among the major global players?

What is the underlying source of many of these changes and challenges in the US–China bilateral economic relationship, which in turn have caused the deepest crisis in the rules-based global economic governance system? Different from much of the existing literature that highlights either the waning of US power and influence, or the scale and magnitude of a "China shock" brought about by a different economic system, I argue here that it is the lack of willingness to 'co-exist' between the two distinct economic systems led by the US and China respectively that has caused conflict between the two largest economies and has placed embedded liberalism under considerable stress. This chapter tries to reject the bifurcated views that the global trade regime must either deepen integration and convergence or decouple along with the rise of new Chinese hegemony by positing a middle course—a hybrid approach for the Western capitalist economies to accommodate the participation of non-Western players in global economy while updating rules of the game and making it more enforceable. This will be a policy return to the modified embedded liberalism of the 1950s to the mid-1970s which accommodates a much wider range of different political-economic governance models, and gradually spreads economic liberalism to the rest of the world.

In this chapter, I first briefly discuss the main perspectives suggested by the neoliberal International Political Economy (IPE) theories on the interest and preferences of domestic actors, bilateral relationships, state behaviors, and on international cooperation. Then I test three main conditions of the neoliberal IPE theories, namely, economic interdependence, rules-based institutions, and domestic pro-cooperation interests and firms in the context of the US–China trade war and economic tensions, and show why they have all failed to deliver continued engagement as the theories suggest. The next section explores what can be done to try to make neoliberalism survive by recognizing the importance of sharing space with non-Western embedded liberalism presented by China and other emerging economies. Finally, I conclude by presenting several ideas about future research agendas to explore possible pathways in order to make these two different economic systems less mutually exclusive in the decades to come.

Main perspectives of the neoliberal IPE theories

We live in the age of neoliberalism when most countries have embraced the concepts and adopted policies to endorse markets, privatization, and deregulation. It became closely associated with two parallel developments, namely, financial deregulation and economic globalization (Rodrik 2017). In the meantime, we have also seen growing reflections and criticisms of liberalism, both its material objectives and ideological beliefs, and both in theory and in practice. As Patrick Deneen argues in his provocative book *Why Liberalism Failed*, liberalism is built on a foundation of contradictions: it trumpets equal rights while fostering incomparable material inequality, its legitimacy rests on consent, yet it discourages civic commitments in favor of privatism; and in its pursuit of individual autonomy, it has given rise to the most far-reaching, comprehensive state system in human history. Liberalism is a system whose success is generating its own failure (Deneen 2018). Similarly, Helen V. Milner points out that global capitalism with its consequent inequality, insecurity, and interdependence seem to be the main source eroding liberal democracy (Milner 2021). While most of these new reflections examine the challenges to neoliberalism from within, it is equally important to study the challenges brought from states previously excluded from, or only weakly integrated into, that order. The focus of this chapter is to examine another weakness of neoliberal institutionalism, that is, its ignorance and incompetence to co-exist and prosper together with countries that do not necessarily share the exact same neoliberal norms (at least in the short and medium run).

This section presents three main theoretical perspectives that are directly derived from the root of neoliberalism and may potentially illuminate the discussions of the US–China trade war and economic decoupling. First, connectedness among national economies through trade, investment, and capital flows fosters bilateral and global interdependence. The concepts of "complex interdependence" and "cascading interdependence" were coined to explain the prospect of international cooperation in an increasingly globalizing world order under anarchy (Keohane and Nye 1977; James Rosenau 1984). A key assumption underlying these arguments is that political conflict damages commercial relations (Keohane and Nye 1977), and that the economic interests (trade and investment in particular) at stake will effectively prevent states from waging or escalating a dispute into a costly lose-lose trade war or escalating into a more serious international confrontation. In the context of the US–China trade war, economic interdependence has been developed between two countries with distinct political and economic systems. This has added an unprecedented level of complexity to the discussion of neoliberalism, as we need to address directly and indirectly related factors such as geo-economic considerations and ideological confrontation. The existing literature has mainly focused on regime type as an explanatory variable to predict the preference of trade liberalization and the likelihood of states developing cooperative trade policies (Mansfield et al. 2002). The impact of regime type on trade relationships between a democracy and an autocracy has not been thoroughly studied, especially in the context of the US–China economic competition.

Second, neoliberal institutionalism builds on neoliberal theory and multilateralism. Proponents of neoliberal institutionalism emphasize the importance of international institutions and negotiated rules and/or treaties in addressing the so-called prisoner's dilemma, which represents a major impediment to international cooperation for states faced with incomplete information in the global system. From this perspective, international institutions encourage cooperation by making the prisoner's dilemma game an iterated one, thereby lengthening the shadow of the future and changing a government's reward structure in favor of cooperation; promoting the use of reciprocity strategies such as tit-for-tat which raise the cost of non-compliance, and facilitate the making of linkages across issue areas, therefore undercutting support for the protectionist status quo and domestic opposition to trade liberalization (Axelrod 1984; Davis 2003; Keohane 1984; Oye 1986). Consequently, international institutions such as the World Trade Organization (WTO) enhance the prospect of reciprocated trade liberalization concessions by offering an unprecedented level of global market access, increasing transparency and providing governments with the information needed to more effectively pursue reciprocity strategies, and offering a legalized forum for dispute resolution, therefore enhancing governments' ability to enforce trade agreements (Bown and Mavroidis 2017). Governments show willingness to cede authority and autonomy to the institutions of other member states in the pursuit of long-term stability and economic gains (Ruggie 1983; Lake, Martin, and Risse 2021). Furthermore, international institutions tend to set boundaries on state behaviors by "socializing" them with embedded norms and values (Johnston 2008). As will be discussed in more detail below, the crisis faced by the WTO in recent years arose mainly because of the challenge to "…integrate the fundamentally different economic systems of Western liberal capitalism and Chinese state capitalism…" (Crowley, 2019). The growing distrust towards the WTO has in turn fed the rise of protectionist impulses, paving the ground for a large-scale tit-for-tat tariff war beginning in 2018 between the two largest economies in the world.

Third, from the liberal perspective frequent economic interactions encourage domestic interests that have benefitted from such relations to lobby against policies that may jeopardize political cooperation (Copeland 1996; Kastner 2007). It seems that the exporting interests of MNCs trumped those of import competing industries in US trade politics, and contributed to the dominance of neoliberal ideas and pro-globalization policies in the US (Milner 1997). The policy preference towards free trade means that in the process of policymaking, governments, especially in the United States, try to insulate the policy process from pressure from protectionist interests as much as possible (Goldstein and Gulotty 2021). By 2000, more than a quarter of the US economy was made up by exports and imports, and trade accounted for over 39 million jobs (White House 2014). Consequently, those who have benefitted from trade should act accordingly to defend free trade, rather than support a trade war or trade denial with China.

However, the US–China trade war seems to contradict established neoliberal IPE theories that predict that economic interdependence will reduce the likelihood of such policies that restrict trade with a high domestic cost. The WTO as global trade governance institution will facilitate cooperation and settle disputes, and the interest groups and MNCs that have benefitted significantly from US–China trade will lobby against such high punitive tariffs imposed on imports of Chinese goods. Why then is decoupling still an option when the two countries have developed such a tightly woven economic network? Why did the WTO fail to settle the long-standing disputes and address the US top concerns against the unfair trade practices adopted by China? Why was the US business community, long considered the ballast in the US–China relationship, not successful in preventing the trade war with China?

US–China economic interdependence: more trade, growing conflict?

China's 2001 entry into the World Trade Organization (WTO) directly connected two polar-opposite economies. China's economy was characterized by high investment, low consumption, high savings, a managed and undervalued currency, low manufacturing costs, and limited trade access, and it was state-driven and highly aggressive in acquiring foreign technology. The US economy on the other hand had low investment, high consumption, low savings, overvalued (for trade purposes) reserve currency, high manufacturing costs, and largely open trade access, and it was market-driven and technology rich. This contrasting set of features made the bilateral trade relationship highly complementary at the beginning of the new century. It has since developed a progressively larger bilateral goods (merchandise) trade imbalance which grew from $83 billion in 2001 to a high of $419 billion in 2018. In 2019, this bilateral deficit on the side of the US receded to $345 billion. The political visibility of this bilateral deficit, as measured by China's share of the total US trade deficit in goods, grew as well; in 2001, it was 20 percent and by 2018 it was 48 percent. The "China shock," as described by American economists to portray the negative impact of trading with China, seems to be both severe and long-lasting. This has mostly been manifested by persistent job losses in the manufacturing sectors. David Autor and his collaborators find that "Labor markets more exposed to import competition from China experienced more plant closures; larger declines in manufacturing employment, employment-population ratios, earnings for low-wage workers, housing prices, and tax revenues; and larger increases in childhood and adult poverty, single-parenthood, and mortality related to drug and alcohol use" (Autor et al. 2013, 2021). This "China shock" has then translated into a "China bashing" trade policy via Republican legislators from import-competing districts blaming China for the economic dislocations and social problems in their districts (Kuk et al. 2018).

More importantly, China, while maintaining its comparative advantage in manufacturing the majority of the labor-intensive products, has successfully moved up the value chain to become competitive in many high-tech sectors and has become a major exporter of high-tech products. It seems that the US and China are now the two major leading countries in emerging technologies, with the potential of positive spillover effects, while the rest of the world lags behind (Hass and Balin 2019). Different from Japan and Germany in the 1980s and 1990s, China is a close match for or even surpasses the US on multiple fronts, including AI, Blockchain, Cyberspace, Data and E-Commerce (ABCDE) (Lee 2018; Ma 2021). For example, of the roughly 4,500 artificial intelligence-involved companies in the world, about half operate in the US and one-third operate in China. According to a widely cited study by PricewaterhouseCoopers, the US and China are set to capture 70 percent of the $15.7 trillion windfall that AI is expected to add to the global economy by 2030 (Hass 2021).

Although neoliberal theory has suggested that economic interdependence will induce international cooperation and mitigate the intensity of trade conflicts, the US–China trade war obviously shows that economic interdependence alone is not sufficient to avert a potential catastrophe, especially when the economic interdependence has been accompanied with fierce geopolitical confrontation, ideological disagreement, and competition in those sectors that are both strategically important and commercially lucrative.

The failure of the WTO and multilateralism?

Beyond the US concerns over the trade deficit and job displacement caused by trading with China, many politicians and scholars alike attribute the problems to China's failure to meet its commitments as a WTO member, and the WTO's failure to bind China's behaviors. In fact, many scholars have emphasized the latter, not the former. It does not seem fair to conclude that China's compliance record—both meeting its market access commitments upon accession, and its implementation of the WTO rulings on the disputes that Beijing lost—is poor. China has been able to meet most of its accession commitments by lowering its tariffs, reducing non-tariff barriers, and removing many trade-restricting administrative regulations, and it was viewed as a "quiet and compliant" new player in its early years in the WTO (Zeng and Liang 2013; Kennedy 2018; Pearson 2006; Lawrence 2006). It seems that China has complied with most of the specific market access commitments, but has done poorly on less verifiable areas such as transparency, IPR enforcement, industrial policy, and agricultural subsidies, etc. (Ezell 2021).

China has successfully lowered its tariffs and removed many trade-distorting regulations, but at the same time it has maintained, and later added, many new non-tariff barriers and trade-distorting regulations to promote exports, protect domestic companies from foreign competition, and provide preferential treatment to the domestic winners chosen by the government. Since Xi Jinping took office in 2013, the Chinese government began to downplay the vital role of market and private firms in the Chinese economy by tightening state control over the economy (Lardy 2019). As part of government efforts, Beijing has carried out ambitious industrial policies to promote ten strategic sectors identified by Chinese bureaucrats in the "Made in China 2025" initiative, including artificial intelligence, information technology, new energy, electrical vehicles, and semiconductors. The government provided billions of dollars in funds to promote these strategic industries that are crucial for China's next phase of development.

China's record on the compliance of WTO dispute settlement rulings also looks good on paper. In most cases, China has complied with the panel (or appellate body) findings that it lost a dispute by changing the domestic measures deemed WTO-inconsistent (Harpaz 2010). Compared with the US and the EU, China's record is technically much better, as in most cases China has genuinely removed the offending measures and, thus, greater access was achieved (Kennedy 2016). But in some cases, the positive change has come too late to matter much, and in others, new (similar) measures have been adopted to substitute the targeted ones. It seems that to many countries, settling a dispute with the WTO won't necessarily solve the structural problems that have led to the disputes with China. This "creative compliance" (Kobayashi 2013) or "paper compliance" (Webster 2014) is where the problem lies, as it reflects China's strategic attempt to be compliant with the written rules instead of the spirit and basic discipline of the WTO (Mavroidis and Sapir 2021).

Moreover, foreign companies have increasingly come to realize that the true barriers they face in terms of market access in China do not fall foul of WTO rules, partly because the current WTO rules were made two decades ago and do not fully reflect the trade reality in the twenty-first century, and partly because the WTO rules were not made to address the fundamental challenges imposed by state capitalism such as China's. Consequently, WTO DSM have been effective in correcting some WTO-inconsistent rules and practices in China, but have failed to tackle China's deeper problems such as its lack of transparency, state subsidies, competition policy, soft loans available to state-owned enterprises, state financing, industrial policy, etc. The US has resorted to both bilateral and multilateral means to address these systemic issues (USTR 2021) but has not been (and probably would not be) able to assimilate China into a free-market economy. As a result, we have seen a wide range of findings when assessing China's WTO compliance in the last two decades which range from compliance, selective compliance and strategic compliance to non-compliance.

Overall, it has become a widely accepted consensus that the WTO, in its current form and operation, cannot effectively function and that a reform is much needed. The US–China rivalry within the WTO has already paralyzed the multilateral institution by undermining its ability to make new rules, settle disputes, and conclude Doha negotiations (Hopewell 2020). Instead, a real breakthrough in WTO reform will require cooperation to reach an agreement between the US and China on how China should be treated within the WTO.

US businesses: no longer a "positive anchor" in the US–China relationship

One important perspective of neoliberal IPE theories is its emphasis on the role played by domestic constraining factors, including pro-free trade interest groups to lobby for avoiding a trade war with the country in which they have vested economic interests at stake. While the US–China trade war has its origins in broader structural forces in the international system, such as rising US–China competition and the decline of the multilateral trading system centered around the WTO, it also grew out of the strong sense of frustration both in the US Congress and in the business community about alleged unfair Chinese trade practices in areas such as intellectual property rights, state-owned enterprises, subsidies, forced technology transfer, and market access. Reviewing the annual members survey conducted by the US–China Business Council, it clearly addresses this paradox: on the one hand, majority member companies that are doing business with and in China have remained successful in the Chinese market and have continued to emphasize the attractiveness of the Chinese market, but on the other hand they have consistently raised concerns about the worsening business environment in China due to unfair regulations and an unlevel playing field (US–China Business Council 2021). Such frustration paved the way for the Trump administration's aggressive market-opening negotiation tactics with China, eventually leading to the unusual decision-making process whereby pro-free trade senators, interest groups in general, and beneficiaries and stakeholders (namely MNCs that have invested heavily in China, gained significant share in the Chinese market, and depend on Chinese raw materials and intermediate parts for domestic production in the US) either did not strongly oppose waging a trade war with China, or failed in preventing it from happening or terminating it sooner. As one seasoned Asian diplomat accurately observed, "[I]t is truly shocking that when President Donald Trump suddenly launched a trade war against China in January 2018, no major American business voices tried to restrain him. Instead, Trump discovered (probably to his surprise) that he received broad and deep bipartisan support. Even leading Democrats supported him" (Mahbubani 2020, pp. 29–30). Major business associations, such as AmCham China and the US–China Business Council, adopted a mixed position by supporting the US policy to pressure for changes in China's business environment while cautioning that tariffs may not be able to serve the purpose. For instance, representatives of the National Association of Manufacturers (NAM) testified before the US–China Economic and Security Review Commission by emphasizing that "our manufacturers have long-faced a wide-range of distortive activities in China, including many extensively documented by this investigation … The NAM urges the administration to seize the moment with a strong solutions-based approach but opposes tariffs because of their unintended impacts on manufacturing" (USCC 2018).

Additionally, under both the Trump and Biden administrations, economic competition/conflict with China has been framed as a "national security" threat, which has made it harder for those stakeholders who support trade with China to lobby for continued economic cooperation as it seems that commercial gains are viewed as marginal in the face of emerging security threats. Trump initiated a series of policy responses to address the cybersecurity and data security concerns posed by Chinese technology companies such as Huawei and social media apps TikTok and WeChat. Though many inherent risks are directly associated with the basic nature of the emerging technologies and the lack of effective government regulation on data protection in general, the Trump administration emphasized solely the risks posed by the governing feature of the Chinese government and the way Beijing would wield power and influence over these technology firms (Williams 2020). Trump defined job displacement and the outsourcing of manufacturing caused by economic globalization as a win–lose game. In his State of the Union Address in 2019, Trump accused China of "the theft of American jobs and wealth," targeting US industries, and stealing US intellectual property (Trump 2019). Similarly, as Biden put it in an article in *Foreign Affairs*,

> The United States does need to get tough with China. If China has its way, it will keep robbing the United States and American companies of their technologies

and intellectual property. It will also keep using subsidies to give its state-owned enterprises an unfair advantage—and a leg up on dominating the technologies and industries of the future. (Biden, 2020)

The description of the US–China economic relationship in Washington from Trump to Biden has tended to securitize and politicize economic and commercial exchanges by emphasizing the ideological differences. This new development has been confirmed by an online survey of more than 2,000 American adults which shows that a large proportion of the surveyed respondents think bilateral trade between the US and China is good but also strongly support the US–China trade war. The survey result suggests that perceptions of the trade war are more closely aligned with political identities/ideologies than with economic interests (Jin et al. 2022). This change of perception from the US president, Congress and the general public has reshaped the cost–benefit calculation among many stakeholders and made corporate lobbyists politically unpopular and ineffective. In many ways, corporations must fight against the political tide (Bade 2021).

Conclusion: what are the implications for neoliberalism?

Three decades of conscious policy choice of economic engagement adopted by Washington towards China, guided by economic neoliberalism, has created interdependence but failed to push convergence (or to Americanize/Westernize) neoliberal economic systems as expected, and instead has dragged the global trade governance into a deep legitimacy crisis. The Chinese government has engaged successfully (so far) in a "delicate balancing act" (Weiss and Wallace 2021) by partially accepting economic liberalism but rejecting political dimensions of that liberalism such as democracy, a free press, and other human rights at the domestic level. China presents a true paradox to the neoliberal economic order as it is the largest trading country in the world (being the largest trading partner of over 130 countries) but it has refused to adopt a fully and transparent market-driven economy. Hence, the trade war launched by the Trump administration and continued by the Biden administration failed to achieve its expected policy goals. The bilateral trade deficit was only marginally reduced. US manufacturing employment was not favorably affected; in fact, it appears the trade war negatively affected the creation of new US manufacturing jobs. China's promise to buy more American goods was mostly in areas where US exports are already strong, and China's further opening to foreign investment in its financial sector comes late; Chinese companies have established strong incumbent market positions in these areas. China has further failed to honor the purchase amount it accepted for the phase one agreement due to the COVID-19 outbreak. Moreover, China's policy of heavily subsidizing its strategic technology and infrastructure industries—highlighted by its "Made in China 2025" initiative—has not changed. China's unwritten policy of holding foreign companies' access to China's market hostage to technology transfer may not be much affected by China's new foreign investment law that formally prohibits it.

What could be the way out? Most authors generally tend to believe that the way forward for the global trading system is to deepen integration and apply pressure for the full adoption of liberal economic policies in the tradition of "Western liberal capitalism," or else "decoupling." Neither will take place easily, or any time soon. Realistically, we should think of the possibility of encouraging a hybrid approach of the "co-existence of two major powers with varying political and economic institutions." The crisis that has been unfolding in neoliberalism over the past two decades is a reflection of the deepening contradictions between the North and South, led by the US and China. Some writers, such as Aaditya Mattoo and Robert Staiger (2019), provide a similar explanation for the US–China crisis and argue that the only resolution to the said crisis will be the inevitable rise of another hegemonic force, such as China (see also Crowley 2019). To the other hand, Rodrik has repeatedly argued that China and other non-Western developing countries, idiosyncratic elements of their economic system notwithstanding, should be accommodated within the current multilateral institutions (Rodrik 2018). This paper posits that the view that the world must choose between only two options: the hegemony of the "US Western liberal capitalist model" and the hegemony of the "Chinese economic model" is erroneous (Obama 2016; Mattoo and Staiger 2019). The future of neoliberalism should focus on seeking alternative approaches to the polarized options of hyper-globalization (convergence) or protectionism (decoupling). The current crisis has provided the world with the opportunity to revisit the limits of neoliberalism and explore a middle ground to accommodate both the developed countries and the emerging economies that have adopted hybrid approaches to developing their national economies.

We are living through an historical crossroads and can reflect upon a few key policy challenges imposed by globalization both domestically and internationally. The competition between the US and China arose not only as an outcome of the conflict of commercial interest, but also due to the disagreement over how China should be treated in a neoliberal economic order. To what extent China should be fully socialized to embrace neoliberal rules and norms, or should be allowed to maintain its not-so-compatible political and economic systems while participating in the current global economic system, is at the center of the debate. Embedded liberalism was adopted in the Bretton Woods system to assure adequate policy autonomy in order to provide "social security and economic stability to make democracy and capitalism compatible" (Ruggie 1982). It was an important compromise to allow governments to deploy necessary social and welfare policies to alleviate the negative impact of globalization (Deese and Biasi 2022). The adopted framework of "embedded liberalism" represented the blending, through compromise, of US ideas and leverage for promoting the liberal multilateral trade system with British and European ideas and insistence on protecting the welfare state. It provided an effective foundation for the Bretton Woods System in the post-WWII era among Western countries (Deese 2008). With the rise and integration of non-Western economies into the globalized world economy, the need for Western countries as well as international institutions to accommodate non-Western type of liberalism was inevitable. Until now, theories of white racial supremacy were part and parcel of widely held theories of the international order, liberal and otherwise. The Western liberal order has already encompassed varieties of liberalisms, including the perspectives of France and of the Americas (Katzenstein 2020). The future of this international order needs to be resilient and fluid in order to embrace more non-Western varieties of liberalism. Today, whether the current system can be integrative and resilient enough to adapt to and from countries that only partially embraced Western neoliberalism will be the real test for US leadership and for the survival of the existing global economic system.

Access to world markets in goods, technologies, and capital is a "must" for economic development and it is now the most desirable policy option for the majority of countries in the world, including China and others that have not wholeheartedly embraced Western neoliberalism, and which is described by Rodrik as "orthodoxy-defying institutional tinkering" but has managed to achieve varied degrees of economic success. Interdependence is the key feature that defines and shapes all nation's economies. Decoupling between the US and China is not only not feasible but is also harmful to both countries. Failure to recognize this interdependence and build necessary resilience and flexibility to engage various capitalist arrangements will make the US and the US-sponsored neoliberal order more fragile. International cooperation through rules-based multilateralism is still the best means to manage interdependence. Both the US and China have to manage and engage their relationships beyond allies and like-minded partners so that neither one will end up worse off. China's phenomenal economic success is largely due to its orthodoxy-defying institutional tinkering.

Bibliography

Autor, David, Dorn, David, and Hanson, Gordon. 2013. "The China Syndrome: Local Labor Market Effects of Import Competition in the United States." *American Economic Review* 103(6): 2121–2168.

Autor, David, Dorn, David, and Hanson, Gordon. 2021, September 8. "On the Persistence of the China Shock." Brookings Paper on Economic Activity. https://www.brookings.edu/wp-content/uploads/2021/09/On-the-Persistence-of-the-China-Shock_Conf-Draft.pdf

Axelrod, Robert. 1984. *The Evolution of Cooperation*. Basic Books.

Bade, Gavin. 2021, September 1. "Corporate America Fights Uphill Battle Against anti-China Push." Politico. https://www.politico.com/news/2021/09/01/business-us-china-trade-508239

Biden, J. 2020, March/April. "Why America Must Lead Again." *Foreign Affairs*. https://www.foreignaffairs.com/articles/united-states/2020-01-23/why-america-must-lead-again

Bown, C., and Mavroidis, P. 2017. "WTO Dispute Settlement in 2015: Going Strong After Two Decades." *World Trade Review* 16(2): 153–158.

Brands, Hal, and Gaddis, John Lewis. 2021. "The New Cold War: America, China, and the Echoes of History." *Foreign Affairs*, November/December.

Copeland, Dale C. 1996. "Economic Interdependence and War: A Theory of Trade Expectations." *International Security* 20: 5–41.

Crowley, Meredith (ed.). 2019. *Trade War: The Clash of Economic Systems Endangering Global Prosperity*. CEPR Press.

Davis, C. L. 2003, August 28–31. "Setting the Negotiation Table: The Choice of Institutions for Trade Disputes." Paper presented at the annual meeting of the American Political Science Association, Philadelphia.

Deese, David. 2008. *World Trade Politics: Power, Principles, and Leadership*. Routledge, Taylor & Francis.

Deese, David, and Biasi, Sam. 2022. "Financial Crises and Trade Wars: Has Globalization Failed to Deliver?" In K. Zeng and W. Liang (eds.), *Research Handbook on Trade Wars*, chapter 3. Edward Elgar Publishing.

Deneen, Patrick J. 2018. *Why Liberalism Failed*. Yale University Press.

Ezell, Stephen. 2021, July 26. "False Promises II: The Continuing Gap Between China's WTO Commitments and its Practices." Information Technology and Innovation Foundation. https://itif.org/publications/2021/07/26/false-promises-ii-continuing-gap-between-chinas-wto-commitments-and-its

Goldstein, Judith, and Gulotty, Robert. 2021. "America and the Trade Regime: What Went Wrong?" *International Organization* 75(2).

Harpaz, Marcia Don. 2010. "Sense and Sensibilities of China and WTO Dispute Settlement." *Journal of World Trade* 44(6): 1155–1186.

Hass, R. 2021, August 12. "The 'New Normal' in US–China Relations: Hardening Competition and Deep Interdependence." Brookings Institution Report. https://www.brookings.edu/blog/order-from-chaos/2021/08/12/the-new-normal-in-us-china-relations-hardening-competition-and-deep-interdependence/

Hass, R., and Balin, Z. 2019, January 10. "US–China Relations in the Age of Artificial Intelligence." Brookings Institution Report. https://www.brookings.edu/research/us-china-relations-in-the-age-of-artificial-intelligence/

Hopewell, Kristen. 2020. *Clash of Powers: US–China Rivalry in Global Trade Governance*. Cambridge University Press.

Jervis, Robert. 2018. "President Trump and International Relations Theory." In Robert Jervis, Francis J. Gavin, Joshua Rovner, and Diane Labrosse (eds.), *Chaos in the Liberal Order*. Columbia University Press.

Jin, Yongai, Dorius, Shawn, and Xie, Yu. 2022. "Americans' Attitudes toward the US–China Trade War." *Journal of Contemporary China* 31(133): 17–37.

Johnston, Alastair. 2008. *Social States: China in International Institutions, 1980–2000*. Princeton University Press.

Kastner, S. 2007. "When do Conflicting Political Relations Affect International Trade." *Journal of Conflict Resolution* 51(4): 664–668.

Katzenstein, Peter. 2020. "Fractures and Resilience of Liberal International Orders." In Chuan Chu (ed.), *From Western-Centric to a Post-Western World: In Search of an Emerging Global Order in the 21st Century*. Routledge.

Kennedy, S. 2016, December 11. "The WTO in Wonderland: China's Awkward 15th Anniversary." CSIS.

Kennedy, S. 2018. *Global Governance and China: The Dragon's Learning Curve*. Routledge.

Keohane, Robert O. 1984. *Hegemony: Cooperation and Discord in the World Political Economy*. Princeton University Press

Keohane, R. O., and Nye, J. S. 1977. *Power and Interdependence*. Longman.

Kobayashi, Yuka. 2013. "China's Creative Compliance in the WTO." In Ka Zeng and Wei Liang (eds.), *China and Global Trade Governance: China's First Decade in the World Trade Organization*, pp. 103–125. Routledge.

Kuk, John, Seligsohn, Deborah, and Jiakun, Jack. 2018. "From Tiananmen to Outsourcing: The Effect of Rising Import Competition on Congressional Voting Towards China." *Journal of Contemporary China* 27(109): 103–119.

Lake, David, Martin, Lisa, and Risse, Thomas. 2021. "Challenges to the Liberal Order: Reflections on International Organization." *International Organization* 75(S2): 225–257.

Lardy, N. 2019. *The State Strikes Back: The End of Economic Reform in China?* Columbia University Press.

Lawrence, R. Z. 2006, October. "China and the Multilateral Trade System." Faculty Research Working Paper Series (RWP06–045), John F. Kennedy School of Government, Harvard University.

Lee, K. 2018. *AI Superpower: China, Silicon Valley and Global Order*. Houghton Mifflin Harcourt.

Ma, V. 2021. *Digital War: How China's Tech Power Shapes the Future of AI, Blockchain, & Cyberspace*. Wiley Press.

Mahbubani, K. 2020. *Has China Won? The Chinese Challenge to American Primacy*. PublicAffairs Books.

Mansfield, Edward, Milner, Helen, and Rosendorff, Peter. 2002. "Why Democracies Cooperate More: Electoral Control and International Trade Agreements." *International Organization* 56(3): 477–513. http://www.jstor.org/stable/3078586

Mattoo, Aaditya, and Staiger, Robert. 2019, April 22. "Trade Wars: What Do They Mean? Why are They Happening Now? What are the Costs?" World Bank Policy Research Working Paper No. 8829.

Mavroidis, Petros, and Sapir Andre. 2021. *China and the WTO: Why Multilateralism Still Matters*. Princeton University Press.

Milner, Helen. 1997. *Interests, Institutions, and Information: Domestic Politics and International Relations.* Princeton University Press.

Milner, Helen. 2021, December. "Is Global Capitalism Compatible with Democracy? Inequality, Insecurity, and Interdependence." *International Studies Quarterly* 65(4): 1097–1110. https://doi.org/10.1093/isq/sqab056

Nye, Joseph. 2020. "'Tough on China' is Not a Strategy. Trump is Scrapping Tools that Keep us Safe and Strong." *USA Today,* August 27. https://www.usatoday.com/story/opinion/2020/08/27/trump-tough-china-but-abandons-soft-power-alliances-immigration-column/3432054001/ (accessed September 9, 2020).

Obama, Barak. 2016. Statement by the President on the Signing of the Trans-Pacific Partnership. https://obamawhitehouse.archives.gov/the-press-office/2016/02/03/statement-president-signing-trans-pacific-partnership

Oye, Kenneth A. (ed.). 1986. *Cooperation under Anarchy.* Princeton University Press.

Pearson, M. M. 2006. "China in Geneva: Lessons from China's Early Years in the WTO." In Alastair Iain Johnston and Robert S. Ross (eds.), *New Directions in the Study of China's Foreign Policy,* pp. 242–275. Stanford University Press.

Rodrik, Dani. 2017. "The Fatal Flaw of Neoliberalism: It's Bad Economics." *The Guardian,* November 14.

Rodrik, Dani. 2018. "The Double Standard of America's China Trade Policy." Project Syndicate, May 10.

Rosenau, J. N. 1984. "A Pre-Theory Revisited: World Politics in an Era of Cascading Interdependence." *International Studies Quarterly* 28(3): 245–306.

Ruggie, Gerard. 1982. "International Regimes, Transactions, and Change: Embedded Liberalism in the Post-War Economic Order." *International Organization* 36: 379–415.

Ruggie, Gerard. 1983. "International Regimes, Transactions, and Change: Embedded Liberalism in the Postwar Economic Order." In Stephen Krasner (ed.), *International Regimes,* pp. 195–231. Cornell University Press.

Segal, Adam. 2020. "The Coming Tech Cold War With China: Beijing Is Already Countering Washington's Policy." *Foreign Affairs,* September/October.

Segal, Stephanie, and Reynolds, Matthew. 2021. "Degrees of Separation: A Targeted Approach to U.S.–China Decoupling." CSIS Report.

Statista. 2020. "Ranking of the Top Trading Partners of the United States for Trade Goods in 2020, by Import Value." https://www.statista.com/statistics/186601/ranking-of-the-largest-trading-partners-for-us-imports-in-2010/Trump, Donald. 2019, February 6. "Remarks by President Trump in State of the Union Address." www.whitehouse.gov/briefings-statements/remarks-president-trump-state-union-address-2/

US–China Business Council. 2021. "Annual Members Survey 2021." https://www.uschina.org/sites/default/files/uscbc_member_survey_2021_-_en_0.pdf

USCC. 2018, June 8. "Hearing on US Tools to Address Chinese Market Distortion." https://www.uscc.gov/sites/default/files/transcripts/Hearing%20Transcript%20-%20June%208,%202018.pdf

USTR. 2021. "2020 Report to Congress on China's WTO Compliance." https://ustr.gov/sites/default/files/files/reports/2020/2020USTRRe portCongre ssChinaWTO Compliance.pdf

Webster, Timothy. 2014. "Paper Compliance: How China Implements WTO Decisions." *Michigan Journal of International Law* 35(3): 525–578.

Weiss, Jessica, and Wallace, Jeremy. 2021. "Domestic Politics, China's Rise, and the Future of the Liberal International Order." *International Organization* 75, Special Issue 2: 635–664.

White House. 2014. "The Economic Benefits of International Trade." https://obamawhitehouse.archives.gov/sites/default/files/docs/cea_trade_report_final_non-embargoed_v2.pdf

Williams, Robert D. 2020, October 30. "Beyond Huawei and TikTok: Untangling US Concerns over Chinese Tech Companies and Digital Security." Brookings Institution Report. https://www.brookings.edu/research/beyond-huawei-and-tiktok-untangling-us-concerns-over-chinese-tech-companies-and-digital-security/

Zeng, K., and Liang, W. (eds.). 2013. *China and Global Trade Governance: China's First Decade in the World Trade Organization*. Routledge.

9. Cyber economic espionage: a framework for future research

William Akoto

Introduction

Espionage typically refers to a government's clandestine efforts to collect classified or otherwise protected information useful in furthering its national security interests and to deal with threats from actual or potential adversaries (Lotrionte, 2015). Information collected typically has to do with military plans, actions and the capabilities of adversaries. In this vein, economic espionage refers to a specific form of espionage that seeks to collect information relevant to a state's economy, particularly information that can be leveraged by domestic firms and industries to boost their economic competitiveness (Wagner, 2011). Information collected in the course of economic espionage could include product design blueprints, prototypes, proprietary software, product development plans and marketing strategies. Economic espionage is about economic competition, often benefitting the domestic private sector while disadvantaging those in other states. Economic espionage is closely related to 'industrial espionage,' which describes efforts by private companies to acquire intelligence on the operations, products and activities of rival firms (Button, 2020). In this sense, economic espionage can be conceptualized as state sponsored industrial espionage.

In espionage, the task of intelligence agencies is to covertly acquire information while keeping targets in the dark about their activities. Many intelligence agencies around the world are adapting classic spy techniques from military and political espionage activities to conduct economic espionage. The end of the Cold War diminished the threat of military confrontation between states. Consequently, intelligence agencies have turned their information collection tools and techniques to target foreign firms (Fialka, 1997). The bulk of economic espionage, particularly those aimed at U.S. firms, comes from Russia,

China and Iran, but there is evidence that many espionage attempts also come from U.S. allies such as France, South Korea and Germany (Promnick, 2017).

Many governments have long considered economic espionage as an important component of national security and economic growth and development. Economic espionage bestows significant benefits on the state. Not only can stolen information help in the domestic development of military and other weapons technology, but the money saved can be re-allocated to fund various socio-economic projects. This could boost the popularity of the regime and help extend its tenure in power.

The study of economic espionage has been spearheaded by legal scholars who are mainly concerned with the legal and legislative aspects of economic espionage. The primary focus is on issues such as how states can legally respond to the theft of intellectual property through cyberspace (Carlin, 2016; Lotrionte, 2015), under what circumstances a state may use countermeasures to deter economic espionage (Danielson, 2008; Rowe, 2020), the legal consequences of economic espionage (Pun, 2017; Reid, 2015), why international law has been ineffective in curbing economic espionage (Anderson, 2017; Banks, 2017), and how to craft legal instruments that pose an effective deterrence to economic espionage while avoiding the potential for escalation into full-scale war (Blinderman & Din, 2017; Crootof, 2018). Despite these efforts, there is a paucity of literature examining the political economy dynamics of economic espionage. This is especially unfortunate because recent technological advances and changing dynamics of interstate economic competition mean there is much scope for a progressive research agenda focused on the political economy of economic espionage.

A research agenda

Given the limited research focus on the political economy of economic espionage and in the spirit of encouraging research in this area, I outline six areas where future research is likely to be most productive. In the subsections that follow, I advocate for studies focused on examinations of the motives of economic espionage, the role that geopolitical rivalries play in driving economic espionage, how states conduct economic espionage operations, analysis of government responses to espionage operations, and explorations of the nexus between economic interdependence (particularly trade) and economic espionage.

The role of geopolitical rivalry

Some analysts argue that economic espionage is partly driven by the level of governmental involvement in a nation's industrial base (Hannas, Mulvenon & Puglisi, 2013; Harris, 2017). Where governments are heavily involved in commercial enterprises, there is a higher likelihood of state involvement in industrial espionage. This thinking goes back to the Cold War-era practices where states relied on their intelligence services for information on the activities and operations of rivals. While many states see no difference between collecting information for military and political purpose and conducting economic espionage, a few states such as the U.S. maintain a distinction (at least in principle) between the two (Promnick, 2017).

For instance, in the former Soviet Union, there was no clear distinction between the state political apparatus and different branches of the economic system. The needs of industry were thus essentially the same as those of the state. Consequently, intelligence gathered by the KGB on defense purchase bids by foreign companies, for example, was passed on to the Soviet Union's defense manufacturers with very little hesitation (Lotrionte, 2015). Similar albeit less pronounced dynamics played out in countries like France where the line between private industry and state enterprise was blurry (Harris, 2017). China, which exhibits a tight integration between the public and private sectors of the economy, is currently one of the most active state sponsors of industrial espionage activities (Geller, 2018).

The current fierce global competition for market share in several sectors provides a powerful strategic incentive for states, even those with some degree of separation between the state and private industry, to get involved in industrial espionage. States have a lot to gain from such activities. Information obtained via espionage may eliminate the need for states to invest in research and development programs, increasing their international competitiveness while disadvantaging attacked states by preventing them from capitalizing on their innovation (Lotrionte, 2015).

Aside from the economic motives, a deeper exploration of the role geopolitical rivalries play in driving economic espionage would also be a fruitful avenue. Previous research suggests that states are more likely to maintain extensive espionage operations against rivals as opposed to their allies (Nasheri, 2005; Pytlak & Mitchell, 2016). For instance, the geopolitical rivalry between the U.S. and China is increasingly taking the form of industrial espionage. U.S. authorities frequently accuse Chinese state intelligence agencies of hacking into computer systems to steal trade secrets, market strategies and other sensitive information which is then passed on to Chinese firms. Chinese state officials in turn routinely levy similar espionage charges against the U.S. government and its intelligence agencies. In contrast, it is exceedingly rare for non-rivalrous states to levy espionage allegations against each other, at least in public.

The conduct of economic espionage

One area of the literature that has received very little attention is efforts to explore exactly how states conduct economic espionage operations. A good understanding of how states conduct their espionage operations is important because reliable attribution of espionage operations to state-sponsors depends on this. Without clear attribution, it is almost impossible to hold states to account. Apart from the scholarly benefits of a better understanding of the relationship between states and their espionage proxies, such efforts are also important for third parties in deciding what actions to take in response. The difficulty of attribution is complicated by the myriad of ways in which states who outsource their espionage operations can organize these outsourcing relationships. For instance, some states can maintain significant control over the activities of their espionage proxies, directing them as to who to target and when. Others can adopt a looser configuration, providing support for the activities of the proxy without necessarily providing specific instructions. Such arrangements may be particularly likely where the interests of the state and the proxy are aligned. Other states may adopt a clean separation between themselves and the proxy, merely providing an enabling environment for the operations of the proxy by turning a blind eye to their activities. In return, the proxy voluntarily passes any useful information it comes across to the state (Maurer, 2018).

Technological advancements and economic espionage

Despite the monumental changes that espionage technology has undergone over the last few years, research analyzing economic espionage has not kept pace. Analysis that focuses on how technological advances have changed the conduct of espionage, and how the actors involved have adapted to this change, is sure to yield valuable insights. For one, recent advances in information and communication technology have greatly facilitated espionage activities of state intelligence agencies. In particular, the centralization of information storage on massive 'cloud' servers has made it comparatively easier to harvest vast troves of data in a single operation.

The rapid advancement in communication technology also creates new avenues for espionage. Vulnerabilities in 5th generation (5G) networks are particularly worrying. 5G networks rely on novel technologies operating at a higher level of complexity than current 3G and 4G networks. These 5G networks are also highly decentralized, making it more challenging to develop and implement robust fault-tolerant systems (Mamolar et al., 2018). State-backed hacker groups can exploit these vulnerabilities in the 5G system to access proprietary information on mobile phones and other internet-enabled devices.

Cyber spies could also take advantage of rapid advancements in Artificial Intelligence (AI) technology. We are quickly approaching a point in AI evolution where the technology can initiate and complete very complex tasks autonomously, ushering in an era of highly customized cyber espionage operations. By analyzing email and other social media communications, AI-powered malware will be able to learn the behavior, language and nuances of key executives within organizations and use this knowledge to replicate the executives' writing style to craft messages that appear highly credible. Because such AI-generated messages may be indistinguishable from genuine communications, they could be used to solicit proprietary information from company employees.

Sampled countries and cases

The expansion of the sample of countries often examined in economic espionage studies is another area of potential improvement. Existing studies have focused almost exclusively on a few large countries (mainly the U.K., U.S., Russia and China), with no broad-based, cross-national analysis. These large economies are not necessarily representative of most states in the international system; thus, this severely limits our understanding of the dynamics of economic espionage beyond these states. Studies that draw on countries not typically studied in the espionage literature, e.g. Eastern European states, countries in Africa and South America, could potentially yield insights that challenge many of our taken-for-granted assumptions and assertions about the motives and conduct of interstate economic espionage.

Pursuing large-N quantitative studies of economic espionage would be a great complement to the more established descriptive approaches in the existing literature. However, compiling such large-N data on espionage activity is fraught with challenges. First, because of language and resource constraints, existing studies are inherently biased towards the analysis of incidents in English-speaking countries. Cybersecurity company reports, which form the bedrock of analysis of cyber espionage activity, are mainly published in English or covered in English-language media. Because of this, many of the countries frequently analyzed in the existing literature – the United States, the United

Kingdom, Australia, Canada, India – are English-speaking. Second, to protect their sources and methods, cybersecurity companies may only provide partial or vague information on cyber breaches. This makes it difficult for researchers to independently confirm the details of cyber espionage attempts, particularly when all the information on an incident is available from a single source.

Government response to espionage operations

There is a paucity of academic literature analyzing government response to espionage. In some ways, this is understandable. Information regarding government action aimed at dealing with espionage is limited or classified because governments are understandably wary of providing adversaries with insights into their counterespionage strategies. Moreover, they are reluctant to be too precise about potential response options to espionage operations in order to avoid setting red lines that, if crossed, might oblige them to take potentially escalatory actions against the alleged sponsor states.

In this regard, there are several policy options that could be considered. For instance, officials of the attacked state could issue public statements condemning the espionage operation. Statements could include an acknowledgment that a cyber breach occurred, and lessons have been learnt and measures put in place to reduce the likelihood of a future breach. This serves to reassure the public, business community and other stakeholders that the government is taking the breach seriously and is taking action to prevent recurrence. It is also useful to reprimand the attacker state and name and shame any hacker groups that took part in the attack. This has the benefit of communicating clearly to the attacker state and hacker groups that their involvement in the attack is known and will not be tolerated.

This is particularly critical given the anonymity that comes with online action and thus the enduring perception that cyber operations are relatively risk free. This has the effect of lowering the threshold for the use of cyber espionage. As highlighted earlier, cyber operations are also difficult to attribute to any specific actor as they are typically performed covertly. It is often not immediately obvious who is behind an espionage incident or its origin. The ubiquity of computer systems and adversaries' constant attempts to penetrate computer systems makes the task of protecting them extremely difficult. Compounding matters, most cyber espionage breaches are undetectable while they are in progress, coming to light weeks, months and even years after the attack. This provides offensive advantage to attackers, who can mount attacks and erase traces before targets become aware. Public condemnations which name attackers help remove their 'cloak of invisibility', an important first step in holding attackers and their state-sponsors accountable.

Another option is to address the cyber breach through diplomatic channels. This can be done in a variety of ways. The attacked state can issue a statement under diplomatic cover to the attacker state protesting the cyber breach and warning of consequences for future breaches. Attacked states could also take a multilateral approach, soliciting condemnatory statements from allies and international organizations aimed at the attacker state. Diplomatic protests could be strengthened by expelling diplomats and other officials representing the attacker state. This kind of diplomatic retaliation, particularly when done multilaterally, could damage the international reputation of the accused state. It has the added benefit of communicating the ability of the attacked state to identify hackers and their sponsors, which helps to deter future attacks. However, this strategy may be damaging to the future diplomatic relations of the states involved, particularly where the accused state responds by expelling diplomats and other representatives of the attacked state.

Finally, as part of the public condemnation strategy discussed earlier, the attacked state could issue criminal indictments against the organizations, individuals and other actors involved in the breach. This goes beyond simply naming and shaming perpetrators and brings criminal charges against them. While it is unlikely that perpetrators, particularly those based in foreign countries, will ever see a day in court, the reputational damage involved may serve as a powerful deterrent for future attacks. However, this strategy entails some risks for the indicting country. As mentioned earlier, it may result in court cases where sensitive intelligence operations could become public during the trial. The evidence presented in court might point to how the intelligence was gathered and the agents involved in the process. This may prove damaging to long-term intelligence gathering efforts. Second, there is the possibility that the alleged attacker state could retaliate with indictments of its own – for example, leveraging falsified charges against companies from the attacked state doing business in the attacker country.

Another response option is political and economic retaliation. This could involve, for example, blacklisting persons and organizations involved in the cyber breach, limiting their ability to conduct international financial transactions and limiting their international travel possibilities. Economic retaliation could take the form of import and export restrictions on goods and services to and from the accused state. For accused countries which strongly depend on trade revenues, such economic sanctions could have a significant deterrent effect. The drawback is that once sanctions have been imposed, the sanctioned state has very little incentive to change its behavior if there are no clear guidelines on when and how the sanctions will be lifted. There is also the risk that the sanctioned state could retaliate with countersanctions of its own. This could be potentially damaging to the attacked state, especially if there are significant economic interrelations between the two states. Future research that focuses efforts on exploring the effectiveness of these and other policy options has the potential to yield valuable insights.

Economic interdependence and espionage

Existing scholarship posits a strategic link between economic interdependence (particularly international trade) and economic espionage. As previously highlighted, trade is an important strategic motive for espionage. However, interstate trade can increase along two distinct dimensions – width and depth. Interstate trade can increase as a result of an increase in the range of products traded between states (i.e. trade widening). Trade can also increase as a result of an increase in the import or export per product for existing products (i.e. trade deepening). Current research has ignored this distinction, particularly how the different dimensions of trade (dis)incentivizes cyber espionage. Future scholars should focus on developing theoretical frameworks that examine how changing the width and depth of trade affects the propensity and frequency of cyber espionage between states. Accounting for this distinction could yield valuable insights into the dynamics of how economic interdependence influences state-sponsored espionage.

Conceptually, trade deepening increases the availability of goods on the domestic market. This increases consumer welfare through the consumption of foreign varieties that would otherwise be unavailable on the domestic market. Cyber espionage activities that come to light can sour relations between trade partners, increasing the probability of confrontation and open hostilities. Trade may suffer and foreign varieties of goods that domestic consumers have become accustomed to may become unavailable. The potential voter effects of this reduction in welfare disincentivizes espionage activity. In addition, politicians who preside over an environment of peace where beneficial trade can thrive are likely to be rewarded with additional terms in office. This incentivizes pacific relations between trade partners (Akoto, Peterson & Thies, 2020; Peterson & Thies, 2012).

On the other hand, trade increases market competition because it carries with it the need for outward expansion. Increased exports from a foreign country into the home state makes the foreign state a bigger economic competitor on the domestic market. As trade is an important component of a state's economic power, increased trade competition increases interstate rivalry to the extent that each state seeks to maximize its relative gains from trade. Trade widening increases the range of products available on the market and thus intensifies interstate competition for market share. This competition is particularly intense for domestic firms whose products directly compete with imported foreign varieties. Since it is typically the most productive foreign firms that can export to the domestic market, these competitors are usually more technologically advanced than domestic ones and have stronger brand loyalty (Kasahara & Lapham, 2013).

Against this background, economic espionage is appealing because it is covert and hard to trace to any particular state, offering easier deniability compared to other policy measures.

In sum, widening trade increases the number of industries the exporter state is active in, making the exporter state a bigger economic competitor in foreign markets. This increases economic rivalry between the states and incentivizes the home state to explore available avenues to gain a competitive edge, including economic espionage. Testing these and other propositions relating to the nexus between international trade and espionage has the potential to yield valuable insights on the link between economic interdependence and state-sponsored espionage activity. There is also room for the exploration of additional dimensions of this issue. For instance, future scholarly work could explore how the effect of trade varies by industry. That is, are economic espionage operations less likely if trade deepens for particular goods, e.g. manufactured products, as opposed to others, e.g. agricultural products? There is also reason to expect that certain domestic firms, such as those in the computer and technology sectors, stand to gain more from espionage than firms in other sectors (see e.g. Akoto, 2021). Cross-national analyses of these industry-level dynamics may provide groundbreaking insights.

Conclusion

This chapter has highlighted areas of the literature that offer the greatest promise for future scholarly contributions to the study of economic espionage. A focus on the areas highlighted above holds the potential to significantly advance the study of economic espionage. It is nonetheless important to highlight that the study of economic espionage poses some unique challenges, particularly in obtaining firm-level data, which is critical for many of the areas highlighted earlier.

For one, studying espionage is challenging because it mostly happens clandestinely, and its success often depends on obfuscation and deception. This complicates the collection and analysis of relevant incidents of espionage. Firms are frequently unaware that their computer networks have been compromised and those that become aware of breaches are often apprehensive about reporting them. Companies certainly do not want perpetrators to go unpunished, but they are concerned about the divulsion of trade secrets during any ensuing criminal trial. To encourage reporting, the U.S. Congress, for instance, mandates that courts take appropriate measures to preserve the confidentiality of any proprietary information during legal proceedings. Nevertheless, there is no guarantee that such information will indeed remain confidential during prosecutions and afterwards.

Successful cyber espionage operations also raise questions about the appropriateness and effectiveness of the targeted firm's cybersecurity policies and procedures. This might create the impression that firm management is not doing its job or IT leadership is failing to keep the firm cyber safe. Moreover, announcing breaches alerts other cyber hackers to the firm's inadequate cybersecurity measures and might invite further attacks. This is a strong incentive for firm leadership to keep espionage breaches quiet. Even where breaches become public, it may take time for a complete and accurate picture of the incident to emerge. The iterative nature of investigations into espionage operations means information about the incidents and actors involved may change as new evidence comes to light. For instance, it is possible that state intelligence agents have masqueraded as non-state actors (or vice versa) and have not been unmasked. Also, attribution of the breach may change, or additional vectors of compromise may emerge as experts investigate deeper into the incident.

Companies also face significant remediation costs in addressing espionage attempts. Espionage could damage company competitiveness and result in lost revenue, sales, business opportunities and disruptions to supply chains. For example, U.S. firm SolarWorld, once the world's leading supplier of solar panels, experienced a successful cyber espionage attempt in 2012. The cyber breach, allegedly carried out by hackers affiliated with the Chinese government, resulted in the theft of designs for new solar panels and other proprietary blueprints. Using this pilfered information, Chinese manufacturers were able to gain a foothold in the competitive solar panels market by flooding the U.S. market with lower-priced alternatives. This resulted in more than US$120 million in lost sales and revenues for SolarWorld. The company went out of business in 2017. Several other U.S. solar manufacturers are also reportedly on the brink of collapse due to intense competition from Chinese and other firms selling products based on stolen trade secrets (Cohen, 2018).

Even if hackers cannot monetize all the stolen information, firms must expend significant resources in dealing with the fallout. Investigating espionage breaches requires forensic analytic activities, crisis management teams and constant communication with both internal and external stakeholders. This can consume a great deal of company resources. Further, companies bear significant additional expenses relating to legal services, new cybersecurity measures and regulatory compliance. The reputation and stock price of companies reporting cyber breaches also tend to suffer (Ettredge, Guo & Li, 2018). These challenges make it difficult to assess the true extent of state-sponsored economic espionage operations, while they also offer a tantalizing opportunity for scholars interested in highlighting these difficulties and proposing possible solutions.

References

Akoto, William (2021) International trade and cyber conflict: Decomposing the effect of trade on state-sponsored cyber attacks. *Journal of Peace Research* 58(5): 1083–1097.

Akoto, William, Timothy M. Peterson & Cameron G. Thies (2020) Trade composition and acquiescence to sanction threats. *Political Research Quarterly* 73(3): 526–539.

Anderson, Paige C. (2017) Cyber attack exception to the foreign sovereign immunities act. *Cornell Law Review* 102(4): 1087–1113.

Banks, William (2017) State responsibility and attribution of cyber intrusions after Tallinn 2.0. *Texas Law Review* 95(7): 1487–1513.

Blinderman, Eric & Myra Din (2017) Hidden by sovereign shadows: Improving the domestic framework for deterring state-sponsored cybercrime. *Vanderbilt Journal of Transnational Law* 50(4): 889–931.

Button, Mark (2020) Economic and industrial espionage. *Security Journal* 33: 1–5.

Carlin, John P. (2016) Detect, disrupt, deter: A whole-of-government approach to national security cyber threats. *Harvard National Security Journal* 7(2): 391–435.

Cohen, Peter (2018) From breach to bankruptcy: How the terminal impact of cyber attacks is accelerating (https://bit.ly/3mko7c3).

Crootof, Rebecca (2018) International cybertorts: Expanding state accountability in cy- berspace. *Cornell Law Review* 103(3): 565–644.

Danielson, Mark E.A. (2008) Economic espionage: A framework for a workable solution. *Minnesota Journal of Law, Science and Technology* 10(2): 503–548.

Ettredge, Michael, Feng Guo & Yijun Li (2018) Trade secrets and cyber security breaches. *Journal of Accounting and Public Policy* 37(6): 564–585.

Fialka, John J. (1997) While America sleeps. *The Wilson Quarterly* 21(1): 48–63.

Geller, Eric (2018) U.S. allies slam China for brazen cyberattacks as Trump administration indicts hackers (https://politi.co/2H3Mvys).

Hannas, William C., James Mulvenon & Anna B. Puglisi (2013) *Chinese Industrial Espionage: Technology Acquisition and Military Modernisation*. Routledge.

Harris, John R. (2017) *Industrial Espionage and Technology Transfer: Britain and France in the 18th Century*. Taylor & Francis.

Kasahara, Hiroyuki & Beverly Lapham (2013) Productivity and the decision to import and export: Theory and evidence. *Journal of international Economics* 89(2): 297–316.

Lotrionte, Catherine (2015) Countering state-sponsored cyber economic espionage under international law. *North Carolina Journal of International Law and Commercial Regulation* 40(2): 443–541.

Mamolar, Ana Serrano, Zeeshan Pervez, Jose M. Alcaraz Calero & Asad Masood Khattak (2018) Towards the transversal detection of DDoS network attacks in 5G multi-tenant overlay networks. *Computers & Security* 79: 132–147.

Maurer, Tim (2018) *Cyber Mercenaries*. Cambridge University Press.

Nasheri, Hedieh (2005) *Economic Espionage and Industrial Spying*. Cambridge University Press.

Peterson, Timothy M. & Cameron G. Thies (2012) Beyond Ricardo: The link between intra-industry trade and peace. *British Journal of Political Science* 42(4): 747–767.

Promnick, Genna (2017) Cyber economic espionage: Corporate theft and the new Patriot Act. *Hastings Science and Technology Law Journal* 9(1): 89–112.

Pun, Darien (2017) Rethinking espionage in the modern era. *Chicago Journal of International Law* 18(1): 353–391.

Pytlak, Allison & George E. Mitchell (2016) Power, rivalry and cyber conflict: An empirical analysis. In Karsten Friis & Jens Ringsmose (eds.), *Conflict in Cyber Space*. Routledge, 81–98.

Reid, Melanie (2015) A comparative approach to economic espionage: Is any nation effectively dealing with this global threat. *University of Miami Law Review* 70(3): 757–829.

Rowe, Brenda I. (2020) Transnational state-sponsored cyber economic espionage: A legal quagmire. *Security Journal* 33(1): 63–82.

Wagner, Robert E. (2011) Bailouts and the potential for distortion of federal criminal law: Industrial espionage and beyond. *Tulane Law Review* 86(5): 1017–1055.

10. Technology and the new geography of trade politics

Gary Winslett

Introduction: bicycles of the mind

Technological advances are driving economic concentration. One of Steve Jobs' favorite stories went something like this: there was a chart in a scientific magazine in which different animals were compared in terms of how much energy they needed to cover a mile (Jobs 2006). The author of the chart had the insight to not just look at a human by themselves (which was in the middle of the pack) but to also look at a human on a bicycle. Once the human and their invention the bicycle were considered, the human was by far the most efficient animal. Jobs said that computers could be like this for cognitive distance covering – they could be bicycles for the mind, and indeed, that is exactly what computers have done. They have made brainy work more productive. That kind of work has historically been located in cities because cities facilitate the generation of ideas and the flow of information. Ergo, the ascent of computers, the internet, more advanced telecommunication and all of the other bicycles of the mind have benefitted cities, especially those cities at the leading edge of technology.

Though there is a robust literature that explains how trade and economic geography affect each other, ongoing technological advances complicate our understanding of that relationship. Technological advances have accelerated and shifted economic agglomeration. This has led to efficiency improvements but also exacerbated inequality along regional and urban–rural lines. This in turn has led to political revanchism. Moreover, this technological explanation stands somewhat in contrast to the China Shock argument.

Geographic agglomeration

The economic clustering seen over the last three decades was fueled by a feed-back loop between computerization and skills. The cities where computers were adopted most quickly in the workplace saw increases in wages, which drew in talent; these places, now abundant in computer-complementary skilled labor, would then adopt computers even faster, further boosting wages (Beaudry et al. 2006, Hendrickson et al. 2018, p. 11). Once these cities possessed greater wealth and tax bases, they had more amenities and more new firms which attracted still more skilled workers (Hendrickson et al. 2018, p. 11). This meant that the cities with the largest share of digital workers saw their share of digital workers grow faster than others (Muro 2017). Again, it bears pointing that this happened in only a relatively small share of places. As a 2016 World Bank report notes, "in the United States, the adoption of advanced internet applications by firms led to substantial wage growth in the 6 percent of counties that were the wealthiest, the most educated, and had an IT-intensive industry, with no effect elsewhere" (World Bank 2016, p. 118).

All of this had an effect on productivity and growth. Starting in the early 1990s, the firms which were the heaviest IT users, which were already somewhat clustered in a few major cities, became much more productive than their more analog counterparts (Brynjolffson and Hitt 1996, pp. 541–548, Stiroh 2002). This trend became even stronger over subsequent years (Jorgenson et al. 2011, Brynjolffson and Hitt 2003). Not only that, but when highly skilled, ambitious employees of innovative technology-oriented firms left those businesses to start their own companies, they tended to do so in the same geographic loca-tions (Moretti 2012, pp. 80–81). With these advantages in hand, new jobs that did not exist until recently tended to show up first in these most educated places, reinforcing those advantages (Lin 2011). Not only that, but whereas manufacturing jobs generate an estimated 1.6 additional jobs in the local economy, jobs in the innovation sector generate an estimated five jobs in the local economy and so the local economy in the cities that the tech sector clus-tered in have boomed (Moretti 2012, pp. 13, 24).

Large cities thus became more productive and saw nearly twice as much private employment growth and greater wage growth as compared to smaller metropolitan areas and non-metro areas (Parilla and Muro 2017, Porter 2017, Hendrickson et al. 2018, p. 8). These areas gained an increasing share of invest-ment, particularly venture capital. In 2016, 75 percent of all venture capital went to just three states: California, New York, and Massachusetts (Townsend 2017). This tech-driven clustering of opportunity into large, dense urban areas is in marked contrast to the geography of manufacturing that took place in large cities, smaller cities, and exurbs (Porter 2017). According to one estimate, across the developed world, for every one job the internet has destroyed, it has created 2.6 jobs but, importantly, the job losses have been geographically spread out while the job gains have most been geographically concentrated (Moretti 2012, p. 65). Superstar firms and cities compete well in and integrate well with global markets and so tend to see greater benefits from international economic integration than other areas and so the same places that benefit from technological advancement also benefit from globalization (Grossman and Rossi-Hansberg 2008, Donaldson 2015, Cosar and Falgelbaum 2013).

The very troubling flipside is that other areas, i.e. smaller metros and rural areas, have largely been left out. This can be seen most starkly in net business creation during the recovery from the three most recent recessions (EIG 2016, p. 21). In the 1992–1996 recovery, 32 percent of net business creation took place in counties with less than 100,000 people, 39 percent in counties between 100,000 and 500,000, and 29 percent in counties with more than 500,000. In the 2010–2014 recovery, 81 percent of net business creation was in counties with over 500,000 in population, 19 percent in 100,000 to 500,000, while counties with less than 100,000 population saw literally no net business growth. The story is similar in jobs. A recent McKinsey report on changes in the U.S. economy between 2017 and 2030 projects that 60 percent of all new jobs will be in the 25 biggest, most prosperous cities while just 3 percent of new jobs are projected to be in low-growth and rural areas, with everywhere else splitting the other 37 percent (McKinsey 2019, p. 50). Advances in AI are projected to add to this trend because they are likely to have a more disruptive impact on the less-educated, less metropolitan places that specialize in low-end services and manufacturing than the more metropolitan, more well-educated places on the coasts (Muro 2019, McKinsey 2019, p. 6).

Meanwhile, rapid progress in IT made it easier for firms to coordinate complicated multinational supply chains and so made it easier for them to locate labor-intensive steps in developing countries (Baldwin 2016). This is an important point to keep in mind. Even when trade is associated with offshoring the enabling cause is technological advancement.

The China Shock and its limitations

Few research veins in trade politics have gained as much public salience as Autor, Dorn, and Hanson's research on the 'China Shock' (Autor, Dorn, and

Hanson 2016). It is not hard to see why. It is well-executed research, on an important topic, and it arrived right when public anxieties about the decline of manufacturing and the rise of China were beginning to fuse.

Their argument went as follows. China's economic policies were calamitous under Mao. That meant that, once China adopted better policies, there was a lot of room to grow, especially given its population size (ibid., pp. 209–211). China's comparative advantage was in labor-intensive manufacturing (ibid., p. 211). China's manufacturing growth thus constituted a large global supply shock for labor-intensive manufacturing and a large demand shock for raw materials (ibid., p. 211). Different industries tend to cluster in different places; this is true in the United States as it is anywhere else. Because of that, different places in the United States experienced different levels of vulnerability to the supply shock in labor-intensive manufactured goods (ibid., pp. 212–213). As some of their earlier works shows, labor-intensive manufacturing is particularly trade exposed and particularly concentrated in a cluster of mostly Southern states (Autor, Dorn, and Hanson 2013, p. 222). The places that were more exposed to this supply shock saw larger declines in manufacturing employment and wages (Autor, Dorn, and Hanson 2016, pp. 224, 229).

These negative effects had big local spillovers, i.e. when labor-intensive manufacturing declined, it undermined demand for other goods and services in that area, corroded tax bases, and contributed to range of other social ills (ibid., pp. 224, 227). Not only that, but contrary to economists' conventional wisdom, people did not tend to move; they stayed put and suffered rather than leaving for greener pastures (ibid., p. 224). In other words, the adjustment costs to this shock were deeper and more scarring than was typically appreciated. The negative impacts were felt most strongly by the least-educated, lowest paid workers; those with higher incomes (implying more education and skills) were better able to transition than those with less income, education, and skills (ibid., pp. 229, 233). When taken at face value and when weaponized by populists, this story painted a damning picture of trade's impact on middle America.

There are, however, several important caveats. The first is that the job losses are probably overestimated. Autor himself has acknowledged that their estimates are the upper-bound (Clement 2016). Other papers have found much smaller effects (Jakubik and Stolzenburg 2018, Caliendo et al. 2019). Multiple studies even find that liberalized trade with China had a *positive* impact on wages and employment (Feenstra and Sasahara 2017, Wang et al. 2018). Some economists contend that Autor, Dorn, and Hanson omitted certain control variables that should have been included and that they underestimated offsetting jobs gains (Feenstra et al. 2017).[1] Additionally, in terms of mobility, Autor, Dorn, and

Hanson's model assumes literally zero geographic mobility (Autor, Dorn, and Hanson 2016, p. 217). Even if they are correct that prior research overestimated mobility, assuming zero mobility (however helpful to the model) is an inaccurate representation of reality and inflates the estimate of jobs lost.

The second caveat is that, even if everything about the China Shock is correct, it is inaccurate to attribute Chinese import penetration to capital-intensive manufacturing decline. As Autor, Dorn, and Hanson point out, some industries like apparel, textiles, and leather are particularly labor-intensive (ibid., pp. 212–213). At the same time, even in the parts of the country that are manufacturing oriented, there is a lot of variation in terms of industry exposure to import competition; Tennessee and Alabama are both strongly manufacturing oriented but Tennessee was a lot more exposed to trade with China because its manufacturing was disproportionately in furniture while Alabama's was in heavy industry (ibid., pp. 223–224). Michael Hicks and Srikant Devaraj's research highlights this same differential between industries (Hicks and Devaraj 2017). Their work suggests that trade only accounted for about 13 percent of manufacturing job losses between 2000 and 2010 (ibid., p. 6). Of the 18 industries they look at, trade was responsible for more jobs lost than productivity increases in *none of them* and was responsible for more than a quarter of job losses in only two of them, apparel and furniture (ibid., p. 6). As they say in their paper, "had we kept 2000 levels of productivity and applied them to 2010-levels of production, we would have required 20.9 million manufacturing workers. Instead, we employed only 12.1 million" (ibid., p. 5). So even if every word of the China Shock literature is true, the bulk of manufacturing jobs that went away did so because we got better at making more stuff with fewer people, not trade shocks, and that statement becomes even more true if one excludes apparel and furniture. Geographically speaking then, even if it makes sense to attribute the decline of furniture and textile towns in the South to the China Shock, it makes no sense to blame the China Shock for the decline of manufacturing jobs in capital-intensive industry.

Not only that but the idea that something is broken in U.S. manufacturing is misleading. Manufacturing is not down; it is manufacturing employment that is down. In 1990, there were roughly 18 million manufacturing jobs in the United States (FRED 2021). By February 2020, there were only 13 million (ibid.).[2] Meanwhile, industrial production nearly doubled (ibid.). Yes, there has been deindustrialization in some places and the people in those places have suffered. They deserve sympathy and help. But it is inaccurate to transition from acknowledging and empathizing with that pain to asserting that manufacturing is in some kind of free-fall.

Third, the China Shock arguments ignore the benefits of imports from China (Lincicome 2019). According to one Federal Reserve study, for every lost job due to the China Shock, there were approximately US$400,000 in consumer benefits (Jaravel and Savier 2019). From 2000 to 2006, the peak years of the China Shock, the price of manufactured goods fell by 7 percent (Amiti et al. 2018). This was not only good for consumers. Because over a third of Chinese imports were intermediate goods, it was good for producers too (Hale et al. 2019). Furthermore, the United States does not just import from China, it also exports goods and services to China as well. Many of the producers of those goods and services would not have had access to the Chinese market were it not for China's integration with the global economy. Those benefits matter too. WTO Accession also promoted some reforms in China albeit not to the level many in the West had hoped for (Tan 2021). Finally, in a more prosaic sense, Chinese people are humans and so the substantial decline in poverty in China, greatly assisted by China's integration into global markets, ought to also count very positively in the moral ledger of increased trade with China.

Fourth, discussions around trade shocks often ignore the costs that accompanied the United States' misguided reactions to it. When President Trump raised tariffs on China and the EU, China and the EU retaliated predictably. American farmers paid the price; agricultural exports targeted by the retaliation were US$8 billion lower in 2018 than they had been in 2017, a 27 percent drop (CRS 2019, p. 7). In 2018 and 2019 combined, the U.S. government bailed out farmers at a cost of US$28 billion (Charles 2019). The damage was wider than just farmers. Just for 2020, President Trump's trade war with China was estimated to cost the average American family over US$1,200 in higher prices and lost productivity (CBO 2020). According to the IMF, the trade war lowered global GDP by 0.8 percent (CRS 2020, p. 3). More broadly than just the trade war, anti-dumping measures on Chinese imports hurt industries that imported the products targeted (and thus the workers in those industries); they raise the cost of production and have significantly negative effects both for employment and wages but do not actually have a positive impact on the industries they were ostensibly protecting (Bown et al. 2021).[3]

Decline and fury: getting punched by automation, punching back at the status quo

With those caveats stated, it is important to recognize that there is a central truth at the core of the China Shock argument that few observers dispute: while the pain of trade liberalization is smaller than the gains, it is very concentrated while the benefits are diffuse. According to one estimate, while the China Shock increased overall welfare, some groups experienced losses five times as high as the average gains (Galle et al. 2017). That central truth stacks on top of another core truth: as discussed earlier, economic gains have been concentrating in cities and increasingly going to the educated, technologically skilled workers that live in them.

As Autor, Dorn, and Hanson show in earlier work, automation exposure is uncorrelated with trade exposure and is geographically more diffuse (Autor, Dorn, and Hanson 2013, pp. 222–223). I would argue, based on the evidence presented here, that much of the decline of rural areas (especially those not connected to textiles and furniture) is due more to the agglomerative effects of technological advancements rather than trade, but it is nevertheless the case that when core industries in an area are negatively affected labor force participation declines, young people leave, property values and local tax revenue drop, and services deteriorate (Feler and Senses 2017). A sad spiral of decline and despair then takes hold.

All of these dynamics are occurring outside of the United States as well. Other countries like Britain and Denmark experienced some version of the China Shock too (Ballard-Rosa et al. 2017, Bo et al. 2019). In the EU, there has been greater urban–rural sorting along educational lines and, at the same time, a lack of geographic mobility has undermined the economic prospects of those remaining in economically underperforming areas (Ehrlich and Overman 2020). Even in the developing world, urban-rural disparities account for roughly half of overall economic inequality within countries (Lagakos 2020).

The hollowing out of middle-skill jobs in rural America is one of the central underpinnings of the cultural pathologies described by Robert Putnam, Charles Murray, and Timothy Carney as well as one of the central drivers of the rise in deaths of despair examined by Anne Case and Angus Deaton (Putnam 2015, Carney 2019, Case and Deaton 2017). Case and Deaton say their explanation of these deaths of despair, and of the broader socioeconomic malaise affecting less educated whites, is a story of "cumulative disadvantage from one birth cohort to the next—in the labor market, in marriage and child outcomes, and in health—[which] is *triggered by progressively worsening labor market opportunities at the time of entry* for whites with low levels of education" (emphasis mine) (Case and Deaton 2017). This dynamic is intimately related to the burgeoning variation in social mobility from one region to the next (Chetty et al. 2017).

Roughly 10 percent of Americans live in smaller metropolitan areas that are stagnating and another 15 percent live in rural areas that are almost all in decline (Muro and Whiton 2018). What makes this worse – and this is something that Autor, Dorn, and Hanson are right about – is that mobility between declining and prospering regions is declining; in 1990, 6.1 percent of Americans moved between states or counties and but in 2017 only 3.5 percent did so (Hendrickson, Muro, and Galston 2018, p. 5).[4] These trends have huge political consequences. Among rural citizens with strong attachments to their local area, scholars have documented a deeply felt, multifaceted, seething resentment toward cities and the institutions associated with them (Cramer 2016, Goodhart 2017, Hochschild 2016). This affects the politics around trade. To the extent that trade is seen as reflecting the cosmopolitan values of educated urban professionals and advancing their interests while leaving rural areas behind, it loses support among rural voters even if the real culprit behind most of their woes is technology. On one level, this makes sense. It is possible to vote against trade deals but there's no easy political response to technological improvements.

These dynamics also gets wrapped in the broader phenomenon of right-wing populism which does not just dislike trade but more generally has a 'draw-bridges up' perspective. Higher declines in manufacturing employment share between 1970 and 2015 were associated with increases in voting for Trump in 2016 (Broz et al. 2019, p. 11). Voters punished incumbents for trade-related job losses (Margalit 2011). In some ways, this was predictable because economic distress is associated with greater xenophobia and in-group bias (Broz et al. 2019, pp. 13–14). This same trend can be seen in Europe where those areas most exposed to trade shocks trended toward the political extremes and populism (Milner 2021). Economic vibrancy continues to concentrate in cities with the lion's share of opportunities going to the young, the educated, and the already affluent. Older, less-educated voters in rural areas are getting left behind and they know it. This leaves them fearful, furious, and eager to lash out at anything, including liberalized trade, that they see to be contributing to their relative decline. Therefore, even if the role that trade has played in exacerbating urban-rural divides has been overstated, especially relative to technology, the geography of support for trade is nevertheless affected by those divides.

Conclusion: will remote work giveth and taketh away?

It is too soon to know what long-term impact the coronavirus pandemic will have on this topic but as with so many other areas of political economy and public policy, it is worth carefully considering how remote work might have an effect. It may be the case that as more workers are allowed to work fully or near-fully remotely that they choose to live much further from central offices located in expensive cities. Rather than pay Newton Massachusetts' real estate prices to be a reasonable daily commute into Boston, it is not hard to imagine a worker who now has the freedom associated with mostly remote work to live in Concord, New Hampshire if they only need to come into the office once or twice a month. If they are fully remote, then the options become even more open. If/when such a worker relocates to Concord, New Hampshire that would spread out the spillover effects of that person's employment. Now, it would be Concord restaurants receiving her business and Concord that would be collecting her property tax. In this manner, it is possible that more workers having the ability to work remotely will alleviate some of the agglomerative impacts of technological change discussed earlier in this chapter thereby spreading prosperity more geographically evenly. Obviously, it is far too early to know if this will or will not come to pass, but it is worth paying attention to.

On the flip side, once work can be done completely remotely, it is possible that more and more white-collar work will be outsourced. After all, once a worker never comes into an office, why would it matter to an employer if the worker is in Kentucky or Kerala? That outsourcing of white-collar work may not help the Indian farmer, but it could provide a further accelerant to the service exports from South India mentioned at the beginning of this chapter. Whether this comes to pass too is not yet knowable, but this is something else relevant to technology, trade, and geography that is worth paying attention to.

References

Amiti, Mary, Mi Dai, John Feenstra, and John Romalis. 2018. "How Did China's WTO Entry Affect U.S. Prices?" National Bureau of Economic Research Working Paper 23487.

Autor, David, David Dorn, and Gordon Hanson. 2013. "The Geography of Trade and Technology Shocks in the United States." *American Economic Review* 103:3: 220–225.

Autor, David, David Dorn, and Gordon Hanson. 2016. "The China Shock: Learning from Labor-Market Adjustment to Large Changes in Trade." *Annual Review of Economics* 8: 205–240.

Baldwin, Richard. 2016. *The Great Convergence: Information Technology and the New Globalization.* Cambridge, MA: Harvard University Press.

Ballard-Rosa, Cameron, Mashail Malik, Stephanie Rickard, and Kenneth Scheve. 2017. "The Economic Origins of Authoritarian Values: Evidence from Local

Trade Shocks in the United Kingdom." *Comparative Political Studies* 54:1: 10.1177/00104140211024296.

Beaudry, Paul, Mark Doms, and Ethan Lewis. 2006. "The IT Revolution at the City Level: Testing a Model of Endogenous Biased Technology Adoption." Federal Reserve Bank of San Francisco Working Paper.

Bo, Dal, Federico Finan, Olle Folke, Torsten Persson, and Johanna Rickne. 2019. "Economic Losers and Political Winner's: Sweden's Radical Right." University of Warwick Working Paper.

Bown, Chad, Paola Conconi, Aksel Erbahar, and Lorenzo Trimachi. 2021. "Trade Protection Along Supply Chains," February 2021. Center for Economic Policy and Research Discussion Paper 15648.

Broz, J. Lawrence, Jeffry Frieden, and Stephen Weymouth. 2019. "Populism in Place: The Economic Geography of the Globalization Backlash." Prepared for a Special Issue of *International Organization* September.

Byrnjolfsson, Erik and Lorin Hitt. 1996. "Paradox Lost: Firm-level Evidence on the Returns to Information Systems," *Management Science* 42:4: 541–548.

Byrnjolfsson, Erik and Lorin Hitt. 2003. "Computing Productivity: Firm-Level Evidence," *Review of Economics and Statistics* 85:4: 793–808.

Caliendo, Lorenzo, Maximiliano Dvorkin, and Fernando Parro. 2019. "Trade and Labor Market Dynamics: General Equilibrium Analysis of the China Trade Shock," *Econometrica* 87:3: 741–835.

Carney, Timothy. 2019. *Alienated America: Why Some Places Thrive While Others Collapse.* New York: HarperCollins.

Case, Anne and Angus Deaton. 2017. "Mortality and Morbidity in the 21st Century." *Brookings Papers on Economic Activity* Spring.

Charles, Dan. 2019. "Farmers Got Billions From Taxpayers in 2019, Hardly Anyone Objected." *National Public Radio.* December 31.

Chetty, Raj, David Grusky, Maximilian Hell, Nathaniel Hendren, Robert Manduca, and Jimmy Narang. 2017. "The Fading American Dream: Trends in Absolute Income Mobility since 1940." *Science* 356:6336: 398–406.

Clement, Douglas. 2016. "Interview with David Autor." Federal Reserve Bank of Minneapolis.

Congressional Budget Office (CBO). 2020. "The Budget and Economic Outlook: 2020 to 2030.

Congressional Research Service (CRS). 2019. "Retaliatory Tariffs and U.S. Agriculture." R45903.

Congressional Research Service (CRS). 2020. "Escalating U.S. Tariffs: Affected Trade." IN10971.

Cosar, A. Kerem and Pablo Falgelbaum. 2013. "Internal Geography, International Trade, and Regional Specialization." NBER Working Paper 19697.

Cramer, Katherine. 2016. *The Politics of Resentment: Rural Consciousness in Wisconsin and the Rise of Scott Walker.* Chicago: University of Chicago Press.

Donaldson, Dave. 2015. "The Gains from Market Integration," *Annual Review of Economics* 7: 619–647.

Economic Innovation Group. 2016. "The New Map of Economic Growth and Recovery."

Ehrlich, Maximilian and Henry Overman. 2020. "Place-Based Policies and Spatial Disparities across European Cities," *Journal of Economic Perspectives* 34:3. 128–49.

Feenstra, Robert and Akira Sasahara. 2017. "The 'China Shock', Exports, and U.S. Employment: A Global Input-Output Analysis." National Bureau of Economic Research Working Paper 24022.

Feenstra, Robert, Hong Ma, and Yuan Xu. 2017. "The China Syndrome: Local Labor Market Effects of Import Competition in the United States: Comment." University of California, Davis.

Feler, Leo and Mine Senses 2017. "Trade Shocks and the Provision of Local Public Goods." *American Economic Journal: Economic Policy* 9:4: 101–143.

Federal Reserve Bank of St. Louis (FRED), n.d. *Economic Data.* https://fred.stlouisfed .org/series/PRS30006013. Last accessed July 12, 2022.

Galle, Simon, Andres Rodriguez-Clare, and Moises Yi. 2017. "Slicing the Pie: Quantifying the Aggregate and Distributional Gains." National Bureau of Economic Research Working Paper 23737.

Goodhart, David. 2017. *The Road to Somewhere: The Populist Revolt and the Future of Politics.* London: Hurst.

Grossman, Gene and Esteban Rossi-Hansberg. 2008. "Trading Tasks: A Simple Theory of Offshoring," *American Economic Review* 98:5: 1978–1997.

Hale, Galina, Bart Hobijnm Fernando Nechio, and Doris Wilson. 2019. "How Much Do We Spend on Imports?" Federal Reserve Bank of San Francisco.

Hendrickson, Clara, Mark Muro, and William Galston. 2018. "Countering the Geography of Discontent: Strategies for Left-Behind Places." Brookings Institution.

Hicks, Michael and Srikant Devaraj. 2017. "The Myth and Reality of Manufacturing in America." Ball State University, Centre for Business and Economic Research. April: 1–7.

Hochschild, Arlie. 2016. *Strangers in the Own Land: Anger and Mourning on the American Right.* New York: The New Press.

Jakubik, Adam and Viktor Stolzenburg. 2018. "The 'China Shock' Revisited: Insight From Value-Added Trade Flows." World Trade Organization, Staff Working Paper ERSD-2018-10.

Jaravel, Xavier and Erick Savier. 2019. "What are the Price Effects of Trade? Evidence from the U.S. and Implications for Quantitative Trade Models." *Finance and Economics Discussion Series 2019-068.* Washington: Board of Governors of the Federal Reserve System.

Jobs, Steve. 2006. "Computers are Like Bicycles for Our Minds" – Michael Lawrence Films. June 1. https://www.youtube.com/watch?v=ob_GX50Za6c

Jorgenson, D.W., M.S. Ho, and J.D. Samuels. 2011. "Information Technology and U.S. Productivity Growth: Evidence from a Prototype Industry Production Account," *Journal of Productivity Analysis* 36:2: 159–175.

Lagakos, David. 2020. "Urban-Rural Gaps in the Developing World: Does Internal Migration Offer Opportunities?" *Journal of Economic Perspectives* 34:3: 174–192.

Lin, Jeffrey. 2011. "Technological Adaptation, Cities, and New Work," *Review of Economics and Statistics* 93:2: 554–574.

Lincicome, Scott. 2019. "A Failure to Adjust." Cato Institute. January 15.

Margalit, Yotam. 2011. "Costly Jobs: Trade-Related Layoffs, Government Compensation, and Voting in U.S. Elections." *American Political Science Review* 105:1: 166–188.

McKinsey. 2019. "The Future of Work in America: People and Places, Today and Tomorrow."

Milner, Helen. 2021. "Voting for Populism in Europe: Globalization, Technological Change, and the Extreme Right." *Comparative Political Studies* 54:13: 2286–2320.

Moretti, Enrico. 2012. *The New Geography of Jobs.* Boston, MA: Mariner Books.

Muro, Mark. 2017. "Tech Empowers, Tech Polarizes." Brookings Institution. November 21.

Muro, Mark. 2019. "Countering the Geographical Impacts of Automation: Computers, AI, and Place Disparities." Brookings Institution. February 14.

Muro, Mark and Jacob Whiton. 2018. "Geographic Gaps are Widening While U.S. Economic Growth Increases." Brookings Institution. January 23.

Parilla, Joseph and Mark Muro. 2017. "Understanding U.S. Productivity Trends from the Bottom-Up." Brookings Institution. March 15.

Porter, Eduardo. 2017. "Why Big Cities Thrive, and Smaller Ones are Left Behind," *The New York Times*, October 10.

Putnam, Robert. 2015. *Our Kids: The American Dream in Crisis*. New York: Simon and Schuster.

Stiroh, K.J. 2002. "Information Technology and the U.S. Productivity Revival: What Do the Industry Data Say?" *American Economic Review* 92:5: 1559–1576.

Tan, Yeling. 2021. "How the WTO Changed China." *Foreign Affairs*. March/April.

Townsend, Tess. 2017. "Steve Case: 47 States Have to Fight for 25 Percent of Venture Capital Dollars." *Vox*, June 1.

Wang, Zhi, Shang-Jin Wei, Xinding Yu, and Kunfu Zhu. 2018. "Re-Examining the Effects of Trading with China on Local Labor Markets." National Bureau of Economic Research Working Paper 24886.

World Bank. 2016. "Digital Dividends." World Development Report.

11. The political economy of local aid: a new research agenda

Emily Scott

Introduction

Since the end of the Cold War, the aid industry has grappled with inequities in the global aid system and the undue influence of aid dollars coming from Western governments on humanitarian and development efforts. Foreign aid refers to the international transfer of goods, services, or capital from donor countries to recipient governments and non-governmental organizations (NGOs) or to UN agencies and international organizations (IOs) (ReliefWeb 2008). Through global aid, donor countries shape the behaviors of recipient governments and organizations, eliciting policy concessions and gaining geo-political influence (Tierney et al. 2011; De Mesquita and Smith 2009; Dunning 2004). The influence of donors in the Global North has grown along with global aid flows over the last half-century. Between 1970 and 2019, global aid given by Organisation for Economic Co-operation and Development (OECD) countries to "developing" nations rose from around 6.5 billion USD to 167.8 billion USD (World Bank 2021). Most of this funding has flowed from governments in the Global North to international actors, inclusive of UN agencies and international non-governmental organizations. Very little has reached local actors—the local NGOs, civil society groups, and populations who are most affected by conflict and crisis, and whose expertise and competencies are essential to relief and development efforts.

At the World Humanitarian Summit in Istanbul Turkey in 2016, some of the world's largest donors and humanitarian organizations signed the Grand Bargain. Responding to gathering evidence that aid is improved through the involvement of local actors (Barbalet and Wake 2020; Ayobi et al. 2017; Tanner and Moro 2016; Dubois et al. 2015; De Waal 1997), major players conceded that the global aid system needed to change. The Bargain struck at the heart of the idea that global interference is needed for effective aid delivery and was a sweeping commitment to "localizing" aid, or to making aid "as local as possible, as international as necessary" (Barbalet 2018, p. 1). Amongst its goals, the Bargain called for recognition of existing local capacities, expertise, and competencies and facilitating local leadership of emergency and development responses (OCHA n.d.). At its core was a promise to move more money, more directly to governments, organizations, and citizens in the Global South, who are most affected by conflict, crisis, and development efforts.

Yet, five years after signing the Grand Bargain, the Global North continues to hold the purse strings—and immense sway—over the direction of aid programming and activities; only 3.1 percent of global humanitarian assistance went directly to local and national governments or organizations between 2016 and 2020 (Development Initiatives 2021). In this chapter, I outline emerging research that often comes from practitioner and expert communities and that shows local actors find it very difficult to enter the global aid community and secure contracts directly with global funders (Gingerich and Cohen 2015; Wall and Hedlund 2016; Khoury and Scott 2021). They are excluded due to a range of factors, inclusive of racism (Barnett 2021; Cornish 2019; Gruffydd Jones 2013), underestimations of local capacities and expertise (Barbalet 2018), and rigorous reporting standards (Slim and Trombetta 2014). They rely on capital from alternative sources, inclusive of remittances, civil society funds, and local government assistance, that is often not counted in studies of global aid but is a key part of any picture of local aid (Willitts-King, Bryant, and Spencer 2019; Bryant 2019). I describe the untested hypothesis that more aid will move to local actors as new, or now more influential, donors emerge, such as China, India, the United Arab Emirates, and Turkey (Mullen 2017; Barnett and Walker 2015). Some expect more recently "developing" members of the Global South to change the way aid is allocated.

To date, political economy of aid research has focused on global aid flows from North to South, the motivations of powerful state donors, and the ways donors constrain and enable, mostly national- or international-level, recipients. Where funding availability is low and numerous actors compete for contracts (Cooley and Ron 2002; Bush and Hadden 2019), recipient nations, organizations, and groups become more likely to make concessions to donor governments and agencies. Studies show that factors like ideology, regime type, or colonial history can influence the discretion major donors give states over how aid dollars are spent (Bush 2015; Fink and Redaelli 2011; Alesina and Dollar 2000). Scholars find that international organizations that receive aid dollars can maintain some independence from donor demands by leveraging their capacities and expertise (Barnett 2009; Hawkins 2006; Pfeffer and Salancik 2003).

Despite these contributions, less is known about how local actors can secure funding, as well as the authority to decide how it is spent. This chapter shows that scholarly study of the political economy dynamics of local aid has a great deal of potential for growth, particularly given new interest among donors and aid organizations in making aid more local.

A research agenda

In this chapter, local aid refers to (1) international aid dollars that are given directly, or as directly as possible, to local actors and (2) resources or capacities that originate in a local community, inclusive of philanthropic, civil society, faith-based, and local government assistance. In the following sections, I outline five areas where new research will advance our understandings of the political economy of local aid. Particularly promising avenues of research include exploring the systems of exclusion keeping local actors out of the global political economy of aid, the role of alternative sources of aid in financing local humanitarian response and reconstruction efforts, the emergence of new regional and global players and the likelihood that they will support localization, the effects of aid on state capacity and development particularly in understudied geographic areas, and where aid goes once it moves subnationally. Research conducted in these areas will help scholars and practitioners to gain a better picture of global aid, as it is experienced and practiced locally.

Systems of exclusion

The global community is falling far short of the targets set in the Grand Bargain. While it set a target of sending 25 percent of global aid directly to local actors by 2020, just over 3 percent of aid dollars went directly to local actors in the five years that followed its signing (Development Initiatives 2021). Scholars have an opportunity to study unequal relationships between Global North funders and local actors in the Global South, how they are perpetuated, and the ways local actors can gain more control over foreign aid. Various roots of inequality have been identified in emerging scholarship. Most insidious and perilous for the aid industry is institutionalized racism. Discourse surrounding who is most competent and therefore able to manage conflict and post-conflict response and reconstruction is racialized (Barnett 2020, 2021; Cornish 2019; Gruffydd Jones 2013). Calls for the decolonization of aid (Konyndyk and Aly, 2020), and for the removal of international intermediaries from the flow and use of global aid funds, outline the ways in which white supremacy and structural racism have become tied into the practice of humanitarianism. Analysis of whether these calls and the mechanisms international donors and organizations adopt in response will effect real change is needed. Scholars might ask, why would the powerful "Humanitarian Club" (Barnett and Walker 2015, p. 131) of elite states, donors, international organizations, and international non-governmental organizations (INGOs) give up power? What are some instances when they have done so and how?

Local actors also face significant barriers to entry that are rooted in beliefs about who has the capacity to do aid work. The legitimacy of foreign interference in the domestic affairs of other nations has long been premised on the idea that international actors are needed when local capacities are lacking or overwhelmed (Pincock, Betts, and Easton-Calabria 2020), and that local actors lack the competencies necessary to deliver aid. The push for global-to-local capacity building has tended to highlight the ways international organizations and aid workers should train local organizations and aid workers. Focus has been on building up local management, governance, and decision-making competencies, as well as local abilities to deliver programs and projects (Barbalet 2018). Global funders tend to demand local actors develop traits commonly associated with international actors, such as global logistical and fundraising abilities, an understanding of donor agency structures and expectations, or know-how surrounding global normative and legal frameworks (Howe, Stites, and Chudacoff 2015; Gingerich and Cohen 2015; Tanner and Moro 2016). As a result, the few local actors that receive aid dollars are often past partners of large international organizations, able to demonstrate familiarity with global systems and structures, and operate in English or French (Willitts-King, Bryant, and Spencer 2019; Wall and Hedlund 2016). When local actors do manage to emulate international organizations or workers, their qualifications and competencies are often still questioned (Benton 2016).

By contrast, the comparative advantages of local actors—their contextual knowledge, abilities to respond rapidly to crises or conflict, or local language capabilities—are not accepted as qualifications to receive donor contracts or discretion over the spending of aid dollars. In fact, promising research by practitioners shows that global actors often do not look for or recognize local capacities. Global funders and international aid organizations consistently fail to map existing capacities and resources, assuming that gaps in local capacities exist and missing opportunities to integrate local actors into planning, coordinating, and delivering aid (Bryant 2019a). Studies also show that mistrust of local actors pervades the aid industry (Barbalet 2019). Scholarly mapping of local capacities and resources would allow for more systematic analysis of the causes of local exclusion, whether a function of prejudice, overwhelmed systems, or other factors.

Another way in which local actors are kept out of the political economy of aid is by increasingly onerous reporting standards, in part due to calls for greater transparency and accountability in the aid industry (Khoury and Scott 2021; Slim and Trombetta 2014). Moreover, funds are rarely provided to local organizations to support their core overhead costs or pay salaries (Dixon et al. 2016; Dichter 2014), undermining their developed capacities and producing heightened dependencies. These costs are often elevated by international non-governmental organizations (INGOs) and international organizations (IOs) that offload risks associated with managing and meeting financial regulations to local NGOs (Stoddard, Czwarno, and Hamsik 2019). These conditions are particularly challenging during complex emergencies or conflict (Howe, Stites, and Chudacoff 2015; Slim and Trombetta 2014) or where global actors expect to find corruption amongst local ones (Rimmer and Hope 2000), whether due to past incidents, concerns over patrimonial traditions, or prejudice. As much of the donor community pushes for greater transparency and accountability as pathways to effective aid delivery there is increasing recognition of the ways resources are being diverted within local organizations to donor relations and away from delivering aid. Building on exciting new analysis by Honig (2018) and Campbell (2018), further research into the tensions between global and local accountability and aid effectiveness is needed.

Alternative sources of aid

Another avenue of new research concerns alternative resource flows, which constitute a significant part of local political economies of aid. There is evidence that as global aid flows fall short of meeting population needs (Moyo 2009; Farmer 2020), more are relying on alternative sources of assistance (Willitts-King, Bryant, and Spencer 2019; Versluis 2014). Resources come from in-kind donation, the private sector, philanthropy, civil society funds, or faith-based and direct giving, as well local government assistance and remittances. These sources of capital bolster local political economies and shape "local conception[s] of assistance" (Willitts-King, Bryant, and Spencer 2019, p. 3). Studies show that community-based assistance can promote community and social cohesion and that *where* or *who* assistance comes from alters its effects (Willitts-King, Bryant, and Spencer 2019; Alik-Lagrange et al. 2021).

While ample research has been conducted on, for example, remittances (Rapoport and Docquier 2006; Giuliano and Ruiz-Arranz 2009; Yang 2011; Levitt and Lamba-Nieves 2011), scholars of aid do not normally count these as sources of aid. Researchers would do well to respond to calls for a redefinition of the concept of aid beyond a traditional "donor-recipient" model to one that accounts for the role of private businesses, charities, and populations themselves in assistance, and in providing financial aid to populations (Adelman 2009). This is particularly the case as the importance of these resources in local economies are highlighted in the wake of localization efforts. Foreign aid is traditionally understood as an international transfer of resources from donor to recipient governments, NGOs, UN agencies, of IOs (ReliefWeb 2008). Scholars might ask, conceptually, why are private or philanthropic donations that move through international organizations or charities counted as aid while remittances are not? What would be gained or lost by expanding the concept of aid to include alternative sources of aid?

Another area of potential scholarly contribution is in improving the data available on alternative sources of assistance. Interest in improving the tracking of these sources is growing, with the UN Secretary-General Report on Humanitarian Financing in 2016 recommending that alternative flows be better tracked (UN Assembled Panel 2016). Yet, scholars acknowledge that issues arise because various "types of financial flows may be defined and measured differently by different countries, and there are imprecisions associated with accounting and reporting. The measurement and reporting of remittance flows, however, is considerably more incomplete than the other types of financial flows" (Gammeltoft 2002, p. 191). Further, these sources are expected to be more significant than international aid flows (Willitts-King, Poole, and Bryant 2018). Study of their relative impact would provide a fuller picture of assistance as it is experienced at the local levels. Direct comparison of the effects of informal, private assistance and foreign, institutionalized aid delivery on humanitarian and development projects would also be an interesting avenue for future research. The notion that private donors will have mostly private effects on private households is questionable and requires further study. In my own work, interlocutors report that private groups are principal investors in social enterprises and civil society efforts in conflict and post-conflict settings. Studies have also shown that these kinds of donors support large-scale infrastructure and investment projects (Bryant 2019b). The study of private–public dynamics in global aid would be fruitful.

The importance of alternative aid is heightened by the unstable, crisis dependent, and short-term nature of traditional humanitarian assistance (Bryant 2019). UN agencies, IOs, and INGOs are highly dependent on these funds. However, alternative sources are often more stable and common sources of assistance to populations. For instance, studies suggest a larger proportion of remittance dollars reach intended recipients than formal aid dollars (ibid.) and, while banks are putting up additional barriers to moving private capital to reduce risks and gain more revenue (Watkins and Quattri 2014), remittances remain a key and growing source of assistance and a tool to alleviate poverty.

Faith-based assistance, such as almsgiving or *zakat* in Muslim nations, is estimated to bring in billions of dollars through formal channels, with even more coming through informal channels (Barnett and Stein 2012; Ager, Fiddian-Qasmiyeh, and Ager 2015; Stirk 2015). Front-line service delivery by local NGOs and civil society groups, the hosting of displaced persons, and moneylending are unofficial sources of domestic assistance, while national and subnational governments often provide programming to populations during crises, only sometimes drawing on global resources (Willitts-King, Poole, and Bryant 2018). Major corporate players like Google and Coca-Cola with large corporate social responsibility arms gain influence through gifts-in-kinds and direct donations (Adelman 2009; Barnett and Walker 2015). Direct giving and crowdfunding are expected to reach almost 100 billion USD in value by 2025, according to the World Bank (Development Initiatives 2021).

The study of these sources under conditions of conflict, siege, or emergencies could be fruitful, given that this can cut off formal aid flows, and because donors are often unwilling to invest in particular initiatives during these times (Majid, Abdirahman, and Hassan 2017). For example, conflict- and crisis-affected populations often prioritize repaying debts to those who helped them flee, access healthcare, or find shelter amongst needs. While cash-transfer is often used for these purposes by recipients, donors do not tend to want to fund this directly (Foster 2015; Wilson and Krystalli 2017). Researchers also find increasing reliance on local and bottom-up funding structures where large-scale infrastructure and investment projects are needed during and after conflict (Bryant 2019b). These are not commonly supported by international funders. Data collection efforts by scholars to understand the sources, scale, and destinations of alternative financial flows would provide the basis for studying their influence, as well as the kinds of relief and reconstruction efforts going on in local spaces but not funded through traditional means. The study of these financiers' motivations would also be an interesting contribution, as investment groups and individual donors are having significant effect in areas of relative insecurity.

Study of alternative sources of assistance may also encourage greater recognition of civilian agency (Baines and Paddon 2012; Krause 2014) and community self-governance (Pincock, Betts, and Easton-Calabria 2020; Crawford et al. 2015). Research suggests that family and kinship ties are essential supports during crisis, and that families may be loaned or given land, information, or social support through these networks. Groups and societies are key sources of lending and assistance (Obaa and Mazur 2017). Expatriate groups who have built lives outside of conflict- or crisis-affected countries often support enterprises in their home country. This suggests that a great deal of community self-assistance is going on and study of their short- and long-term effects is needed.

Emerging players

New players are emerging as major foreign aid donors and changing the shape of humanitarian and development finance. There are avenues open to study whether they will increasingly regionalize, or even localize, aid. Some former "developing" nations are now giving aid (Dreher, Nunnenkamp, and Thiele 2011) and the relative donations of non-OECD nations more broadly are increasing. As China, India, and Turkey, the Gulf states, and others gain influence, a common question has become, will "new" donors change the political economy of aid? Some have suggested these donors will undermine commitments within the aid industry to environmental protection, support rogue states, and re-indebt highly indebted poor countries (HIPC) (see Woods 2008). However, others suggest that, as more recent recipients, these donors will be more attuned to the on-the-ground difficulties that recipient nations face (Mullen 2017). Academic scholarship could be advanced by research looking at whether emerging donors will be more supportive of local aid actors or more responsive to local needs.

New donors have been found to be more regionally focused, with some "rising states" like South Africa and India viewing themselves as giving to "Southern partners" based in principles of solidarity (Chin and Quadir 2012, p. 494) and others choosing to support their close neighbours (Dreher, Nunnenkamp, and Thiele 2011). Some emerging donors are giving funds based on religious and ideological ties (Kavakli 2018), shifting away from the colonial or historical legacies that ruled for many donors in the Global North. Scholars have suggested that, because of their more regional or close-to-home focus, new donors are likely to be more responsive (Barnett and Walker 2015). Given these initial expectations, I suggest a new fruitful avenue for research would investigate whether these new donors will recognize and reward the capacities and expertise of more local or regional actors. And, will the growing influence of donors from or near the Global South move more money directly into the hands of actors *in* the Global South?

New countries, contexts, and local and state capacity

Scholars have not reached a consensus on whether the effect of aid on state capacity and development is positive or negative. Some argue that aid has made the poor poorer and states weaker (Moyo 2009). Others suggest that assistance by foreign actors leads citizens to demand new services from the state (Campbell, DiGiuseppe, and Murdie 2019; Murdie and Hicks 2013) or that aid is effective in states with good fiscal and monetary policies (Burnside and Dollar 2000). Still others suggest there is no significant relationship (Young and Padilla 2019). What these studies do agree on is that various states and local actors respond to aid differently.

And yet, despite all we know about how varied the effects of aid can be, studies have been limited by locality and geographic context. Most of our datasets exclude key geographic areas (Kandil 2009), particularly where data availability and limited access for researchers diminishes the number of studies that take place (Robinson, Hartley, and Schneider 2006). Case study research also tends to be based in low-income countries in sub-Saharan Africa. These contexts are not representative of where new aid is flowing or where more influence is being exerted. For example, more aid dollars are going to the Middle East and to Asia, as well as to low-to-middle-income countries and low-and-middle-income contexts in wealthier countries (Fabre 2018; Glennie 2011; Development Initiatives 2021). An expanded scope of research to include these countries and contexts will help scholars to better understand relationships between aid and local and state capacity. For example, there is the possibility that higher-income countries with larger bureaucracies and more developed socioeconomic and legal infrastructures will be more resistant to the influence of donors, and so respond differently to the constraints of foreign aid. Populations from low-to-middle-income contexts in various country contexts are likely to present with different needs, expectations, capacities, and competencies, and respond to assistance efforts differently. They may be less likely to turn to community self-assistance and more likely to rely on foreign assistance if improved financial circumstances undermined communal societies and self-protection.

Aid *below* the state

Understanding aid flows to local and national actors is difficult because most data on aid stops at the level of the state. Filling this gap is an important next step in academic scholarship. A problem of "over-aggregation" was identified a decade ago (Tierney et al. 2011) and suggests that we can know only so much about foreign aid flows because we do not have a clear picture of how it flows within states, governorates, or provinces. Databases on foreign aid tend to focus on aid aggregated to country level (Findley et al. 2011). While important inroads have been made over the last decade to follow aid dollars as they move below the state, barriers remain. The United Nations Financial Tracking Service (UNFTS) added data on recipients of aid but also noted that "data beyond first-level recipients is not yet reported comprehensively" (ALNAP

2018, p. 84) At AidData, a GeoQuery function now allows users to explore data at the provincial or district level (AidData 2021a) and a great deal of work has been done to show the Chinese "global development footprint" down to a project level (AidData 2021b). This is a welcome step given that non-DAC countries and emerging donors are broadly underrepresented in these data-sets. The World Bank is also increasingly geocoding its data.

However, because these are new and resource-intensive efforts, most sub-national data collection efforts have been focused on a few regions and sub-Saharan Africa, in particular. Efforts also tend to focus on a few major donors that collect geo-referenced data, like USAID or the World Bank. Emerging donors are not commonly included, more disaggregated data are less common for regions, such the Middle East, and data on low-to-middle-income country recipients are lacking. Importantly, new data collection efforts focused on the movement of aid below the state would create new opportunities to explore substate and project-level hypotheses. This level of analysis is essential to gaining an understanding of the effects of aid on households and communi-ties, the equity of allocation and distribution below the state, as well as the dif-ferent ways foreign governments, diaspora communities, private international citizens, industry, or informal aid shape local spaces.

As scholars expand ideas about what constitutes aid, we also face the challenge of accounting for informal and alternative aid flows. These are more difficult to track because they often originate with private citizens and move to house-holds, they are subject to hidden costs and changing exchange rates, and can transfer without documentation, or informally (for example, in a *hawala* or *zakat* systems) (Bryant 2019). Much of this money moves outside of govern-ment or national systems (Stirk 2015). Meeting this very difficult challenge would produce immense new possibilities for knowledge creation.

Conclusion

This chapter brings attention to areas of research with the potential to contrib-ute significantly to the study of local political economies of aid. Scholars who advance knowledge in these areas will move the study of the political economy of aid forward, while helping to redefine what is considered and studied *as* global aid. Doing so will be challenging. Systems of exclusion are often part of a hidden curriculum that is meant to keep certain local actors out without implicating those in the "club" (Barnett and Walker 2015) for doing so; alter-native and informal aid flows are, by nature, difficult to track; and emerging players are playing by rules that are not familiar to scholars and so may not be easily unpacked using existing concepts and theories. Meanwhile, to study subnational aid flows and previously understudied countries and contexts, researchers will need to do a great deal of resource-intensive work to develop new datasets, relationships, and research networks.

These endeavours are, however, worthwhile. Global aid is changing and demands for aid to move more directly to local actors, and with fewer strings attached, are louder. In 2016, the Secretary-General of the UN called for humanitarian action to be made "as local as possible, as international as necessary." Almost five years later, the Charter for Change Coalition, made up of 450 national and local organizations around the world, called on the international community to accelerate "the flow of funding to national and local organisations at the frontlines of the Covid19 crisis" (Charter for Change 2020). Scholars who work to understand these aid flows, and the constraints and opportunities they place on local actors, will produce knowledge with real-world applications. They will also propel forward the study of the political economy of local aid.

References

Adelman, Carol. 2009. "Global Philanthropy and Remittances: Reinventing Foreign Aid." *The Brown Journal of World Affairs* 15 (2): 23–33.

Ager, J., E. Fiddian-Qasmiyeh, and A. Ager. 2015. "Local Faith Communities and the Promotion of Resilience in Contexts of Humanitarian Crisis." *Journal of Refugee Studies* 28 (2): 202–21. https://doi.org/10.1093/jrs/fev001

AidData. 2021a. "GeoQuery: Filter and Aggregate Data to Provinces or Districts without Code or Mapping Software." https://www.aiddata.org/geoquery

AidData. 2021b. "Mapping China's Global Development Footprint: AidData's Geocoded Global Chinese Official Finance Dataset." https://www.aiddata.org/china-project-locations

Alesina, Alberto, and David Dollar. 2000. "Who Gives Foreign Aid to Whom and Why?" *Journal of Economic Growth* 5 (1): 33–63. https://doi.org/10.1023/A:1009874203400

Alik-Lagrange, Arthur, Sarah K. Dreier, Milli Lake, and Alesha Porisky. 2021. "Social Protection and State–Society Relations in Environments of Low and Uneven State Capacity." *Annual Review of Political Science* 24 (1): 151–74. https://doi.org/10.1146/annurev-polisci-041719-101929

ALNAP. 2018. State of the Humanitarian System. London: ALNAP/ODI. https://sohs.alnap.org/

Ayobi, Y.A., A. Black, L. Kenni, R. Nakabea, and K. Sutton. 2017. *Going Local: Achieving a More Appropriate and Fit-for-Purpose Humanitarian Ecosystem in the Pacific*. Melbourne: Centre for Humanitarian Leadership, Fiji National University, Humanitarian Advisory Group.

Baines, Erin, and Emily Paddon. 2012. "'This Is How We Survived': Civilian Agency and Humanitarian Protection." *Security Dialogue* 43 (3): 231–47. https://doi.org/10 .1177/0967010612444150

Barbalet, Veronique. 2018. *As Local as Possible, as International as Necessary: Understanding Capacity and Complementarity in Humanitarian Action*. London: Overseas Development Institute. www .odi .org/ publications/ 11238 -local   -   possible-international-necessary-understanding-capacity-and-co mplementarity-humanitarian

Barbalet, Veronique. 2019. *Rethinking Capacity and Complementarity for a More Local Humanitarian Action*. London: Overseas Development Institute. www.odi.org/publications/11471-rethinking-capacity-and-complementarity-more - local-humanitarian-action

Barbalet, Veronique, and Caitlin Wake. 2020. "Inclusion and Exclusion in Humanitarian Action: The State of Play." HPG Working Paper. Humanitarian Policy Group and Overseas Development Institute. https:// cdn .odi .org/ media/ documents/ Inclusion _and_exclusion_in_humanitarian_action_the_state_of_play.pdf

Barnett, Michael. 2009. "Evolution without Progress? Humanitarianism in a World of Hurt." *International Organization* 63 (4): 621–63.

Barnett, Michael. 2020. "The Humanitarian Global Colour Line." *ALNAP* (blog). https://www.alnap.org/blogs/the-humanitarian-global-colour-line

Barnett, Michael. 2021. "Humanitarian Organizations Won't Listen to Groups on the Ground, in Part Because of Institutionalized Racism." *Washington Post*. https://www .washingtonpost.com/ politics/2021/06/08/humanitarian-organizations-wont-listen -groups-ground-part-because-institutionalized-racism/

Barnett, Michael, and Janice Stein. 2012. *Sacred Aid: Faith and Humanitarianism*. Oxford University Press. https:// doi .org/ 10 .1093/ acprof: oso/ 9780199916023 .001 .0001

Barnett, Michael, and Peter Walker. 2015. "Regime Change for Humanitarian Aid: How to Make Relief More Accountable." *Foreign Affairs* 94 (4): 130–41.

Benton, Adia. 2016. "African Expatriates and Race in the Anthropology of Humanitarianism." *Critical African Studies* 8 (3): 266–77. https:// doi.org/ 10.1080/ 21681392.2016.1244956

Bryant, John. 2019. *Remittances in Humanitarian Crises*. London: Overseas Development Institute. https://cdn.odi.org/media/documents/12638.pdf

Bryant, J. 2019a. *Mapping Local Capacities and Support for More Effective Humanitarian Response*. London: Overseas Development Institute. https:// www .alnap .org/ help -library/ mapping -local -capacities -and -support -for -more -effective -humanitarian -responses

Bryant, J. 2019b. "The Humanitarian Response in Iraq: Support beyond International Assistance in Mosul." HPG Working Paper. https://cdn.odi.org/media/documents/ 12782.pdf

Burnside, Craig, and David Dollar. 2000. "Aid, Policies, and Growth." *American Economic Review* 90 (4): 847–68.

Bush, Sarah Sunn. 2015. *The Taming of Democracy Assistance: Why Democracy Promotion Does Not Confront Dictators*. Cambridge University Press.

Bush, Sarah Sunn, and Jennifer Hadden. 2019. "Density and Decline in the Founding of International NGOs in the United States." *International Studies Quarterly*, 63 (4): 1133–1146. https://doi.org/10.1093/isq/sqz061

Campbell, Susanna P. 2018. *Global Governance and Local Peace: Accountability and Performance in International Peacebuilding*. Cambridge University Press.

Campbell, Susanna, Matthew DiGiuseppe, and Amanda Murdie. 2019. "International Development NGOs and Bureaucratic Capacity: Facilitator or Destroyer?" *Political Research Quarterly* 72 (1): 3–18. https://doi.org/10.1177/1065912918772941

Charter for Change. 2020. "Charter for Change Statement on the Revised UN Global Humanitarian Response Plan on Covid19." Charter4Change. https://charter4change .org/ 2020/ 05/ 07/ charter -for -change -statement -on -the -revised -un -ghrp -on -covid19/

Chin, Gregory, and Fahimul Quadir. 2012. "Introduction: Rising States, Rising Donors and the Global Aid Regime." *Cambridge Review of International Affairs* 25 (4): 493–506. https://doi.org/10.1080/09557571.2012.744642

Cooley, Alexander, and James Ron. 2002. "The NGO Scramble: Organizational Insecurity and the Political Economy of Transnational Action." *International Security* 27 (1): 5–39.

Cornish, Lisa. 2019. "Q&A: Degan Ali on the Systemic Racism Impacting Humanitarian Responses." *DevEx* (blog). June 20. https://www.devex.com/news/q-a-degan-ali-on -the-systemic-racism-impacting-humanitarian-responses-95083

Crawford, Nicholas, John Cosgrave, Simone Haysom, and Nadine Walicki. 2015. "Protracted Displacement: Uncertain Paths to Self-Reliance in Exile." https://cdn.odi .org/media/documents/9851.pdf

De Mesquita, Bruce Bueno, and Alastair Smith. 2009. "A Political Economy of Aid." *International Organization* 63 (2): 309–40.

De Waal, Alexander. 1997. *Famine Crimes: Politics & the Disaster Relief Industry in Africa.* African Issues. London: African Rights & the International African Institute in association with James Currey, Oxford & Indiana University Press, Bloomington.

Development Initiatives. 2021. "Global Humanitarian Assistance Report 2021." Global Humanitarian Assistance. https:// devinit .org/ resources/ global -humanitarian -assistance-report-2021/

Dichter, Thomas. 2014. "Capable Partners Learning Agenda on Local Organization Capacity Development." USAID. https:// usaidlearninglab .org/ library/ capable -partners-learning-agenda-local-organization-capacity-development

Dixon, Steven Joe, Elsa Romera Moreno, Amal Sadozai, and Ahmed Haj Asaad. 2016. "Localisation of Humanitarian Response in the Syrian Crisis." *Confluences Méditerranée* 99 (4): 109–21.

Dreher, Axel, Peter Nunnenkamp, and Rainer Thiele. 2011. "Are 'New' Donors Different? Comparing the Allocation of Bilateral Aid between NonDAC and DAC Donor Countries." *World Development* 39 (11): 1950–68.

Dubois, M., C. Wake, S. Sturridge, and C. Bennet. 2015. *The Ebola Response in West Africa: Exposing the Politics and Culture of International Aid.* London: Overseas Development Institute. www.odi.org/ publications/9956-ebola-response-west-africa -exposing-politics-culture-international-aid

Dunning, Thad. 2004. "Conditioning the Effects of Aid: Cold War Politics, Donor Credibility, and Democracy in Africa." *International Organization* 58 (2): 409–23.

Fabre, Cyprien. 2018. "Crises in Middle-Income Countries: World Humanitarian Summit Putting Policy into Practice." The Commitments into Action Series. https:// www.oecd.org/development/humanitarian-donors/docs/Crises_in_middle_Income _Countries_OECD_guideline.pdf

Farmer, Paul. 2020. *Fevers, Feuds, and Diamonds: Ebola and the Ravages of History.* Farrar, Straus and Giroux.

Findley, Michael G., Josh Powell, Daniel Strandow, and Jeff Tanner. 2011. "The Localized Geography of Foreign Aid: A New Dataset and Application to Violent

Armed Conflict." *World Development* 39 (11): 1995–2009. https://doi.org/10.1016/j .worlddev.2011.07.022

Fink, Günther, and Silvia Redaelli. 2011. "Determinants of International Emergency Aid—Humanitarian Need Only?" *World Development* 39 (5): 741–57. https://doi .org/10.1016/j.worlddev.2010.09.004

Foster, Jillian. 2015. "Impact of Multipurpose Cash Assistance on Outcomes for Children in Lebanon." Improving Cash-Based Interventions Multipurpose Cash Grants and Protection. UNHCR, Lebanon Cash Consortium, Save the Children. https://reliefweb.int/sites/reliefweb.int/files/resources/erc-save-the-children-action -research-web.pdf

Gammeltoft, Peter. 2002. "Remittances and Other Financial Flows to Developing Countries." *International Migration* 40 (5): 181–211. https:// doi .org/ 10 .1111/ 1468–2435.00216

Gingerich, Tara R., and Marc J. Cohen. 2015. "Turning the Humanitarian System on Its Head: Saving Lives and Livelihoods by Strengthening Local Capacity and Shifting Leadership to Local Actors." Oxfam Research Reports. Washington, D.C: Oxfam.

Giuliano, Paola, and Marta Ruiz-Arranz. 2009. "Remittances, Financial Development, and Growth." *Journal of Development Economics* 90 (1): 144–52.

Glennie, Jonathan. 2011. *The Role of Aid to Middle-Income Countries: A Contribution to Evolving EU Development Policy*. London: Overseas Development Institute.

Gruffydd Jones, Branwen. 2013. "'Good Governance' and 'State Failure': Genealogies of Imperial Discourse." *Cambridge Review of International Affairs* 26 (1): 49–70. https://doi.org/10.1080/09557571.2012.734785

Hawkins, Darren G. (ed.). 2006. *Delegation and Agency in International Organizations*. Political Economy of Institutions and Decisions. Cambridge University Press.

Honig, Dan. 2018. *Navigation by Judgment: Why and When Top-down Management of Foreign Aid Doesn't Work*. Oxford University Press.

Howe, Kimberly, Elizabeth Stites, and Danya Chudacoff. 2015. "Breaking the Hourglass: Partnerships in Remote Management Settings–The Cases of Syria and Iraqi Kurdistan." Tufts University, Feinstein International Center. https://fic.tufts .edu/publication-item/organization-partnerships-remote-settings/

Kandil, Magda. 2009. "Determinants of Institutional Quality and Their Impact on Economic Growth in the MENA Region." *International Journal of Development Issues* 8 (2): 134–67. https://doi.org/10.1108/14468950910997693

Kavakli, Kerim Can. 2018. "Domestic Politics and the Motives of Emerging Donors: Evidence from Turkish Foreign Aid." *Political Research Quarterly* 71 (3): 614–27. https://doi.org/10.1177/1065912917750783

Khoury, Rana B., and Emily K.M. Scott. 2021. "Going Local without Localization? Humanitarian Responses to the War in Syria." Working Paper Presented at ISA 2021.

Konyndyk, Jeremy, and Heba Aly. 2020. "Decolonizing Aid: Rethinking Humanitarianism." The New Humanitarian. https:// www .cgdev .org/ blog/ decolonizing-aid-rethinking-humanitarianism-episode-7

Krause, Monika. 2014. *The Good Project: Humanitarian Relief NGOs and the Fragmentation of Reason*. University of Chicago Press.

Levitt, Peggy, and Deepak Lamba-Nieves. 2011. "Social Remittances Revisited." *Journal of Ethnic and Migration Studies* 37 (1): 1–22.

Majid, Nisar, Khalif Abdirahman, and Shamsa Hassan. 2017. "Remittances and Vulnerability in Somalia: Assessing Sources, Uses and Delivery Mechanisms." Rift Valley Institute. https:// documents1 .worldbank .org/ curated/ en/

633401530870281332/ pdf/ Remittances -and -Vulnerability -in -Somalia -Resubmission.pdf

Moyo, Dambisa. 2009. *Dead Aid: Why Aid Is Not Working and How There Is a Better Way for Africa.* Macmillan.

Mullen, Rani D. 2017. *India in Afghanistan: Understanding Development Assistance by Emerging Donors to Conflict-Affected Countries.* JSTOR. https://www.jstor.org/stable/pdf/resrep10798.pdf

Murdie, Amanda, and Alexander Hicks. 2013. "Can International Nongovernmental Organizations Boost Government Services? The Case of Health." *International Organization* 67 (3): 541–73.

Obaa, Bernard B., and Robert E. Mazur. 2017. "Social Network Characteristics and Resource Access among Formerly Displaced Households in Lira, Uganda." *Disasters* 41 (3): 468–86. https://doi.org/10.1111/disa.12210

OCHA. n.d. "Grand Bargain (Hosted by the IASC)." IASC. https://interagencystandingcommittee.org/content/grand-bargain-hosted-iasc

Pfeffer, Jeffrey, and Gerald R Salancik. 2003. *The External Control of Organizations: A Resource Dependence Perspective.* Stanford University Press.

Pincock, Kate, Alexander Betts, and Evan Elise Easton-Calabria. 2020. *The Global Governed? Refugees as Providers of Protection and Assistance.* 1st ed. Cambridge Asylum and Migration Studies. New York: Cambridge University Press.

Rapoport, Hillel, and Frédéric Docquier. 2006. "The Economics of Migrants' Remittances." *Handbook of the Economics of Giving, Altruism and Reciprocity* 2: 1135–98.

ReliefWeb. 2008. "Glossary of Humanitarian Terms." https:// reliefweb .int/ sites/ reliefweb .int/ files/ resources/ 4F 99A3C28EC3 7D0EC12574 A4002E89B4 -reliefweb _aug2008.pdf

Rimmer, Douglas, and Kempe Ronald Hope. 2000. "Aid and Corruption." Edited by Goran Hyden, Rwekaza Mukandala, Bornwell C. Chikulo, Patrick Chabal, and Jean-Pascal Daloz. *African Affairs* 99 (394): 121–28.

Robinson, Michael D., James E. Hartley, and Patricia Higino Schneider. 2006. "Which Countries Are Studied Most by Economists? An Examination of the Regional Distribution of Economic Research." *Kyklos* 59 (4): 611–26. https://doi.org/10.1111/j.1467–6435.2006.00352.x

Slim, Hugo, and Lorenzo Trombetta. 2014. "Syria Crisis Common Context Analysis: Report Commissioned by the IASC Inter-Agency Humanitarian Evaluations Steering Group as Part of the Syria Coordinated Accountability and Lessons Learning Initiative." New York: OCHA.

Stirk, Chloe. 2015. "An Act of Faith: Humanitarian Financing and Zakat." Development Initiatives. https://devinit.org/resources/humanitarian-financing-and-zakat/

Stoddard, Abby, Monica Czwarno, and Lindsay Hamsik. 2019. "NGOs & Risk: Managing Uncertainty in Local-International Partnerships." InterAction and Humanitarian Outcomes. https:// www .interaction .org/ wp -content/ uploads/ 2019/ 03/Risk-Global-Study.pdf

Tanner, L., and L. Moro. 2016. "Missed out: The Role of Local Actors in the Humanitarian Response in the South Sudan Conflict." https://www.oxfam.org/en/research/missed-out

Tierney, Michael J., Daniel L. Nielson, Darren G. Hawkins, J. Timmons Roberts, Michael G. Findley, Ryan M. Powers, Bradley Parks, Sven E. Wilson, and Robert L. Hicks. 2011. "More Dollars than Sense: Refining Our Knowledge of Development

Finance Using AidData." *World Development* 39 (11): 1891–1906. https://doi.org/10
.1016/j.worlddev.2011.07.029
UN Assembled Panel. 2016. "High-Level Panel on Humanitarian Financing Report
to the Secretary-General: Too Important to Fail – Addressing the Humanitarian
Financing Gap." United Nations.
Versluis, Anna. 2014. "Formal and Informal Material Aid Following the 2010 Haiti
Earthquake as Reported by Camp Dwellers." *Disasters* 38 (s1): S94–109. https://doi
.org/10.1111/disa.12050
Wall, Imogen, and Kerren Hedlund. 2016. "Localisation and Locally-Led Crisis
Response: A Literature Review." http://www.local2global.info/wp-content/uploads/
L2GP_SDC_Lit_Review_LocallyLed_June_2016_final.pdf
Watkins, Kevin, and Maria Quattri. 2014. *Lost in Intermediation: How Excessive Charges
Undermine the Benefits of Remittances for Africa.* London: Overseas Development
Institute. https://gsdrc.org/document-library/lost-in-intermediation-how-excessive
-charges-undermine-the-benefits-of-remittances-for-africa/
Willitts-King, B., J. Bryant, and A. Spencer. 2019. *Valuing Local Resources in
Humanitarian Crises.* London: Overseas Development Institute. www .odi .org/
publications/11480-valuing-local-resources-humanitarian-crises
Willitts-King, Barnaby, Lydia Poole, and John Bryant. 2018. "Measuring the Iceberg:
The Opportunities and Limits of Better Tracking of Resources beyond International
Humanitarian Assistance." HPG Working Paper. Overseas Development Institute.
https://cdn.odi.org/media/documents/12540.pdf
Wilson, Kim, and Roxani Krystalli. 2017. *The Financial Journey of Refugees.* Medford:
The Henry J. Leir Institute for Human Security at the Fletcher School of Law
and Diplomacy. https:// fic .tufts .edu/ wp -content/ uploads/ Financial -Journeys -of
-Refugees.pdf
World Bank. 2021. "Net Official Development Assistance and Official Aid Received
(Current US$)." stats.oecd.org
Woods, Ngaire. 2008. "Whose Aid? Whose Influence? China, Emerging Donors and
the Silent Revolution in Development Assistance." *International Affairs* 84 (6):
1205–21. https://doi.org/10.1111/j.1468–2346.2008.00765.x
Yang, Dean. 2011. "Migrant Remittances." *Journal of Economic Perspectives* 25 (3):
129–52.
Young, Andrew T., and Estefania Lujan Padilla. 2019. "Foreign Aid and Recipient
State Capacity." In *Lessons on Foreign Aid and Economic Development*, edited by
Nabamita Dutta and Claudia R. Williamson, 169–86. Cham: Springer International
Publishing. https://doi.org/10.1007/978–3–030–22121–8_8

PART V

Resetting the IPE research agenda

12. Feminist theory in international political economy

Corinna Dengler and Hanna Völkle

Introduction

In 1997, Fiona Robinson asserted that one "of the most interesting things about the literature on gender and/or feminism and International Political Economy (IPE) is the relative lack of it" (Robinson 1997, p. 773). In this chapter, we discuss to what extent this claim still holds true 25 years later. Starting from the assumption that including gender as a dummy variable in IPE analyses is not enough, we introduce the field of feminist international political economy (FIPE). We draw upon the three themes of (1) money, (2) care, and (3) climate to first illustrate that FIPE ventures beyond mainstream IPE in deploying an intersectional approach to gender(ed) injustices, which allows for a (more) holistic and integrated understanding of debates on money and care. However, we hold that against the background of multiple and inter-linked ecological crises such as climate change and biodiversity loss, which remain relatively marginalized in both IPE and FIPE, we need to move towards an ecofeminist international political economy (EFIPE) that sees destructive societal relationships with nature as inseparable from other power relations, such as extractive capitalism, patriarchy, and coloniality. In perceiving society and economy as embedded in a specific context and embodied through the material reality of our lifelong shaped and vulnerable bodies, we sketch out a future research agenda and point towards promising pathways already being explored in (E)FIPE.

From gender in IPE towards an ecofeminist IPE

International political economy (IPE) emerged in the 1970s at the interface of international relations (IR) and economics. It is a diverse discipline with some scholars putting their emphasis on the *political,* while others put it on the *economic* part of IPE (Cohen 2007; Watson 2017). Mainstream IPE and some of the more critical IPE approaches share the assumption that measuring and quantifying are the single most useful way of capturing complex structures and systems (Griffin 2007). When feminists started to demand a comprehensive consideration of gender inequalities in IPE, "adding gender/women" as an empirical category was seen as a relatively comfortable solution (Elias and Rai 2019). As various feminist IPE scholars have pointed out, the "easy adding solution" to rather complex gender questions in IPE misses epistemological implications, interdependencies, and materially manifesting impacts that gender has on global political economies (Peterson 2005; Waylen 2006; Elias and Rai 2019). As gender is not a monolithic category, an empirical answer fails to acknowledge the manifold intersections of gender injustices with other systems of oppression such as racism, classism, or ableism (Crenshaw 1989; Goodley 2014; Collins and Bilge 2016; Tilley and Shilliam 2018). Hence, in this chapter, we are interested in contributions that venture beyond gender as an empirical category.

Based on Aysel Yollu-Tok and Fabiola Rodríguez Garzón's (2018) distinction of "gender economics" and "feminist economics," we distinguish "gender IPE" from "feminist IPE" (FIPE) along the lines of their epistemological assumptions. While gender IPE refers to "women" as an empirical facticity and regularly remains rather shallow in its analyses, FIPE is epistemologically dedicated to (de-)constructivist positions that regard gender as socially constructed, and/or materialist positions that consider gender as a structural category, thereby fundamentally challenging mainstream IPE's "problematic premises – of positivism, modernism and masculinism" (Peterson 2018, p. 23).

Feminist international political economy (FIPE) is a flourishing and diverse field with multidisciplinary roots in, for example, Marxist feminism (Hartmann 1979; Federici 2020), feminist economics (Ferber and Nelson 1993; Berik and Ebru 2021), postcolonial feminisms (Mohanty 2003; Bhambra 2021), and Black feminist scholarship (Davis 1981; Banks 2020). The *Signs: Journal of Women in Culture and Society* special issue *Feminists Theorize International Political Economy* (Rai and Bedford 2010) was an important milestone in the development of FIPE. Other landmark publications, such as the *Handbook on the International Political Economy of Gender* (Elias and Roberts 2018) or the recent *Review of International Political Economy* special issue on *Feminist Global Political Economies of Work and Social Reproduction* (Mezzadri, Newman, and Stevano 2021) show that FIPE covers a broad spectrum of topics. These range from critical feminist approaches to development (e.g., Kothari 2002; Rai 2018) and the international political economy of surrogacy (e.g., Vertommen and Barbagallo 2020) to feminist analyses of global care chains (e.g., Ehrenreich and Hochschild 2002; Safri and Graham 2010; Wichterich 2020), digitized economies (e.g., Adams-Prassl and Berg 2017; Schor et al. 2020), and global finance (e.g., Keating, Rasmussen, and Rishi 2010). These FIPE analyses resemble each other in their critical starting point of questioning power hierarchies within capitalism, while focusing on different facets of these power asymmetries.

Despite being often labeled as the most pressing global crisis of the 21st century, climate change arguably is a rather marginalized topic both in IPE and FIPE (Paterson 2021). Koch and Buch-Hansen (2020, p. 376) hold that while "IPE research has dealt with environmental policy issues, the major theoretical perspectives and debates defining the field are not oriented towards the impact of economic processes on the environment." Similarly, the FIPE landmark volumes and special issues referred to above remain surprisingly silent on the matter. This is especially startling because of the rich literature at the intersection of feminisms and the environment: Materialist ecofeminism (e.g., Mies 1986; Plumwood 1993; Gaard 2017), feminist ecological economics (e.g., Perkins 1997, 2021; O'Hara 1997, 2009; Dengler and Strunk 2018), and feminist political ecology (Rochelau, Thomas-Slayter, and Wangari 1996; Mollett 2017; Bauhardt and Harcourt 2019), among others, share the general outlook that the monetized economy is only "a small part of a much greater sustaining whole" (Mellor 2009, p. 253). The non-monetized "economy of socio-ecological provisioning" (Dengler and Lang 2022) can be metaphorically described as the invisible underwater part of an iceberg (Mies 1986), entailing social reproduction/unpaid care work and ecological reproduction/ecosystem functions. Every production process in the monetized economy fundamentally relies on, but at the same time invisibilizes, devalues (in the case of unpaid care work), and destroys (in the case of ecosystem functions) its invisible foundation. IPE analyses that focus on the monetized tip of the iceberg often confuse monetary value with value creation and social recognition. This "productivist bias" (Mezzadri, Newman, and Stevano 2021) has been problematized in FIPE, which centers around social reproduction, yet often conceptualizes it disembedded from the natural environment. The integrating perspective of an ecofeminist international political economy (EFIPE), inspired by, for example, the work of Mellor (2005, 2016), considers how the monetized economy is indissolubly entangled with the sphere of both social and ecological reproduction.

Money, care, climate: topical interventions of an (eco-) feminist IPE

In their call for a "mission-oriented approach" (Mazzucato 2021) or an "inter-ested pluralism" (Dobusch and Kapeller 2012) that is "ontologically reflexive" (Bigo and Negru 2008), ever more authors argue that we need to put topics rather than schools of thought at the centre of political economy analyses. The following section discusses three such topics, namely (1) money, (2) care, and (3) climate, and shows how a feminist-ecological understanding of these topics enhances the chances to design socially just, environmentally sound, and hence intra- and intergenerationally responsible economics systems.

Money

The monetized economy is currently at the center of economic systems on a global level. Money equals, at least through a mainstream lens, value. From the very beginning of IPE as a distinctive scholarly field, money and related topics such as monetary policies, trade, or international finance have been a key field of interest (Kirshner 2003). Up until today, most IPE analyses dealing with the economy remain within the narrow field of monetized econo-mies. FIPE has contributed to IPE's account of money in two ways, namely in showing (a) that money is deeply gendered and (b) that social reproduction/unpaid care work, though non-monetized, is the invisibilized foundation for production processes in the monetized economy. Referring to (a), institutions like money, independent from the topic they might be concerned with, are no neutral entities but are themselves highly dependent on human biases and embedded in prevailing gendered, class-related, and/or racialized power structures and asymmetries. FIPE scholars criticize, for example, the capitalist assumption that the "free" market is the most efficient way to distribute priva-tised money (Çağatay, Elson, and Grown 1995; Mellor 2010). The 2007/2008 global financial crisis has demonstrated the insufficiencies of the logic of a free, neutral finance market and vividly illustrated the consequences of a lack in gender-sensitive perspectives (Seguino 2011; Walby 2015).

Thus, coming to (b), crisis-driven austerity politics for the Eurozone such as cutbacks in public spending impact gender inequality through shifting the work of reproduction from the public to the private sphere (Braunstein 2013; Rubery 2015; Young 2018). More generally, institutionalized "deficit hysteria" (Nersisyan and Wray 2010) seems to prohibit investing public money into the sphere of social provisioning and hence into the fields of education, public health systems, or future-fit social infrastructures. FIPE scholars argue that a change in perspective that centers social provisioning instead of money production allows for central bank policies that choose public investments instead of cutbacks. As Mellor (2016, p. 194) points out:

> This is the choice between debt and democracy. It is the choice between a privatised money system based on debt, for which the public is ultimately responsible, and a debt-free, democratically controlled money system as the framework for socially just and ecologically sustainable sufficiency provisioning.

This feminist provisioning perspective, which is closely linked to questions of care dealt with in the subsequent section, links macroeconomic theory, insights of gender-aware public finance, and the courage to elaborate systemic alternatives to a structurally un-caring system (Palmer 1995; Mellor 2010).

Care

The concept of care work is a central topic for FIPE. Care work refers not only to the monetized economy/paid care work, but also to the sphere of unpaid care work/social reproduction. Very broadly, care work describes how people provide for themselves, their families, friends, and communities through closely interlinked paid and unpaid economic activities (Power 2004). Although the COVID-19 pandemic has vividly reminded us that care work is "essential work" that provides the foundation of our societies, it is also work that lacks economic and social recognition (e.g., Stevano, Ali, and Jamieson 2021): While paid care work is systematically underpaid and often performed under precarious working conditions (Folbre 2006), unpaid care work often remains invisible in mainstream IPE analyses. Both paid and unpaid care work are highly gendered spheres, which are up until today mainly performed by women (Bakker 2007; Budlender 2010; ILO 2018). Taking a life cycle approach, the gendered division of labor, via a gender pay and gender care gap, results in a striking gender pension gap that lies at the core of the feminization of old-age poverty (Yollu-Tok and Rodríguez Garzón 2018).

The transnationalization of care work is a central topic for FIPE. Arlie Hochschild (2000, p. 130) figuratively describes a global care chain as "an older daughter from a poor family who cares for her siblings while her mother works as a nanny caring for the children of a migrant nanny who, in turn, cares for the child of a family in a rich country." The so-called "care drain" (Hochschild 2003) or "care extractivism" (Wichterich 2020) often starts from rich countries, where dual-career couples outsource "their" caring responsibilities through purchasing power via market transactions to other carers. In Germany, where both chapter authors are located, a common example is precariously employed Polish 24-hour elderly care nurses with live-in arrangements (Lutz and Palenga-Möllenbeck 2010), who then again sometimes hire Ukrainian migrant workers to compensate for the emerging care deficit in Poland (Goździak 2016, for other examples see Ehrenreich and Hochschild 2002). Similar relocation processes can be retracted on surrogacy and global fertility chains (Jana and Hammer 2021; Vertommen and Barbagallo 2020). Global care chains are complex and cannot be grasped by empirics alone, as the "moral harm" (Kittay 2014) and the reproduction of intersectional inequalities along the lines of the race-class-gender nexus requires an in-depth analysis of global power asymmetries.

Taking a feminist approach to IPE, we argue, requires a shift in languages of valuation. Rather than analyzing the topic of care through an IPE lens, the "economic" and "political" should center around care, thereby overcoming the "deep separation structure in economics" (Biesecker and Hofmeister 2010) that artificially separates the sphere of production from the sphere of reproduction. Biesecker and Hofmeister (ibid.) have coined the term "(re)productivity" as a mediation category that overcomes the structural separation between the two spheres, thereby socially and economically revaluing the formerly invisibilized spheres of unpaid care work and the natural environment. While, as we have shown in this chapter, social reproduction/unpaid care work is a key topic in FIPE, the question of how the economy, politics, and social reproduction are embedded in the natural environment remains largely underresearched in both IPE and FIPE.

Climate

It is undeniable that climate change is the most pressing crisis of the 21st century, threatening the survival of the human species as such (Steffen et al. 2015; IPCC 2021). The climate crisis as well as interlinked other ecological crises such as biodiversity loss or ocean acidification are social-ecological in the sense that they reify and reinforce social and also gender injustices both inter- and intragenerationally (Agarwal 1992; Harvey 2003; Roser and Seidel 2013). The climate crisis is also inherently global, as climate change knows no national borders. Quite to the contrary: Climate change (re-)produces the double global injustice that the world regions and social strata that have contributed least to the environmental problems of the 21st century are affected most by them.

Paterson (2021, p. 395) argues that despite some IPE work on, for example, international climate politics or climate finance, the overarching and more foundational questions of how we analyze climate change and what this means with regard to the depth of the required transformation remain a white spot. For example, the idea of meeting international climate agreements through emission trading following the polluter-pays principle is a strategy anchored in mainstream IPE and its sole focus is on the monetized tip of the iceberg (MacKenzie 2009). The logic of granting value by commodifying and trading environmental pollution on transnational markets remains within narrow mainstream economic boundaries and misses the chance to integrate more complex analysis of how power relations and global inequalities link to the climate crisis (Spash 2010). Matulis (2014, p. 157) points out that:

> Economic valuation reduces complex management decisions to simple economic accounting and denies the politics of inherently political activities. Who decides how resources are managed and who benefits from those decisions are questions central to justice in environmental management. Choosing a particular course of action because it 'makes the most economic sense' evades responsibility for unjust and inequitable outcomes.

From an ecofeminist IPE perspective, the strategy of shifting formerly non-monetized ecosystem functions or unpaid caring activities to the monetized economy by means of monetization and/or commodification has little transformative potential (Dengler and Lang 2022). While "putting a price-tag on" grants visibility in our current economic system, it also reinforces the capitalist growth paradigm by giving social recognition only to what is included in the monetized economy (ibid.; Salleh 2009). Taking a feminist-ecological stance, we need instead a radical questioning of the ontological and epistemological underpinnings of our current economic system, thereby focusing on alternatives to growth rather than growth alternatives. An ecofeminist international political economy aligns with research on relational values in ecological economics (Muraca and Himes 2018) and discusses the incommensurability of nature, pointing out that carbon markets commodify and sell the "right to pollute" instead of finding more holistic ways of valuing nature (Spash 2010; Gómez-Baggethun and Ruiz-Pérez 2011).

Outlook

Which future research agenda thus needs to be developed further and which promising pathways do already exist and point towards an ecofeminist international political economy (EFIPE)? Instead of ever differentializing more adjectives such as "feminist," "ecological," or "global," we suggest the integration and acknowledgment of already existing and promising pathways in IPE. From FIPE, the set of in-depth analysis and derived questions to tackle structural inequalities are essential to be capable of finding holistic solutions for the crisis of care and social reproduction. From feminist-ecological scholars, the set of relevant and pressing ecological topics which require global and intersectional IPE perspectives can be embraced to fill the white spot of specific (F)IPE research. These are necessary steps to (a) contribute to the "political" claim in IPE and (b) meet the responsibility of a social science discipline in the 21st century that acknowledges the complex dynamics of intertwisted processes of global social-ecological (re)production. However, EFIPE needs to thrive further than to simply integrate the above-mentioned analyses and topics through relocating the boundaries of the iceberg by commodifying/ monetizing everything and everyone.

To do so, (F)IPE can learn from materialist ecofeminism that has long emphasized the necessity to challenge culturally embedded conceptual binaries such as nature/culture, production/reproduction, or human/non-human that are deeply inscribed into capitalist civilization (Merchant 1980; Plumwood 1993; Bauhardt 2013; Gaard 2017). A promising pathway in this regard is the work of scholars who thrive for destabilizing these dualisms by integrating a queer perspective into the field of IPE (Peterson 2017; Gore 2021). Moreover, EFIPE must overcome the prevailing male-dominated, monetized boundaries in economics without reproducing them at different, even more marginalized, edges as in the case of global care chains. This requires a fundamental change in the language of valuation, from a language that only values what is counted in monetary terms to plural and relational values that are sensitive for feminist and decolonial perspectives on social-ecological transformations (Martinez-Alier 2008). A future-oriented research agenda of IPE needs to embrace queer instead of binary, (re)productive instead of productive, decolonial instead of colonial, global instead of North biased, embedded and embodied instead of disembedded and disembodied perspectives to construct a common pathway towards a more socially just and ecologically sound system.

Conclusion

Summarizing this overview of feminist theory in IPE, we do see some promising changes and developments in the scholarly field. The flourishing field of FIPE thrives for perspectives that are aware of structural inequalities and its academic reproduction. Coming back to Robinson (1997) and her analysis that IPE lacks a gender-sensitive perspective, we conclude that this does not hold true today. There is a broad range of research that focuses on international social reproduction processes and their intertwined relations to the monetized part of the global economy. What is still missing is an integrating perspective that captures the fundamental ecological embeddedness of our society. Feminist-ecological perspectives to IPE provide existing approaches and emerging theory for how to overcome the disembedded and disembodied male-stream of IPE. They elaborate on cornerstones for a socially just and environmentally sound economic system that is embedded in environmental processes and embodied through the material reality of human bodies. For future research agendas of EFIPE this means an acknowledgment and integration of feminist IPE and diverse scholarship at the intersections of feminisms, decoloniality, and the environment. Overcoming different conceptual grammar and fostering an ontologically reflexive, interested pluralism as well as interdisciplinary methodology is an important stepping stone for these ecofeminist IPE futures.

References

Adams-Prassl, Abi and Janine Berg (2017). When Home Affects Pay: An Analysis of the Gender Pay Gap Among Crowdworkers. Available at SSRN: https://ssrn.com/abstract=3048711 or http://dx.doi.org/10.2139/ssrn.3048711

Agarwal, Bina (1992). The gender and environment debate: Lessons from India. *Feminist Studies* 18(1), 119–158.

Bakker, Isabella (2007). Social reproduction and the constitution of a gendered political economy. *New Political Economy* 12(4), 541–556.

Banks, Nina (2020). Black women in the United States and unpaid collective work: Theorizing the community as a site of production. *Review of Black Political Economy* 47(4), 343–362.

Bauhardt, Christine (2013). Rethinking gender and nature from a material(ist) perspective: Feminist economics, queer ecologies and resource politics. *European Journal of Women's Studies* 20(4), 361–75.

Bauhardt, Christine and Wendy Harcourt (eds.) (2019). *Feminist Political Ecology and the Economics of Care: In Search of Economic Alternatives*. London/New York: Routledge.

Berik, Günseli and Kongar Ebru (eds.) (2021). *The Routledge Handbook of Feminist Economics*. London/New York: Routledge.

Bhambra, Gurminder K. (2021). Narrating inequality, eliding empire. *British Journal of Sociology* 72, 69–78.

Biesecker, Adelheid and Sabine Hofmeister (2010). Focus:(Re) productivity: Sustainable relations both between society and nature and between the genders. *Ecological Economics* 69(8), 1703–1711.

Bigo, Vinca and Ioana Negru (2008). From fragmentation to ontologically reflexive pluralism. *Journal of Philosophical Economics* 1(2), 127–150.

Braunstein, Elissa (2013). Central bank policy and gender. In Deborah M. Figart and Tonia Warnecke (eds.), *Handbook of Research on Gender and Economic Life*. Cheltenham, UK and Northampton, MA, USA: Edward Elgar Publishing, 345–358.

Budlender, Debbie (2010). *What Do Time Use Studies Tell Us About Unpaid Care Work? Evidence From Seven Countries.* London/New York: Routledge.

Çağatay, Nilüfer, Diane Elson, and Caren Grown (1995). Introduction. *World Development* 23(11), 1827–1836.

Cohen, Benjamin (2007). The transatlantic divide: Why are American and British IPE so different? *Review of International Political Economy* 14(2), 197–219.

Collins, Patricia Hill and Sirma Bilge (2016). *Intersectionality.* Cambridge/Malden: Polity Press.

Crenshaw, Kimberle (1989). Demarginalizing the intersection of race and sex: A black feminist critique of antidiscrimination doctrine, feminist theory and antiracist politics. *University of Chicago Legal Forum*, 1, 139–167.

Davis, Angela (1981). *Women, Race and Class.* New York: Random House.

Dengler, Corinna and Miriam Lang (2022). Commoning care: Feminist degrowth visions for a socio-ecological transformation. *Feminist Economics* 28(1), 1–28.

Dengler, Corinna and Birte Strunk (2018). The monetized economy versus care and the environment: Degrowth perspectives on reconciling an antagonism. *Feminist Economics* 24(3), 160–183.

Dobusch, Leonhard and Jakob Kapeller (2012). Heterodox United vs. Mainstream City? Sketching a framework for interested pluralism in economics. *Journal of Economic Issues* 46(4), 1035–1057.

Ehrenreich, Barbara and Arlie Hochschild (2002). *Global Woman: Nannies, Maids, and Sex Workers in the New Economy.* New York: Metropolitan Books.

Elias, Juanita and Shirin M. Rai (2019). Feminist everyday political economy: Space, time, and violence. *Review of International Studies* 45(2), 201–220.

Elias, Juanita and Adrienne Roberts (eds.) (2018). *Handbook on the International Political Economy of Gender.* Handbooks of Research on International Political Economy series. Cheltenham, UK and Northampton, MA, USA: Edward Elgar Publishing.

Federici, Silvia (2020). *Revolution at Point Zero. Housework, Reproduction, and Feminist Struggle.* Oakland, CA: PM Press.

Ferber, Marianne A. and Julie Nelson (eds.) (1993). *Beyond Economic Man. Feminist Theory and Economics.* London/Chicago: The University of Chicago Press.

Folbre, Nancy (2006). Measuring care: Gender, empowerment, and the care economy. *Journal of Human Development* 7(2), 183–199

Gaard, Greta (2017). *Critical Ecofeminism.* Lanham, MD/London: Lexington Books.

Gómez-Baggethun, Erik and Manuel Ruiz-Pérez (2011). Economic valuation and the commodification of ecosystem services. *Progress in Physical Geography* 35(5), 613–628.

Goodley, Dan (2014). *Dis/Ability Studies: Theorising Disablism and Ableism.* London/New York: Routledge.

Gore, Ellie (2021). Understanding queer oppression and resistance in the global economy: Towards a theoretical framework for political economy. *New Political Economy.* DOI: 10.1080/13563467.2021.1952558.

Goździak, Elzbieta M. (2016). *Trafficked Children and Youth in the United States.* New York: Rutgers University Press.

Griffin, Penny (2007). Refashioning IPE: What and how gender analysis teaches international (global) political economy. *Review of International Political Economy* 14(4), 719–736.

Hartmann, Heidi I. (1979). The unhappy marriage of Marxism and feminism: Towards a more progressive union. *Capital & Class* 3(2), 1–33.

Harvey, David (2003). *The New Imperialism*. Oxford: University Press.

Hochschild, Arlie R. (2000). Global care chains and emotional surplus value. In Anthony Giddens and Will Hutton (eds.), *Living with Global Capitalism*. London: Jonathan Cape, 130–146.

Hochschild, Arlie R. (2003). *The Commercialization of Intimate Life: Notes from Home and Work*. Berkeley: University of California Press.

ILO (2018). *Care Work and Care Jobs for the Future of Decent Work*. Geneva: ILO.

IPCC (2021). *Climate Change 2021: The Physical Science Basis. Contribution of Working Group I to the Sixth Assessment Report of the Intergovernmental Panel on Climate Change*. Cambridge: Cambridge University Press.

Jana, Madhusree and Anita Hammer (2021). Reproductive work in the Global South: Lived experiences and social relations of commercial surrogacy in India. *Work, Employment and Society*. DOI: 10.1177/0950017021997370.

Keating, Christine, Claire Rasmussen, and Pooja Rishi (2010). The rationality of empowerment: Microcredit, accumulation by dispossession, and the gendered economy. *Signs: Journal of Women in Culture and Society* 36(1), 153–176.

Kirshner, Johnathan (2003). Money is politics. *Review of International Political Economy* 10(4), 645–660.

Kittay, Eva Feder (2014). *The Completion of Care—With Implications for a Duty to Receive Care Graciously: Care Professions and Globalization*. New York: Palgrave Macmillan, 33–42.

Koch, Max and Hubert Buch-Hansen (2020). The IPE of degrowth and sustainable welfare. In *The Routledge Handbook to Global Political Economy*. London/New York: Routledge, 375–390.

Kothari, Uma (2002). Feminist and postcolonial challenges to development. In Uma Kothari and Martin Minogue (eds.), *Development Theory and Practice: Critical Perspectives*. London: Palgrave Macmillan, 35–51.

Lutz, Helma and Ewa Palenga-Möllenbeck (2010). Care work migration in Germany: Semi-compliance and complicity. *Social Policy and Society* 9(3), 419–430.

MacKenzie, Donald (2009). Making things the same: Gases, emission rights and the politics of carbon markets. *Accounting, Organizations and Society* 34(3–4), 440–455.

Martinez-Alier, Joan (2008). Languages of valuation. *Economic and Political Weekly* 34(48), 28–32.

Matulis, Brett (2014). The economic valuation of nature: A question of justice? *Ecological Economics* 104, 155–157.

Mazzucato, Mariana (2021). *Mission Economy. A Moonshot Guide to Changing Capitalism*. Dublin: Penguin Random House.

Mellor, Mary (2005). Ecofeminist political economy: Integrating feminist economics and ecological economics. *Feminist Economics* 11(3), 120–126.

Mellor, Mary (2009). Ecofeminist political economy and the politics of money. In Ariel Salleh (ed.), *Eco-Sufficiency and Global Justice*. London: Pluto Press, 251–267.

Mellor, Mary (2010). *The Future of Money. From Financial Crisis to Public Resource*. London: Pluto Press.

Mellor, Mary (2016). *Debt or Democracy. Public Money for Sustainability and Social Justice*. London: Pluto Press.

Merchant, Carolyn (1980). *The Death of Nature: Women, Ecology, and the Scientific Revolution*. San Francisco: Harper & Row.

Mezzadri, Alessandra, Susan Newman, and Sara Stevano (2021). *Feminist Global Political Economies of Work and Social Reproduction*. Special Issue, *Review of International Political Economy*. DOI: 10.1080/09692290.2021.1957977.

Mies, Maria (1986). *Patriarchy and Accumulation on a World Scale: Women in the International Division of Labour*. London: Zed Books.

Mohanty, Chandra Talpade (2003). *Feminism without Borders*. Durham, NC: Duke University Press.

Mollett, Sharlene (2017). Gender's critical edge: Feminist political ecology, postcolonial intersectionality, and the coupling of race and gender. In Sherilyn MacGregor (ed.), *Routledge Handbook of Gender and Environment*. London/New York: Routledge, 146–158.

Muraca, Barbara and Austin Himes (2018). Relational values: The key to pluralistic valuation of ecosystem services. *Current Opinion in Environmental Sustainability* 35, 1–7.

Nersisyan, Yeva and Randall L. Wray (2010). Deficit hysteria redux? Why we should stop worrying about U.S. government deficits. *Real-World Economics Review*, 53, 109–128.

O'Hara, Sabine (1997). Toward a sustaining production theory. *Ecological Economics*, 20(2), 141–154.

O'Hara, Sabine (2009). Feminist ecological economics: Theory and practice. In Ariel Salleh (ed.), *Eco-sufficiency and Global Justice: Women Write Political Ecology*. London: Pluto Press, 180–196.

Palmer, Ingrid (1995). Public finance from a gender perspective. *World Development* 23(11), 1981–1986.

Paterson, Matthew (2021). Climate change and International Political Economy: Between collapse and transformation. *Review of International Political Economy* 28(2), 394–405.

Perkins, Patricia E. Ellie (1997). Introduction: Women, ecology, and economics: New models and theories. *Ecological Economics* 20, 105–106.

Perkins, Patricia E. Ellie (2021). Commoning and climate justice. In Prateep Nayak (ed.), *Making Commons Dynamic: Understanding Change through Commonisation and Decommonisation*. Routledge Studies in Environment, Culture, and Society Series. London/New York: Routledge, 123–137.

Peterson, Spike V. (2005). How the (meaning of) gender matters in political economy. *New Political Economy* 10(4), 499–521.

Peterson, Spike V. (2017). Towards queering the globally intimate. *Political Geography* 100(56), 114–116.

Peterson, Spike V. (2018). *Revisiting Gendered States: Feminist Imaginings of the State in International Relations*. Oxford: Oxford University Press.

Plumwood, Val (1993). *Feminism and the Mastery of Nature*. London/New York: Routledge.

Power, Marilyn (2004). Social provisioning as a starting point for feminist economics. *Feminist Economics* 10(3), 3–19.

Rai, Shirin (2018). Gender and development. In Juanita Elias and Adrienne Roberts (eds.), *Handbook on the International Political Economy of Gender*. Cheltenham, UK and Northampton, MA, USA: Edward Elgar Publishing, 142–158.

Rai, Shirin and Kate Bedford (2010). *Feminists Theorize International Political Economy*. Special Issue, *Signs: Journal of Women in Culture and Society*, 36(1), 1–18.

Robinson, Fiona (1997). Feminist IR/IPE theory: Fulfilling its radical potential? *Review of International Political Economy*, 4(4), 773–781.

Rocheleau, Dianne, Barbara Thomas-Slayter, and Esther Wangari (eds.) (1996). *Feminist Political Ecology: Global Issues and Local Experiences*. London/New York: Routledge.

Roser, Dominic and Christian Seidel (2013). *Ethik des Klimawandels. Eine Einführung.* Darmstadt: Wissenschaftliche Buchgesellschaft.

Rubery, Jill (2015). Austerity and the future for gender equality in Europe. *ILR Review*, 68(7), 715–741.

Safri, Maliha and Julie Graham (2010). The global household: Toward a feminist post-capitalist international political economy. *Signs: Journal of Women in Culture and Society*, 36(1), 99–125.

Salleh, Ariel (2009). *Eco-Sufficiency and Global Justice: Women Write Political Ecology.* London/Melbourne: Pluto Press and Spinifex Press.

Schor, Juliet B., William Attwood-Charles, Mehmet Cansoy et al. (2020). Dependence and precarity in the platform economy. *Theory and Society* (49), 833–861.

Seguino, Stephanie (2011). The global economic crisis, its gender and ethnic implications, and policy responses. In Ruth Pearson and Caroline Sweetman (eds.), *Gender and the Economic Crisis*. Warwickshire: Practical Action Publishing, 15–36.

Spash, Clive (2010). The brave new world of carbon trading. *New Political Economy* 15(2), 169–195.

Steffen, Will, Wendy Broadgate, Lisa Deutsch, Owen Gaffney, and Cornelia Ludwig (2015). The trajectory of the Anthropocene: The Great Acceleration. *Anthropocene Review* 2(1), 82–98.

Stevano, Sara, Rosimina Ali, and Merle Jamieson (2021). Essential for what? A global social reproduction view on the re-organisation of work during the COVID-19 pandemic. *Canadian Journal of Development Studies* 42(1–2), 178–199.

Tilley, Lisa and Robbie Shilliam (2018). Raced markets: An introduction. *New Political Economy* 23(5), 534–43.

Vertommen, Sigrid and Camille Barbagallo (2020). The in/visible wombs of the market: The dialectics of waged and unwaged reproductive labour in the global surrogacy industry. *Review of International Political Economy*. DOI: 10.1080/09692290.2020.1866642.

Walby, Silvia (2015). *Crisis*. Hoboken, NJ: John Wiley & Sons.

Watson, Matthew (2017). The nineteenth-century roots of theoretical traditions in global political economy. In John Ravenhill (ed.), *Global Political Economy*. Oxford: Oxford University Press, 26–51.

Waylen, Georgina (2006). You still don't understand: Why troubled engagements continue between feminists and (critical) IPE. *Review of International Studies* 32(1), 145–164.

Wichterich, Christa (2020). Who cares about healthcare workers? Care extractivism and care struggles in Germany and India. *Social Change* 50(1), 121–140.

Yollu-Tok, Aysel and Fabiola Rodríguez Garzón (2018). Feminist economics—A critique of mainstream economics. *List Forum* 44, 725–762.

Young, Brigitte (2018). Financialization, unconventional monetary policy and gender inequality. In Juanita Elias and Adrienne Roberts (eds.), *Handbook on the International Political Economy of Gender*. Cheltenham, UK and Northampton, MA, USA: Edward Elgar Publishing, 241–251.

13. Decolonizing labor, land, and the Global South

Aaron Schneider

There has been a widening call for the decolonization of development theory and practice. This chapter seeks to move decolonization one-step further by focusing on core functions of colonialism and neo-colonialism – the ongoing exploitation of labor and land. To decolonize meaningfully, the chapter first traces the history of colonization in terms of its relation with racism and capitalism, intertwined with development in the Western European core and reflected in peripheral territories through conquest. The integration of race, capital, and colonialism infected development thinking as it matured after World War II, constraining paradigms to elitist approaches and condemning the field to limited and negative impacts over decades.

The very concept of decolonization became more precise through Aníbal Quijano's 1990s innovation of the concept of "coloniality" (Quijano, 2007). Coloniality and capitalism were twin traits of Western modernity, the hierarchical assertion that "other cultures are different in the sense that they are unequal, in fact inferior, by nature" (Quijano, 2007: 174). For Quijano, the label of coloniality was especially important to distinguish from decolonization of the 1960s and 1970s, which ended colonialism but not capitalism, with local elites capturing independence but continuing the exploitation of labor and land.

Decolonizing development requires replacing the system of coloniality at the level of knowledge, practice, and social relations. Fortunately, embryonic alternatives already exist, and these reflect authentic knowledge from below, built on the unevenness of peripheral experiences with development and resistance. Resistance blends global integration with local class struggle and cultural traditions. While the specific combinations of global and local vary, they share a relational approach in terms of coherent community interactions with the natural world and the global system. Unlike elite strategies of development, decolonization does not require the exploitation of labor and land, opting instead for a practice of development built on local traditions of resistance.

Race, capitalism, and colonialism

Perhaps the clearest observation of the close link between race, capitalism, and colonialism comes from Cedric Robinson's concept of "racial capitalism" (Robinson, 2000). Robinson differs from those who argue that racism and colonialism represent inefficient and pre-capitalist prejudices, destined to erode with the evolution of markets. Robinson argues that racism and colonialism were central to the emergence and operation of capitalism.

He argues that the seeds of racism and capitalism were planted within feudalism. "From its very beginnings, this European civilization, containing racial, tribal, linguistic, and regional particularities, was constructed on antagonistic differences" (Robinson, 2000: 10). Western European feudalism established various gradations based on ethnic, national, and other dimensions to organize social relations. The original word for slave came from the Slavs, the populations of Eastern Europe forced into serfdom, shifted like property when land changed hands, treated as appendages to the land in service to landlord extraction. Other European ethnicities and religious minorities, such as Jews and gypsies, were also considered sub-human, undeserving of the same dignity afforded to dominant populations (Robinson, 2000: 42). Further, persecution of women as witches and other myths of female threat cloaked the stripping of their rights, creating an entire subclass based on gender (Federici, 2000).

Feudal hierarchies of status justified treating certain populations as less than human, and these distinctions transferred to capitalist social relations to define certain people's labor and land as commodities available for appropriation (Polanyi, 2001). By taking advantage of available distinctions of ethnicity, region, religion, and gender, capitalism could tear people from their pre-existing social relations and establish social relations of property and wage. Capitalism extrapolated these social relations further, minoritizing whole populations by organizing production along ethnic lines. Thompson describes the Irish working class, uprooted and forced to migrate to UK industrial cities. Once they entered English society, they were defined as another race, attributed sub-human characteristics, denied rights, and relegated to the most exploitative working and living conditions "By the 1830s, whole classes of work had passed almost entirely into the hands of Irishmen since the English either refused the menial, unpleasant tasks or could not keep up with the pace" (Thompson, 1963: 434).

To extend capitalism across the world, the cultural innovation of race extrapolated further, now defined in global terms, such that all outside the privileged and constructed ethnicity of the core could be othered and available for exploitation. Racism was not just difference but superiority, denying rights to those defined as non-white. Practices such as the African slave trade, the genocide of indigenous peoples, and the land grab of colonialism were justified by racism in the service of extending capitalism. Said observed,

> Arabs, for example, are thought of *as* camel riding, terroristic, hook-nosed, venal lechers whose undeserved wealth is an affront to real civilization. Always there lurks the assumption that although the Western consumer belongs to a numerical minority, he is entitled either to own or to expend (or both) the majority of the world resources. Why? Because he, unlike the Oriental, is a true human being. (Said, 1979: 108)

The utility of racism in weaving together early capitalism and colonialism defies those who might argue that racism and colonialism were aberrant hold-overs doomed to disappear, rather they were essential to jumpstart industrialization. The explosion of the European slave trade and extension of European colonialism to every continent coincided with the onset of capitalist social relations throughout Western Europe. For Marx, this was no coincidence, as the super-profits available through the "primitive accumulation" of colonialism provided the initial capital needed to finance industrialization. Extraction of this sort could only be justified by denigrating and dehumanizing the societies being colonized, revealing in "naked" form "the inherent barbarism of bourgeois civilization" (Marx, 1853).

Further, both racism and colonialism survived over time in service to renewing capitalism at its various crises. Luxembourg noted the utility of the global periphery during the downswings in international boom-bust cycles. Available and necessary super-profits could be found in the markets, investment opportunities, raw materials, and labor outside the core, in what she labels pre-capitalist modes of production. "From the aspect both of realizing the surplus value and of procuring the material elements of constant capital, international trade is a prime necessity for the historical existence of capitalism – an international trade which under actual conditions is essentially an exchange between capitalistic and non-capitalistic modes of production" (Luxembourg, 1951: 359).

David Harvey extends Luxembourg's analysis to "accumulation by dispossession," in which capitalism renews itself by entering areas previously outside the market, such as through neoliberal privatization, marketization, and deregulation (Harvey, 2005: 185–186). As an economic geographer, Harvey emphasizes the geographic logic to capital circulation and accumulation, in which capital "displaces crises" rather than resolving them (Harvey, 2011). Each round of hyper-profits requires ideological justification, and race and other markers of difference excuse thinly veiled patterns of colonial and post-colonial intervention, regime change, and extraction.

There is still work to be done on how intertwining racism and colonialism shaped the character of capitalism in the core, as well its possible future evolutions. In particular, how have racism and colonialism been recreated as capitalism evolves, from industrialization to globalization to financialization to today's "platform capitalism" (Srnicek, 2016)? The next section addresses the question of how racial capitalism operating in the core projected outwards in even more brutal fashion in the periphery. As Frantz Fanon observed, "in the colonial context the settler only ends his work of breaking in the native when the latter admits loudly and intelligibly the supremacy of the white man's values" (Fanon, 2005: 43).

Hierarchies and binaries in development theory and practice

The way race, colonialism, and capitalism work together plays out in development theory and practice. Race and other hierarchies of difference operate as binaries; the Global North as archetype and endpoint of development, and the Global South as a diminished subtype or backwards version. By constraining development thinking in this way, development practice followed elitist models, reinforcing the presumed authority and hierarchy of those educated by, operating from, and originating in the Global North. As a result, development interventions have had limited success, with the most significant advances in those regions, such as East Asia, that avoided Northern prescriptions, and the least progress made in regions where elitist models dominated, such as Africa and much of Latin America.

For Escobar (2011), the racial capitalist framework that guided colonialism updated in post-World War II North and South relations to maintain exploitation of labor and land. The binary construct of developed and undeveloped presumed development required application of science to increase wealth and productivity. "The key to greater production is a wider and more vigorous application of modern scientific and technical knowledge" (as cited, Escobar, 2011: 13). Yet, science and knowledge valued Western technological solutions to development problems, constraining "forms of knowledge that refer to it and through which it comes into being and is elaborated into objects, concepts, theories, and the like; the system of power that regulates its practice; and the forms of subjectivity fostered" (ibid.: 10).

Binary thinking in which the West is the bearer and the endpoint of modernity validates an elitist conceit in which development is something brought from the core to developing countries. Selwyn describes this as an "elite subject-subordinate object conception of development," empowering elites with access to knowledge and capital and "legitimate[ing] elite repression and exploitation of the poor politically and economically, especially when the latter contest elite-led development" (Selwyn, 2016: 782–783). In effect, an elitist and binary approach to development excludes the non-West, non-white, poor majority of the world as obstacles to be overcome.

Yet, the results have been exactly opposite to that promised. Seven decades of development practice have produced "massive underdevelopment and impoverishments, untold exploitation, and oppression" (Escobar, 2011: 4). The combination of racism, colonialism, and capitalism was born of feudal origins, implanted in European industrialization, and updated in the second half of the twentieth century in an elitist development practice. The updates preserved a model of binaries and hierarchies to exploit labor and land in the Global South, with devastating and unsustainable impacts on the environment and on society. A few countries, particularly the newly industrialized countries of East Asia, achieved a degree of development in the postwar period, but even their success requires additional inquiry into the negation of humanity outside the developed core.

Negation of the negation

Decolonizing development seeks to recover dignity for those excluded from elitist models of development by altering the social relations of the international system. If elitist development strips people of their humanity, decolonizing development "negates the negation" of that stripping. Decolonization asserts the humanity of the poor, non-white, and Global South. Further, it charts a path forward towards a system that does not rest on the hyper-exploitation of land and labor, doing so by combining the modern abundance of global production with local traditions of community and resistance. While these local cultures vary by context, they share a relational view of society, differing fundamentally from the binary and hierarchical view of coloniality.

The concept of negating the negation is central to decolonizing development and draws on Hegelian ideas identified with the black radical tradition. Kelley notes that

> over the centuries, the liberation projects of men and women in Africa, the Caribbean, and the Americas acquired similar emergent collective forms in rebellion and marronage, similar ethical and moral articulations of resistance; increasingly they merged as a function of what Hegel might have recognized as the negation of the negation in the world system. (Kelley, in Robinson, 2000: xxxii)

In negating the negation of humanity, colonial and post-colonial resistance is forward-looking. It does not reject modernization; rather, decolonization rejects a version of modernity interwoven with exploitation and environmental destruction. The response is not one of rage but rather the expression of an alternative humanity. In observing the Haitian revolution, the only successful slave rebellion of modern times, C.L.R. James observed, "When history is written as it ought to be written, it is the moderation and long patience of the masses at which men will wonder, not their ferocity" (James, 1989: 138). Rebellious Haitian slaves, despite centuries of cruelty and inhuman treatment, walked the plantation owners and colonial authorities to the docks and packed them back to France. That act showed the goal of revolution not simply to flip hierarchies and binaries of the West, but rather to establish a new social relation of humanity for all.

New social relations are what gives decolonization its liberating potential. In winning the dignity of the colonized, decolonization also potentially frees the colonizer from the binaries and hierarchies that lock them into exploitative social relations. Thus, decolonization promises not just to replace the colonizers with the colonized, it offers something new and transformative, a new set of social relations. This was clear in one of the very first colonies, Ireland.

> If you remove the English army tomorrow and hoist the green flag over Dublin Castle, unless you set about the organization of the Socialist Republic your efforts would be in vain. England would still rule you. She would rule you through her capitalists, through her landlords, through her financiers, through the whole array of commercial and individualist institutions she has planted in this country and watered with the tears of our mothers and the blood of our martyrs. (Connolly, 1897/1988: 124)

Decolonizing development

The decolonization of development depends on three elements: relationalism, local and indigenous worldviews, and the combination that comes from the mix of international advances and local class and cultural struggles. Relationalism stands in contrast to the individualism of Western, liberal capitalism, and builds on the communal practices in which people connect to one another and to nature. What is important in relationalism is the relation between actors, rather than the specific actor attributes or resources. This worldview is typical of indigenous and local traditions, and provides both a source of resistance to the binaries and hierarchies of colonialism and an alternative, more humane future. The nature of that future will vary by context, as it will be the outcome of the very uneven and combined nature of development, in which advanced capital interacts with the class structures and cultural traditions operating in each place. Decolonizing development lifts these combinations, echoing outwards and joining them globally to structure new social relations that do not depend on forms of difference to exploit labor and land.

Relationalism refers to a worldview, an ontology, in which the relationship among entities becomes paramount. A common example might be a family, in which the relations among members (mother, son, daughter, cousin, and so forth) tell us much of what we need to know about them, their identities, and the way they are likely to interact. International relations has increasingly elaborated relational approaches, in which the specific characteristics of actors (such as countries) can be read and understood through "connections, ties, transactions, and other kinds of relations among entities" (Jackson and Nexon, 1999: 2). In contrast to Western liberalism and most development thinking, relational views see the world made up of relations between things rather than seeing the things themselves as primary; entities only take on their reality when arranged in relation to other entities. Thus, we can understand the world by knowing where entities are positioned and the interactions of positions in a system.

The emphasis on relations is common within indigenous worldviews, in which people exist in social relation to their community and to the land on which they live. The indigenous relation with the land is a particular distinction from notions of land as property and commodity; rather, land is akin to a relative, due respect, care, and rights. Indigenous social relations encompass human and environmental relatives, not as external entities but inseparable from communal life. On the indigenous nations of North America, Nick Estes writes, "Ancestors of Indigenous resistance didn't merely fight against settler colonialism; they fought for Indigenous life and just relations with human and nonhuman relatives, and with the earth" (Estes, 2019: 248). He contrasts this with settler notions of property to be bought and sold, "land as spatial and commodity form replaces and re-signifies value through the elimination of Native title and populations. This process of effacing Native meaning from landscapes is economic, political, legal, and material in nature" (Estes, 2013: 197).

In many parts of the Americas, this relational approach extends even further, connecting people, community, land, and the spirit world, labeled a "cosmos." All dimensions of human life exist in relation to each other and cannot be compartmentalized or separated (Mignolo and Walsh, 2018). To establish property relations in land and wage relations for labor, capitalist social relations attempted to negate the totalizing cosmos, tear people from their relationships, and make land and labor available for exploitation. This required the coercion of colonialism and the binary hierarchy of race and other forms of difference, and the indigenous response was to reassert relational views defending the dignity of people and their unbreakable relationship with nature.

Yet, this resistance is not a millenarian backwards-looking attempt to return to a prior moment. Rather, resistance comes directly from the uneven character of international capitalism, as more developed areas come into contact with less developed areas. Trotsky highlights this unevenness in his theory of uneven and combined development. "The development of historically backward nations leads necessarily to a peculiar combination of different stages in the historic process. Their development as a whole acquires a planless, complex, combined character" (Trotsky, 1977: 27). The combination that results depends on the particular class struggles and patterns of cultural resistance in each place.

Combination means that the decolonization of development occurring in any given context reflects two elements. First, all developing countries experience the sharp edge of the international economy – capitalism, colonialism, and racism. Second, their response is rooted in a relationalism reasserting their humanity and charting a way forward. The path charted in each context depends on the class struggles and patterns of cultural resistance produced by the encounter with unevenness. More work is required to explore these commonalities, how do we understand these shared experiences of developing countries? The next section explores the commonalities of their resistance. As developing contexts face elite strategies of development that negate their humanity, they negate that negation by reasserting a relational approach and articulating an alternative future social relation. "Whereas past revolutionary struggles have strived for the emancipation of labor from capital, we are challenged not just to imagine, but to demand the emancipation of earth from capital. For the earth to live, capitalism must die" (Estes, 2019: 257).

Constructing decolonized development

African combinations of capitalist modernization and local cultures of resistance articulate some of the most elaborate proposals for decolonized development. Mbembe observes the particular brutality of colonialism in Africa, including genocide and slavery, as well as an ideological project dehumanizing Africans and their culture. In pursuing this project, Europeans asserted their own difference and superiority. "Africa as an idea, a concept, has historically served, and continues to serve, as a polemical argument for the West's desperate desire to assert its difference from the rest of the world" (Mbembe, 2001: 2).

This ideological project negated African humanity and justified Western exploitation and extraction. The impact for Africans was to strip them of their history. "Africa thus stands out as the supreme receptacle of the West's obsession with, and circular discourse about, the facts of 'absence,' 'lack,' and 'non-being,' of identity and difference, of negativeness – in short, of nothingness" (Mbembe, 2001: 4).

This reinforced an elite approach following Western prescriptions but blind to the true complexity of African life. "One consequence of this blindness is that African politics and economics have been condemned to appear in social theory only as the sign of a lack, while the discourse of political science and development economics has become that of a quest for the causes of that lack" (Mbembe, 2001: 8). Elite development reflects and reinforces patterns of colonialism and post-colonialism, leaving a dead end of poverty and misgovernment, and missing an opportunity for an alternative future.

> Whether produced by outsiders or by indigenous people, end-of-the-century discourses about Africa are not necessarily applicable to their object. Their nature, their stakes, and their functions are situated elsewhere. They are deployed only by replacing this object, creating it, erasing it, decomposing and multiplying it. Thus, there is no description of Africa that does not involve destructive and mendacious functions. (Mbembe, 2001: 242)

Yet, Mbembe demands and points to the possibility of an alternative. Centuries of stripping Africans of their history and of elitist development created a paradoxical fertility of innovations. African subjects were so far outside of European humanity that it was possible to create new spaces of solidarity and humanity. Especially because of the diaspora of slavery and the ongoing dislocation and mixing of migration and instability, Africa can be the site of constructing an alternative social relation rooted in humanity. "It is this song of shadows, its metamorphoses, its sight, hearing, sense of smell, taste touch – in short, its expressive power – to which we have given the ultimately meaningless name of postcolony" (Mbembe, 2001: 242).

The need for African innovations is especially relevant under new forms of technological capitalism that require fewer workers and therefore must discipline, surveil, and potentially discard the rest.

> The last decades of the twentieth century have been marked by the universalization of the market principle. Capital, in particular finance capital, having reached its maximal capacity for velocity, circulation, and flight, is now more than just dictating its own temporal regime. It now seeks to reproduce itself on its own, in an infinite series of structurally insolvent debts. If yesterday's drama of the human subject was exploitation by capital, the tragedy of the multitude today is that they are unable to be exploited at all. (Mbembe, 2019: 111)

Because capitalism and democracy have come to this contradictory impossibility, it is through the resistance of decolonized struggle that new social relations can be born. For Mbembe, decolonized development includes a new social relation not just among people, but also between humans, nature, and even technology. "Neoliberalism has created the conditions for a renewed convergence, and at times fusion, between the living human being and objects, artifacts, or the technologies that supplement or augment us and are in the process transfigured and transformed by us" (Mbembe, 2019: 108). By engaging in what Fanon labeled "a relation of care," we can construct a new social relation of people embedded in community. "Humanity in effect arises only when a gesture – and thus the relation of care, is possible; when one allows oneself to be affected by the faces of others" (Mbembe, 2019: 176). Mbembe imagines a future guided by the ethics of the passer-by, "This experience of presence and distance, of solidarity and detachment, but never of indifference – let us call it the ethics of the passerby" (Mbembe, 2019: 188).

What is notable about Mbembe's version of decolonized development is the centrality of relational approaches. Colonized reality established binary and distant relations of colonized and colonizer, human and non-human object – "proximity without reciprocity" (Mbembe, 2021: 79–99). Yet, at the edges of empire, in the weakest links of uneven global capitalism, these binaries are at their most fuzzy, creating zones of possibility in which a blurring of binary opposites occurs. In these spaces of possibility, a "new creole and, in many ways, cosmopolitan urbanity" takes shape (Mbembe, 2021: 145). The social relations erected by colonial and post-colonial hierarchy dominate in the periphery, but weak institutionalization in states and ongoing colonial subservience of leading factions of the bourgeoisie mean they cannot be hegemonic, in the sense of consensus among the dominant and dominated groups. As a result, the periphery offers the possibility of heightened cultural mixing and class struggle. Africa uniquely mixes African, European, and American cultures, and presents heightened class struggle because of the weakness of post-colonial national bourgeoisies and their states.

Together, the potential for cultural and class innovation from below make Africa a site to construct decolonized development built on a new set of cosmopolitan social relations. He describes these relations as "Afropolitanism ... As a matter of fact, the destiny of our planet will be played out, to a large extent, in Africa. This planetary turn of the African predicament will constitute the main cultural and philosophical event of the twenty-first century" (Mbembe, 2021: 222). By breaking down the binaries and hierarchies of colonialism, racism, and capitalism, the social relations of property and wage transform into a liberatory future for all. "The message of joy in a great universal future equitably open to all peoples, all nations, and all species ... pulled up and created over the course of struggles" (Mbembe, 2021: 229).

Notable in these new relations is the necessity of liberation for both colonized and colonizer. The colonial negation of humanity not only dehumanized Africans, it also dehumanized Europeans, establishing racial and other hierarchies that undermined Western pretenses of liberalism. Similar to the cases of plantation and colony, the West now makes excuses for operating wholly undemocratic practices outside liberal norms to house immigrants, suspend the rights of suspected terrorists, imprison large subpopulations, and otherwise exacerbate a security state that makes life unlivable for large swathes of humanity. How is it that Western liberalism appears to be doubling down on its illiberal practices, now more than ever?

Mbembe labels this determination of life and death "necropolitics," an exaggerated form of biopower – the "ultimate expression of sovereignty resides, to a large degree, in the power and the capacity to dictate who may live and who must die" (Mbembe, 2003: 11; Mbembe, 2019). "Recovering the humanity of those who were colonized also recovers the humanity of colonizers, establishing a new social relation that encompasses both colonized and colonizers, indeed the entirety of humanity and its relation to nature, spirituality, and beyond" (Mbembe, 2021: 187).

Decolonizing development practice

Decolonizing development offers a framework to construct an alternative, more humane future and inspires new development practices. Some of the most interesting can be found in Latin America, drawing on a history of anti-imperial resistance, working-class and peasant mobilization, and the persistence of powerful and evolving indigenous movements.

One trajectory of resistance can be traced to the works of Mariátegui in the Andes. Writing in the 1920s and experiencing a period of exile in Europe, he famously called for an authentic version of anti-colonial and working-class organizing, reflective of the indigenous and agrarian reality of his home country of Peru. "We certainly do not wish socialism in America to be a copy and imitation. It must be a heroic creation. We must give life to an Indo-American socialism reflecting our own reality and in our own language" (Mariátegui, 1928/2011: 130). Two aspects of Mariátegui's statement stand out. First, he notes the necessity of an "Indo-American socialism," calling attention to the history of colonialism, the ongoing realities of uneven capitalist development, and the persistent exclusion of anti-indigenous racism. Second, Mariátegui also calls for "heroic creation," which various observers have interpreted as an indicator of romantic revolutionary theory (Löwy, 1998). Romanticism reacts to the dehumanizing impact of capitalism that compartmentalizes and individualizes economic, political, and social life. To restore humanity, Mariátegui highlights the relational aspects of pre-conquest and pre-capitalist indigenous and peasant Latin American cosmovision, connecting people, their communities, nature, and the cosmos.

Contemporary Andean movements draw on this heroic creation in the practice of Buen Vivir (living well). Used to describe local and national practices in Peru, Ecuador, and Bolivia, Buen Vivir fits within the decolonizing development framework for its relational approach and its combination of advanced development and indigenous communal traditions. In some instances, the approach has been applied to fairly mundane policies, "questioning the practice of corporations ... blowing the whistle on companies that pollute ... pedestrian zones ... or cash transfer programs for the poor" (Gudynas, 2015: 201). More significantly, it appears in post-capitalist development and indigenous relational cosmovision, such as "'republican bio-socialism' in Ecuador, or as 'integral development in Bolivia'" (Gudynas, 2015: 201). The varieties of Buen Vivir share a view of "modernity as a particular ontology that in the last centuries determined the division between nature and society, a colonial distinction between modern and non-modern indigenous peoples, the myth of progress as a unidirectional linear path, and a strong confidence on Cartesian science" (Gudynas, 2011: 447).

Decolonization rejects the presumed binary and hierarchy of elite development approaches. Buen Vivir does "not accept the concept of progress and its derivatives (particularly growth) or the idea that welfare depends only on material consumption" (Gudynas, 2015: 202). Instead, it argues for a relational approach, in which an expanded notion of community includes human and natural worlds. Buen Vivir also draws on Western feminism and mirrors Fanon's and Mbembe's "ethic of care," as well as ecological justice versions of environmentalism, including the "rights of Nature," expressed in the Ecuadoran and Bolivian constitutions (Gudynas, 2011: 444).

One version of Buen Vivir appears in practices in some Aymara communities in Bolivia, oriented towards suma qamaña, a fulfilled life, "which can only be achieved by deep relationships within a community," in which the community includes "other living beings and elements of the environment located within a territorial framework (ayllu)" (Gudynas, 2015: 202). In these ayllu, "well-being encompasses not only persons, but also crops and cattle, and the rest of Nature" (Gudynas, 2011: 444). In Ecuador, the approach can be seen in sumac kawsay, a welfare system that is "not only material but ... also expressed within extended communities, both social and ecological" (Gudynas, 2015: 203). Further versions are recognizable among the Mapuche in Chile and Guaraní in Paraguay. Especially in Bolivia and Ecuador, Buen Vivir has been used to guide "reforms in legal forms, introduction of environmental accounting, tax reforms, dematerialization of economies and alternative regional integration within South America" (Gudynas, 2011: 446).

Because Buen Vivir depends on the particular ways in which indigenous cosmovision interacts with global processes, its application varies according to the operation of community, nature, and spiritual worlds in each place. Yet, all versions of Buen Vivir are relational, focusing on the embeddedness of these worlds. All versions of Buen Vivir are also ongoing creations, engaging Western versions of modernization while drawing on indigenous relational worldviews. "'Buen Vivir' should not be understood as a return to a distant, Andean past, pre-colonial times. It is not a static concept, but an idea that is continually being created" (Gudynas, 2011: 443).

It is worth reflecting on the geography of decolonization, as each site of resistance stitches together particular combinations of class conflict and cultural resistance. In terms of class conflict, the size, composition, and relation among class factions depends on the insertion of each country into international capitalism. Natural resource exporters will have different class structures than textile exporters, with particular implications for the size and organizational forms of lower classes, as well as the potential for alliances with factions of the national bourgeoisie. Resistance is further shaped by cultural traditions, as local actors blend international and local values in particular ways. Andean relations to the land are different from African relations to the land.

Still, local struggles for decolonization cannot oppose globalized capitalism if they do not also globalize. Globalizing decolonization means understanding both the particularities and the universality – class struggle and cultural resistance do not operate in the same way everywhere, but they are constant in their opposition to the exploitation of labor and land, their relational approach to community, production, and nature, and their forward-looking desire to negate the negation of their humanity. This kind of globalized decolonization was identified by Paul Ortiz as "emancipatory internationalism," found in "antislavery, anticolonial, pro-freedom, and pro-working-class movements against tremendous obstacles ... a political culture where the pursuit of liberty outranks nationalism or commercial imperialism" (Ortiz, 2018: 1).

In noting the connections between abolition struggles in the US, slave-revolt in Haiti, and anti-colonial struggle in Latin America, "Black speakers and their audiences articulated the idea that their individual rights were intimately connected with the rights of oppressed people in Latin America, the Caribbean and other parts of the world. This was an ideology based on the harsh experience of seeing slavery and racial capitalism extinguishing liberty everywhere it went" (Ortiz, 2018: 74). Ortiz's historical analysis signals the need for greater research into solidarity across decolonizing movements.

Conclusion

This chapter has argued for decolonizing development as a relational, forward-looking, and liberatory strategy. Examples of decolonizing development practice, such as Buen Vivir, and decolonizing development thinking, such as Afrocosmopolitanism, share these qualities and potentially transform the international system. Unlike elite development strategies as brought by Northern actors, decolonizing development is relational, emphasizing the relations among entities as prior to and constitutive of those entities. The North and South exist because of the social relation between them, in which binary and hierarchical relations combine racism, colonialism, and capitalism to make the land and labor of the South available to further Northern accumulation. Instead, decolonizing development draws on cultural traditions and class struggles specific to each context to outline an alternative modernity that combines (1) the progress of modernity with the relational worldviews of the South and (2) productive relations that do not depend on the hyper-exploitation of land and labor. The resulting combination is forward-looking and liberatory, as it makes possible an alternative future that liberates not only those in the South, but also those in the North.

Several things have to happen for an alternative future to take shape, including ongoing research inspired by the decolonizing tradition. In particular, we need more studies of the particular combinations resulting from the unevenness of the international system. What are the ways in which relational thinking in the South adapts modernity to local cultural and historical traditions? Further, in what ways are class struggle manifest and waged in response to particular incorporations into the international economy? How do the resulting combinations shape the trajectories of national development? These combinations vary across different geographies and over time, and it is worthwhile to gather such case studies, celebrate, and contribute to them.

Finally, we have yet to articulate the way in which various alternative modernities might combine internationally. This is not to say that universal alternatives are necessary or even possible. Still, patterns of resistance learn from those that have come before and those operating in other parts of the world. The nature of learning, diffusion, and collaboration among resistance movements, and the ways they combine to create additional innovations, pose an opportunity for new and necessary insights.

Bibliography

Connolly, James. 1897/1988. "Shan Van Vocht." Reprinted in P. Beresford Ellis (ed.), *James Connolly – Selected Writings*. Chicago: Pluto Press.

Escobar, Arturo. 2011. *Encountering Development*. Princeton, NJ: Princeton University Press.

Estes, Nick. 2013. "Wounded Knee: Settler Colonial Property Regimes and Indigenous Liberation." *Capitalism Nature Socialism* 24:3: 190–202.

Estes, Nick. 2019. *Our History is the Future: Standing Rock versus the Dakota Access Pipeline and the Long Tradition of Indigenous Resistance*. New York: Verso.

Fanon, Frantz. 2005. *The Wretched of the Earth*. New York: Grove Press.

Federici, Silvia. 2000. *Caliban and the Witch*. New York: Autonomedia Press.

Grosfoguel, Ramón. 2011. "Decolonizing Post-Colonial Studies and Paradigms of Political Economy." *Transmodernity* 1:1: 1–37.

Gudynas, Eduardo. 2011. "Buen Vivir: Today's Tomorrow." *Development* 54:4: 441–447.

Gudynas, Eduardo. 2015. "Buen Vivir." In G. D'Alisa, F. Demaria, and G. Kallis (eds.), *Degrowth: A Vocabulary for a New Era*. New York: Routledge.

Harvey, David. 2005. *The New Imperialism*. New York: Oxford University Press.

Harvey, David. 2011. *The Enigma of Capital and the Crises of Capitalism*. New York: Oxford University Press.

Jackson, P.T., and Daniel Nexon. 1999. "Relations before States." *European Journal of International Relations* 5:1: 291–332.

James, C.L.R. 1989. *Black Jacobins: Toussaint L'Ouverture and the San Domingo Revolution*. New York: Random House.

Langdon, Jonathan. 2013. "Decolonizing Development Studies." *Canadian Journal of Development Studies* 34:3: 384–399.

Löwy, Michael. 1998. "Marxism and Romanticism in the Work of José Carlos Mariátegui." *Latin American Perspectives* 25:4 (101): 76–88.

Luxembourg, Rosa. 1951. *The Accumulation of Capital*. London: Routledge and Kegan Paul.

Mariátegui, J.C. 1928/2011. "Anniversary and Balance Sheet." In Harry E. Vanden and Marc Becker (eds.), *José Carlos Mariátegui: An Anthology*. New York: Monthly Review Press.

Marx, Karl. 1853. "The Future Results of British Rule in India." *New York Daily Tribune*, August 8.

Mbembe, Achille. 2001. *On the Postcolony*. Berkeley: University of California Press.

Mbembe, Achille. 2003. "Necropolitics." *Public Culture* 15:1: 11–40.

Mbembe, Achille. 2019. *Necropolitics*. Durham, NC: Duke University Press.

Mbembe, Achille. 2021. *Out of the Dark Night*. New York: Columbia University Press.

Mignolo, Walter D., and Catherine E. Walsh. 2018. *On Decoloniality: Concepts, Analytics, Praxis*. Durham, NC: Duke University Press.

Ndlovu-Gatsheni, Sabelo. 2018. *Epistemic Freedom in Africa: Deprovincialization and Decolonization*. New York: Routledge.

Ortiz, Paul. 2018. *An African American and Latinx History of the United States*. Boston, MA: Beacon Press.

Pailey, Robtel Neajai. 2019. "Decentering the White Gaze of Development." *Development and Change* 51:3: 729–745.

Polanyi, Karl. 2001. *Great Transformation*. Boston, MA: Beacon Press.

Quijano, Aníbal. 2007. "Coloniality and Modernity/Rationality." *Cultural Studies* 21:2: 168–178.

Robinson, Cedric. 2000. *Black Marxism*. Chapel Hill: University of North Carolina Press.

Said, Edward. 1979. *Orientalism*. New York: Vintage Books.

Selwyn, Benjamin. 2016. "Theory and Practice of Labor-Centered Development." *Third World Quarterly* 37:6: 1035–1052.

Srnicek, Nick. 2016. *Platform Capitalism*. Hoboken, NJ: Wiley Press.

Sultana, Farhana. 2019. "Decolonizing Development Education and the Pursuit of Social Justice." *Human Geography* 12:3: 31–46.

Thompson, E.P. 1963. *The Making of the English Working Class*. New York: Vintage Books.

Trotsky, Leon. 1977. *History of the Russian Revolution*. Chicago: Haymarket Books.

White, Sarah. 2002. "Thinking Race, Thinking Development." *Third World Quarterly* 23:3: 407–419.

Index

Printed and bound by CPI Group (UK) Ltd, Croydon, CR0 4YY

16/04/2025

14658490-0002